The Far Country

The Far Country

Paul Twitchell

Illuminated Way Publishing

P.O. Box 28130 • Crystal, Minnesota 55428

The Far Country

Copyright © 1971 ECKANKAR

Printed in U.S.A.
ISBN: 0-914766-91-0
Library of Congress Catalog Card Number: 87-82674

Cover design by Lois Stanfield
Cover special effects photo by Richard Hartman

First 📖 Printing – 1990

Dedicated to

the ECK

CONTENTS

INTRODUCTION

There comes a time in the spiritual history of man when he must meet with crises like those today which are devastating to him both in Soul and consciousness.

The deep concern which I have for the human race and the individual has brought about this book The FAR COUNTRY. I have tried to lay down the patterns of the most breathtaking and far reaching esoteric teachings known to man. The contents should settle many of the problems which man faces in the spiritual and material climax of these times.

Rebazar Tarzs, the great ECK Master, from the eastern region of Tibet, is the moving figure in this book. He went through a complete series of dialogues with me, about the whole works of ECKANKAR, the ancient science of Soul Travel. He also included in these discourses the planes beyond the physical senses. Hence the title The FAR COUNTRY, meaning those worlds which are generally invisible to man and his outer facilities.

Rudyard Kipling once wrote a short story with the same title. It was about a man who had a vision of the world beyond his physical senses as a child, and again when a soldier dying on the battlefield.

The FAR COUNTRY is a matchless piece of literature of divine wisdom. There are few sacred writings in the world today which can equal it in its beauty and revelation of the God worlds and what is contained within them. This manuscript gives the ways of reaching God, the various planes and what are on them, the philosophy and doctrine of ECKANKAR. It contains almost everything within it that is needed for the God seeker to have in his hands to find the heavenly kingdom.

Whoever reads and studies The FAR COUNTRY becomes an inspired person for the relationship between the ECK chela and the MAHANTA, the Living ECK Master is clearly outlined. In pursuit of the God-Consciousness it is shown how the jigsaw puzzle of life will fall logically into place. Any one piece, even a small one, may bring about revolutionary results if left out of the pattern of life for the individual ECK chela.

As the theme of God-Realization is developed in this manuscript, one becomes aware that there is a constant revelation of the greater results of Soul Travel with each trip into the inner worlds. Rebazar Tarzs never lets up with the reader, who is considered the chela, the God seeker, but keeps him always aware of the tangible insight between free will and fate, and the understanding of human conflicts as well as those of karma and non-karma patterns.

It is quite certain that if the reader will spend anytime at all in the study of this manuscript he will come to know that ECK is the highest of all paths to God. That there is no other way to gain spiritual enlightenment.

Paul Twitchell

Chapter 1

THE FAR COUNTRY

The Far Country is a vast world lying beyond what the human race calls the earth planet and which apparently has not been explored by either the scientists or politicians for materialist glory.

It is a magnificent series of spiritual universes where the Tuza* goes, following the disposal of its earthly body in that phenomena called death, and where so many travel in their Atma-Sarup† body from this earth plane.

The Far Country has many names. The Greeks called it the Elysian fields, or the Isles of the Blessed, Happy Isles, Fortunate Isles, and the Garden of Hesperides; the Scandinavians give it the names, Valhalla and Asgard; the American Indians knew it as the Happy Hunting Grounds, and the Hebrews as Canaan, or the Promised Land.

The Buddhists call it Nirvana and the Christians know it as Paradise or Heaven. Other religions have various names for this afterworld where all disembodied entities live.

Rudyard Kipling wrote a story of a boy who had a glimpse of this Far Country. Occasionally he would see the vision as he progressed into manhood. He yearned to enter that Far Country but had no way except through death. When dying from a wound received in battle during World War I, he sees the vision of the Far Country and knows at last he is ready to enter. The short story was called The Far Country and is one of Kipling's best.

Those who have had a glimpse of the Far Country are always unhappy with their existence on this earth planet. Unless they learn the art of Soul Travel, these people become

---

*Tuza—the Soul in ECKANKAR terminology.

†Atma Sarup—the Soul body.

extremely restless. Some will commit suicide in hope of reaching it, but they only defeat their purpose.

Tom Lea, well known author, did a novel called The Wonderful Country. It was the story of a range rider who restlessly searched the southwest on his magnificent, black stallion, for that world which exists but could never be found.

Many people have a knowledge of The Far Country, although they are neither fortunate enough to witness it in vision nor can they travel through the esoteric planes in the Atma Sarup body like those who have the knowledge and ability to leave their bodies at will.

Those explorers of the Far Country, Rebazar Tarzs, Kabir, Yaubl Sacabi, Guru Nanak, Sudar Singh, Zoroaster, Buddha, Tulsi Das, Shamus-i-Tabriz, Fubbi Quantz, and others have been the pioneers of the Far Country. They left a living saga which must be studied and admired for its adventurous spirit.

These great ones have given us a philosophy to live by, but much of it has been misused and often employed for individual gain, instead of for the universal cause of mankind.

One of the bolder spirits who constantly explores the Far Country is Rebazar Tarzs, the great Master of ECKANKAR, living in the wildest region of the Himalayas near the Afghanistan and Kashmir borders, where they are joined by the Hindu Kush range.

He gave me additional knowledge of the Far Country, adding to that which Sudar Singh at his ashram in Allahabad, India had already given me. After extensive exploration of Sach Khand,* Sudar Singh granted me permission to proceed on my own through the spiritual worlds.

It was through Sudar Singh while traveling in the Soul body, that I met Rebazar Tarzs and intensified the study of the world called The Far Country, during a lengthy visit with him in the Himalayas above Darjeeling.

Later, with Gail, my wife, I came to know Rebazar Tarzs

---

*Sach Khand—Fifth spiritual plane.

better. He talked several times to us. I began to leave the body at night and meet with him at his mud and brick hut in the Himalayas.

Rebazar Tarzs is a man who looks to be in his middle thirties, but many, including Yaubl Sacabi, say that he is well over five hundred years old in his physical body. He is approximately six feet in height, covers his muscular 185 pounds with a maroon colored robe, walks with a springy, youthful stride and generally carries a five foot, wooden staff.

Tarzs' black hair is cropped closely, and is curly enough not to bother him in the fierce winds from the icy mountains. His beard is coal black and trimmed close. His eyes are shining coals of dark fire, his lips purple and his speech a clipped style as he barks words to emphasize points he is making. His flesh is dark, swarthy from the hot sun and winds.

His hands are noticeable. They are square with long, blunt fingers, and restless. He uses the forefinger of his left hand frequently to emphasize a point. His hands are also swarthy from the weather of those high climes.

His feet are large, generally encased in sandals, but he often goes barefooted through the rocks and sand. They are as dark as walnut stain.

Rebazar Tarzs lives alone in his little, mud-brick hut high on a cliff above a torrential blue river, roaring out of the high glaciers across the valley into the plains to feed the teeming millions, six hundred miles to the south in the vast sweltering midlands.

The view is breath-taking. Miles across the valley lie the wild outposts of Afghanistan. Due north, beyond the flat, monotonous plains, rise the jagged ranges of the Hindu Kush, the snow white tip of Tirich Mir, rising 25,263 feet above all the smaller peaks. Falah, Sar and Monhil, at 1900 feet are dwarfed beside it. The mountains are dust-colored by day, indigo by night, layer upon layer like a succession of steps in a vast staircase that leads, via the Himalayas, to the roof of the world.

11

From far below echoes the perpetual thunders of the Swat River, hurrying to join the giant Indus, whose valleys have rung to the march of the invader from time immemorial. Three hundred and twenty-seven years before Christ an army that marched proudly, with the arrogance of countless conquests, plumed, helmeted, striking terror everywhere, the Army of Alexander the Great, came through these cold passes into the soft, warm world of the south.

In this spot lives Rebazar Tarzs. It is a way station between the Earth planet and the Far Country, where the Tuza can find its guide and a path to make the cross-over into the world beyond.

Often leaving his physical body on the rude cot inside the hut, Rebazar Tarzs goes to the Tuza who needs his help, or to teach in one of the temples in the Far Country. He is always busy helping others, in or out of the physical body.

I came to his little hut early in the afternoon, one day, to discuss with him the doctrine of ECKANKAR. Above the canyons filled with blue spruce, silver fir and walnut trees and the roar of the raging river, I learned more about the Far Country.

*   *   *

We sat in lotus fashion on the hard earth floor. He began by asking a series of questions, while puncturing the cool air with a forefinger, to emphasize each question.

"What lies beyond the Earth plane?" His voice was sharp and caustic. "How many worlds make up the Far Country?"

He jabbed a finger in my chest. "Where does it lie? How much do the physical scientists know about it?"

"Nothing!" He barked with his black eyes glowering. "The materialists look at the heavens with objective eyes, and make use of the canopy of air for the purpose of scientific progress for the worship of the commercial Gods of mankind.

12

"The scientists start from the outside and work inwardly toward the center of things. The ECK Masters* start from the center of things and work outwardly through the same planes. They see much, and with realistic eyes.

"The materialist claims there are five layers in the atmosphere lying upward from this world and that we are like the primitive savage standing on the shores of an ocean and wondering how far the water stretches beyond the setting sun.

"They call these regions or layers the troposphere, tropopause, stratosphere, ionosphere and the unknown. The travelers give them the following names: Sukhsham Desh, Brahm Lok, Daswan Dwar, Bhanwar Gupha, Sach Khand and beyond these five are hundreds of others, but mainly three known as Alakh Lok, Agam Lok and the nameless world, often called Anami Lok, the highest where dwells the SUGMAD.†

"The Vedantists know them as the Astral, Mental, Wisdom, Bliss and God plane.

"The objective side of these planes is studied by the scientists and the subjective by the spiritual travelers. Another advantage the latter has is, they come and go at will to any plane desired.

"A comparison of the five planes as seen by both the materialist scientists and spiritual travelers is of interest," he said breaking off here. "Let's have some tea!"

*　*　*

We seated ourselves again on the floor and silently drank the buttered yak tea for awhile. When we had finished, he began again.

"The first of these planes is the troposphere, that which encompasses the Earth planet. It is about five miles thick at

---

*ECK Masters—Those who leave their physical body and travel through the Far Country in the Atma Sarup body.

†SUGMAD—Name for God in Far Country.

the poles and ten miles or so at the equators. It is a region of rapid climatical changes and quite turbulent.

"A layer of storms here, calms there, polar cold and tropic heat; a layer in which the temperature falls steadily about 1 degree Fahrenheit for every 300 feet until a low of 67 degrees below zero Fahrenheit is reached.

"Eighty percent of the air by weight is packed into the troposphere. Do you understand this?" He fixed a cold glare in my direction.

"I doubt if you do, although you've traveled with Sudar Singh in many planes of the Far Country!"

He sipped his tea and stared through the open door at the vast world outside and the shining, white peaks in the distance.

Finally he spoke again. "This is ordinarily called the Astral world, though we know it as the Sukhsham Desh, or the Anda, the lowest plane of the Far Country. It lies nearest the physical world.

"The lower part of this world is the gross material of the universe of the planets and stars, including the Earth planet. Coarse matter dominates all but a few mana(s) * and some Tuzas!

"This region embraces all the suns and planets, known or unknown to human astronomy. It extends out into space, without the knowledge of the physical scientists, far beyond the reach of any telescope.

"The adept returns to this lower region again and again to help those who wish to untangle themselves from the darkness of this negative world.

"The capital of this world is at the top of the Astral region, a plane often called the Turiya Pad, by the Sufis. The city is named Sahasra dal Kanwal, which means thousand petalled lotus, the center which all yogis strive to reach inwardly for spiritual perfection.

"The ruler of this region is Jot Niranjan, the being en-

---

* Mana (s)—Mind.

14

dowed with the negative power. This power is essential, for it creates matter in the lower world.

"He is the center of this power, the thousand petalled lotus, the great cluster of lights, these magnificent lights which the traveler views when approaching the higher Astral planes. Here is the actual powerhouse of the physical universe, what the scientists seek to understand.

"They have discovered the duality of the atom which turns from its spiritual refinement, to gather with the coarser to make matter, a process that physical science is studying like school children.

"Out of this powerhouse flows the current of lights which has created and sustains all the worlds in the universe. These lights are of all shades and tints, but basically made up of seven colors, black, red, green, orange, blue, yellow and white.

"These flow off into streams of rays throughout the universes, and each have their different aspect to assist physical life on the planets of this universe. For example, green is the individualizing ray which shows the growth of Soul in man's aura, for the rays touch every aura in every living thing throughout these worlds.

"Black is the pure color of the darker or negative side, while white is the opposite, or highest. Red is the shade of human love, orange the ray of life, called Prana by the Hindus. Blue is the intellectual ray from which all great thinkers and creative artists receive their inspiration and yellow is the spiritual ray.

"If you will take closer scrutiny of the colors in clothes worn by a person, it will somewhat tell you about the dominating astral rays in their aura.

"The great Astral city lies just below a shining mountain. This is where the powerhouse of lights are caught up from the current flowing down from the plane above it.

"The city is often called the City of Lights. Here dwells many of the earth's renowned people, from all ages of history. Many religious figures live here because they believe that this is the heaven that they wanted to reach in the afterlife.

"This is the home of Jot Niranjan who lives in a great castle within the shining mountain. The ECK* here is the bell and the conch.

"The Astral region is the negative pole of the whole spiritual universe. Life here is so long, that many of its inhabitants believe they have reached immortality. All the work done by these dwellers pertains to some form of creative activity.

"The Astral world is always wiped out after several million years, in the same manner as the lower material universes are, and following a long period of equal darkness, a new creation of the region is begun.

"All who live in the Astral and physical worlds are put into a deep sleep and drawn up to the next region higher, called the Brahm Lok, or the mental plane.

"When the creation is finished and a new Astral and lower physical universes are re-established, the Souls are sent back to their former worlds, where old threads of existence are picked up again."

With this he got up again and refilled the cups with tea. While we drank the hot liquid and shuddered against the wind which whistled down from the high slopes, he appeared to sleep.

*   *   *

After a while Rebazar Tarzs aroused himself and started his discussion again.

"Now for the second region.

"The scientist thinks of this as a no-man's land lying above the troposphere or Astral plane. They call this world, the Tropopause. We give it the name of the Brahm Lok, or the mental plane.

---

*ECK—Music of the audible life current known to the spiritual travelers.

"According to the materialists this region is a thin layer in which the temperature ceases to fall with increasing altitude.

"It lies many miles above the earth plane and has not yet been very well explored by the material scientists.

"Sometimes the spiritual travelers call this region the Brahmanda,* which means the egg of Brahm, and refers to the name of its Lord, Brahm. This Deity is supposed to be the supreme being of all creation by the Yogis. This is the highest world known to practically all faiths, including Christianity.

"If the yogi or other holy man claims to be a master and declares that Brahman† is the highest of all creators, that this is the supreme heaven, he is not a master in the sense that we know. He is only a humble seeker under the supreme ruler of this plane, Brahman.

"This is the top of the three worlds, the physical, lower and upper Astral. It is called the first grand division of the universes.

"This is the world of the spiritual-material essence, because spirit dominates it.

"This is the region of the universal mind, whose power is called AUM. Hence the word Omkar, the power on this plane, which is still the negative force. The lower part of this region is that known as the Home of the Universal Mind. It is from here that all individual minds are derived, and to that region all minds must return when they are discarded during the upward flight of Soul.

"An ECK Master takes you through this world, into the next region, for only a master can be the guide, and know the path, thorny as it is. He is the recognized Lord of all.

"All other lords, rulers and peoples on every plane pay homage to Him.

"When you arrive at the border of this region the sound of

---

*Brahmanda—the third grand division.
†Brahman—Lord of Brahm Lok plane.

17

Omkar is heard continuously resounding, like a great drum. You go up a hill and open a gate, enter a crooked tunnel, pass on through to the other side. Then you cross high and low hills where the vision appears to be reversed. It's as if you are traveling in reverse.

"You pass through a fortlike region which is the home of the ruler, Omkar, and halt, for Soul to become adorned with the attributes of devotion and faith.

"The seeds of the traveler's karma are burned and destroyed here.

"The color of this region is that of a beautiful, setting sun. Above it is another part of the world of Omkar where you find deserts, mountains and gardens. Flowers are arranged in artistic designs everywhere.

"You will be intoxicated with joy, wandering through a splendid region of canals and streams, before coming to an ocean of water over which you can cross by bridge to the other side where there are three mountain peaks named Mer, Sumer and Kailash.

"This is a halting place for many spiritualists and mystics. Some yogis believe this to be their heaven. The miracles of the mind are performed from this section of Brahm Lok, e.g., stopping of trains, filling dry wells and healing the sick.

"This world is extremely vast, despite what the scientists assert when comparing it with the physical world or the Astral plane.

"There are six planes within Brahm Lok, and many subdivisions. The chief city here is called Mersumer Kailash, named after the three peaks of Brahm Lok.

"This region is controlled by Brahm whose chief duty is to channel the great power, AUM, into the region and the worlds below.

"The function of AUM, a part of the great sound current, is to create, maintain and destroy the universes below it. It is the center of creation of the material and Astral worlds.

"Many of the great scriptures have sprung from this region, including the Vedas, Christian scriptures, Buddhist texts, to name a few. Lord Krishna as well as many other spiritual leaders make their home here.

*   *   *

Rebazar Tarzs paused for a moment to finish his tea. He wiped his mouth with the sleeve of his left arm and continued.

"Now for the third plane," he said.

"The physical scientists know this layer or world as the stratosphere which extends for miles into the sky. It is a region of steady, gentle winds, beautiful clouds and steadily rising temperatures.

"This is what might be called the ozone layer. Beyond that is very little physical air.

"The subjective side of this plane is a region called Daswan Dwar. It is filled with a brilliant light. Soul can bathe itself in the lake of nectar called Mansarover, and join the swans, those Tuzas known as the Hansas; hence the name, used by many Hindu holy men, the Parahansas. The Tuza gives up all its bodies, physical, astral, mental, and is purified.

"The lord of this region is known as Ramkar. He is the power supply station for all the worlds below this one. The light of your Tuza becomes equal to the light and radiance of twelve suns, and the happiness and bliss experienced by It at this stage is beyond physical description.

"While on this plane you are capable of performing grand miracles, such as giving sight to the blind, sometimes raising the dead and the ability to travel through the ether in the physical body.

"Here the Tuza beholds itself as pure spirit stripped of all materiality. It becomes self-realized.

"The color ray in this world is the orange hue, the stream of the life-giving forces.

"Very few Souls will attempt to leave this realm for the worlds above. Yet their understanding of the Far Country

19

is wondrous, for they have an exceedingly good knowledge of the worlds still further beyond their world.

"If the Master takes you to the top of this region you may hear its sounds, those of the violins. Here you cross the Tribeni, a place where three streams meet, hence the Kumba Mehla, a religious fair held every twelve years in India. It is only a reflection of this place in the third heaven.

"Then you enter the region of Maha Sunna, where you find all the secret knowledge of the worlds.

"This area is many vast earth miles in circumference and in the center pitch darkness. Four sound currents are heard emanating from invisible sources; the jhankar* predominates and is indescribable in human words.

"Here you are entranced by their music and must force yourself to leave or you may stay forever.

"Also here are the five egg-shaped worlds, full of a variety of creations and each permeated and governed by a Brahm. Each has its predominating color like green or yellow or even white. They are quite vast in comparison with which the entire universe below appears very insignificant.

"He who has gained or attained this region will have increasing powers and understanding in proportions, as this region is vast beyond description, when compared with those you have been through to reach it.

"But there is increasing difficulty as you go higher in giving expression to anything relating to the upper regions. The very ideas in these upper regions are beyond the grasp of man's thoughts, until he has traveled them and has the experience. Even then he cannot put his words into earthly language."

*   *   *

Rebazar Tarzs paused for a few minutes to catch his breath. I looked out the open window at the rocks where a

---

*Jhankar—another name for melodies of the lower worlds. A musical instrument.

frenzy of violent forces were causing a great upheaval of slate, limestone, lava, granite and sandstone, mixing all into strange patterns.

The cliffs across from the mud hut showed formations twisted and turned into gigantic whorls. I was looking at these, wondering why the SUGMAD had let nature run wild, when Tarzs spoke again.

"The fourth region," he said sharply, gathering my attention instantly, "is that which the scientists call the ionosphere. Here the physical air is so thin that there is a constant electrically excited condition which stimulates the atoms. In this condition the atoms are called Ions.

"There are several layers in this objective side of the region that serve as reflectors of radio or mental waves. One layer reflects long waves, the other reflects short waves. Some short waves pass through the planes below, like sharp knives cutting through materials. The mind and radio waves are like light waves, traveling in a straight line.

"The curvature of the earth would prevent us from transmitting and receiving radio messages and even psychic impressions, if it weren't for the Ionosphere region.

"The electrical mirror in the sky reflects waves back to the earth, and the earth sends them up again and so they finally reach their destination.

"Hence, if you send out a strong desire for something it goes through the same process and returns to you materialized.

"The spiritual travelers call this region the fourth plane, or the land of Bhanwar Gupha. It is the home of the Lord Sohang, through whom the great power current flows into this region and downwards.

"This divine being lives in a city of great light called Arhirit. He is filled with majestic beauty and grandeur. When the Tuza sees Him, Its consciousness is filled with overwhelming joy. It says to Itself, 'I am that!'

"This is the meaning of the word, Sohang.

"At this moment of sublime realization, you know that

you are part of the Supreme! In union with me, the self, and master!

"This is why the Occultists call it the Bliss plane!

"To reach this plane you must cross the pass above the Hansni tunnel and enter another tunnel, the Rukmini tunnel, where you see a strange and beautiful structure. Here the faculties of the power to hear and the power to see are greatly enhanced giving peace and satisfaction.

"To your right are bright islands, and to your left many continents covered with palaces, appearing as if made of pearls, having their roofs covered with rubies and studded with emeralds and diamonds. Only the brave can venture this far. That is why Sudar Singh told you that only the courageous, the daring and the enterprising would have the SUGMAD.

"This is the city that St. John saw in his revelations, which were written and passed down through the Christian New Testament.

"In the distance are the Bhanwar Gupha mountains. The Sohang ECK* is easily heard. The sound is like that of a keen flute. You see the sun above with an immense light and find the world most beautiful, sweet and full of light.

"The Tuzas living here exist on the sound current as their food. The roads are sometimes filled with those groups of Hansas who have been fortunate enough to penetrate this region, followed by the devotees. They are trying to reach the regions above.

"There are numerous plains and worlds with a variety of creations, inhabited by millions of Tuzas living on the nectar of Bani. Kabir said there are eighty thousand continents in this world, with beautiful homes on each for their inhabitants.

"The color of this region is blue, for it is often spoken of as the Home of Truth, and is the plane of true miracles, from which all things can happen. But woe to him who misuses this power.

----

*The sound heard on this plane.

"The physical scientists say there is nothing beyond their fourth layer. They admit to the theory of something beyond it, but their physical instruments have yet to record anything to give them material proof."

He paused a moment, then continued, "On the spiritual side the approach to the fifth region is guarded by a zone of such deep, dense darkness that none but the pure can cross it.

"Only he who has the light and power may tread here in the world of Sach Khand. Here you find dwelling Sat Nam, the lord of all, above and below. His brilliance is so great that even one hair on his body, if there were any, would radiate a light equal to that of many millions of suns combined.

"This is the true home of Soul. It is the grand headquarters of all creation and the reign of immortality. It is changeless, perfect and deathless. It is called the God or Soul plane by the Occultist. It is untouched by dissolution or reconstruction. This is the world of the ECK saints, where they live.

"The fifth region is the jumping off place for the Tuza into the great worlds of pure spirit. Its citizens are only of the highest order, and in such countless numbers that you couldn't estimate them.

"They live in a joy so great that you couldn't conceive or measure it.

"Within the Soul plane is a fort-like place where is situated the throne of the Lord of the worlds. You know Him as the true Lord.

"Soul is now taken by the MAHANTA* to a great park where the scenery is indescribable. There is also a huge reservoir here, like those on the earth plane, from which flows the most delicious nectar through canals to supply the distant regions of this great world.

---

*MAHANTA—one possessing the highest of all states of consciousness.

23

"Golden palaces are set in open fields of silvery light. The landscape is beyond human description and the beauty of the saints living here is incomprehensible, the brilliancy of each equal to the combined light of sixteen suns and moons.

"You reach the real entrance of the city. The watchers at the gates are saints, who pass you through into the palace of the Lord and you are greeted by Sat Nam.

"He is the first, definitely limited manifestation of the all Supreme formless SUGMAD. He is the power, the light, the great Master flowing down and out into all creation, to create, govern and sustain all regions, like a gigantic stream of water.

"This is the shabda, the sound current which permeates all systems of the Far Country. This is the positive pole of the spiritual regions.

"Above the world of Sach Khand are worlds beyond worlds, beyond physical description. Those living in these worlds are under the supreme being we call the formless one, the Advaita, which is the real name for the formless. The SUGMAD is that which is so beyond all the worlds that we can hardly conceive that IT exists.

"This Advaita is not a being, nor anything but life itself, a living force that is called the ECK. Your imagination begs to be relieved of trying to image what lies beyond the fifth plane.

"When you come to face Sat Nam, you become aware that 'I Am He!'

"Love is the holy bond that holds all the worlds together. Only a saint can reach this region and travel into those worlds above. Then he is called a Param Sant.

"All the ECK power, coming down from the far regions above, come to a perfect manifestation for the first time in Sat Nam, as the first actual or complete personification of the Supreme One. He is the great Father of all, to worship and love with complete devotion. He is so fathomless and impersonal you cannot approach Him, even in thought. He sits between the infinite light and the created universes, and

24

so in time when purged of every imperfection you will approach Him as the Father and receive His gracious welcome home.

"While still in the lower regions of the Astral Plane and that of Brahm Lok, Soul is often compelled to return to the earth plane for rebirth and death, or what Buddha called the Wheel of the Eighty-Four.

"But when the Soul reaches the pure region of Alakh Lok, the first of the planes in the first grand division of the Far Country, there is no returning to earth except as a redeemer.

"The Tuza becomes a saint himself, and the mission of Its Master is over. But the Tuza has yet to travel into the most sublime and beautiful part of his spiritual journey to the SUGMAD.

"Above Sach Khand are three other planes of inconceivable splendor known to the saints. Here the Lord of the fifth world, Sat Nam, has taken over and guides Soul toward the goal of reaching the nameless splendor of all splendors.

"First, the Tuza becomes united with the very essence of the Sat Nam in a mystical sense, and so, becomes a part of Him, partaking in all Sat Nam's marvelous attributes. Then the Tuza advances to the three remaining known planes.

"First is the Alakh Lok, presided over by the Alakh Purusha, and after this is the Agam Lok plane presided over by the Agam Purusha, or lord. Finally Soul reaches the end of Its journey, the region of the nameless One, Advaita, the formless, that which is the first you know about the SUGMAD, the feeling or the understanding of the Divine.

"Eventually you come to the SUGMAD in the vast worlds above.

"No words can describe IT. No thought can embrace IT. IT is formless, the All Embracing One.

"IT is the impersonal, infinite ocean of love.

"From IT flows all life and spirituality, all truth, all reality. IT is all wisdom and love and power. All visible lords of all regions are ITS manifestation. IT takes forms, many forms, in order that ITS purposes might be carried out

25

in all creations. They are all ITS forms; but none of them express ITS totality.

"IT may take millions of forms, but IT, ITSELF, remains formless, impersonal, all pervading. IT is universal spirit, universal life.

"In the literature of the sacred, this divine formless spirit is expressed by many names, such as ECKANKAR, Nirankar, Akal, Nirala, Anami, Agam, Alakh, Sat Purusha, Prabhu, Prabhswami, Akashar, Paramakshar, Purusha.

"All of these words have been coined in an effort to convey to human intelligence some idea of what the Saints think of the SUGMAD or Lord God, the highest power.

"ECKANKAR means the one oneness, the body of oneness, All, or Totality—this is the secret name of God or the SUGMAD which will be creeping into these talks between us as I go deeper into this philosophy.

"Nirankar means without body or form. Advaita, Soami, or Swami means the all pervading Lord.

"Akal means timeless: Nirala, peerless, having none like Him; Anami, without name; Agam, inaccessible; Sat Purusha, true Lord, the real Lord, as distinguished from all hypothetical gods. That which is not Sat does not really exist. Sat means truth, reality, existence. Hence the fundamental idea of truth is existence. The untrue does not exist; the true does. Truth and existence are synonymous terms. Purusha implies being, and being implies creative energy, the predominating and presiding Lord, the source of creative energy. Prabhu means Lord, having power and control.

"Prabhswami means all-pervading Lord, having power. Akashar means the Lord who has real power, the actual king of all, like Sat Purusha. This is used in contradistinction to Dharam Ray, the negative power, who controls the Three Worlds. It implies law and order. Remember the more law and order there is in a society, the more negative it is—the more it is under the control of the Dharam Ray. Dharam is law, order, system, and it is used to also designate religion, or any religious system.

"Akashar is Sat Purusha, or Akal Purusha, while Dharam Ray is Kal* Purusha, or Kal or Brahm.

"The whole universe is considered as One, the true ECKANKAR. There is perfect oneness in the universe, which is also co-existent with God, infinite, unlimited. Hence the SUGMAD is Nirankar, i.e. formless.

"As such, he is without personality, without name. He cannot be said to be anywhere, as he is everywhere. Since He is everywhere, all and everything, he must be impersonal. Of course, He may assume any number of forms; but none of these forms embrace his entire being, any more than one sun embraces the sum total of physical matter.

"When the SUGMAD limits ITSELF to some extent, however slightly, IT becomes Agam Purusha. If a little more limited, Alakh Purusha, and when IT takes a definite form for the purpose of administrating the affairs of the universe, the SUGMAD becomes Sat Purusha, or Sat Nam.

"Sat Nam is the first, definitely limited, manifestation of the Supreme Being. But IT is not limited, except to form only. Sat Nam, true name, is that which defines ITS individuality, and points definitely to the first personal manifestation of the Infinite One.

"The names of the SUGMAD, in other languages than the Sanskrit and Hindi, are as many as are the ideas of IT. God is Anglo-Saxon adaptation of good. IT is the chief good, or the sum total of God. Deus is the Latin name, signifying something like supreme emperor. Theos is the Greek appellation, meaning the chief of those august powers who sat upon Mount Olympus and ruled the world.

"Adonai, or Elohim, or Yahveh, are some of the Hebrew names assigned to the god who was first a tribal deity of the Jews, but later proclaimed lord over all gods and worlds. He was the supreme law-giver, the commander of all the armies of Israel. He was the majestic warrior whose wrath was so much to be feared. Love was not in his makeup until later.

---

* Kal—means negative.

27

"We have others, for example, Allah, the Merciful of Islam. Varuna, the greatest of all ancient Hindu gods, outstanding in the Vedas. Brahm, Rama, Brahma, Vishnu and Shiva, and a host of others in the Indian sacred books.

"Zarathustra spoke of Ormuzd and the Norseman had his Thor. The North American Indian worshipped their Manitou and each primitive tribe and nation had a being to adorn, admire, and to protect them.

"The ECK travelers know the great SUGMAD by many names. For names are only labels. They care so little for the knowledge of who IT might be, but are seeking to know what IT is and where IT is found."

He finished, stood up and looked around. Outside the mountains had turned a pinkish color and then green. It was time to go and I left knowing that on the morning, Rebazar Tarzs would start again on his discussions of the Far Country.

I would be back.

Chapter 2

THE SEARCHLIGHT ON RELIGION

The Hindu Kush is a high mountain range which penetrates Afghanistan in the northeast corner and runs across
the nation in a west-by-southwest course.

Hindu Kush means Killer of Hindus. The bloody events
of the past which have happened in this beautiful range of
mountains has given it this ominous name.

The range in its northwestern end has peaks above 20,000
feet, with Tirich Mir reaching 25,263. The passes are some
of the highest in the world, that of Lowarai, 10,200 feet;
Darkot, 15,400 feet; and Baraghil, 12,400. Not the highest
passes, they are among those which reach the top scale in
heights in the Himalaya mountains.

It was a perfect summer day with only a few fleecy clouds
in the sky. The view from the front of Rebazar Tarzs' mud
and brick hut was one of grandeur.

At a distance the Tirich Mir seemed more imposing than
it had at any other time. It is a cold, rough spire of snow
and ice, reaching into heights where mountains are not supposed to be. I felt, as if I were looking into another world.
This peak, like Everest, Kanchenjunga, Godwin Austen,
Nanga Parbat, and Annapurna, reaches far above the abode
of man into the supernal land, the Far Country.

Sitting there and watching, one becomes lost in thoughts of
the supernatural. One soon learns that this is the world of
spirits and gods and the mysterious forces of life. In those
mountains are the ECK masters and teachers, as also in the
Karakoram range and the Himalayan mountains.

We ate a mixture of what tasted like honey and meal, drank
the buttered tea, then Rebazar Tarzs began.

"Today, I will turn the spotlight upon religion. There are
several great forces of religion in the world today. When I
use the word great, I speak of numbers in each varied sys-

29

tem of faith. Buddhism is the largest in the world, followed by Christianity, Mohammedanism, and Hinduism. The other various religions make up the fringe in memberships, mainly Confucianism and Taoism.

"The destruction of lives in the name of a holy being has been the bane of this earth. The fight between materialistic organizations, calling themselves religious faiths under the banner of a true God, is the worst of the conditions man has invented.

"No savior who came to this world intended to propagate a faith. Instead he wanted to give a few simple truths learned in the Far Country, and have them passed along to those who would listen.

"The ancient masters followed this method. They hardly wrote anything, for none of their followers had the ability to read nor write. They passed the word by mouth. Once they initiated a person into the holy path which they were following, then they would turn to another.

"None had a clinging, social teaching as you find today in many of the organized churches. Therefore you find that religion is simply a social institution, demonstrably true of the western religions, and woven through those in the Oriental countries.

"Name one religion which is in existence today and I will show you that it is a product of the social conscience, instead of the Truth of the SUGMAD. All laws, which are called the Law of God, are hardly anything except the evolution of the social conscience from the Law of Manu, the Code of Hammurabi, the Law of Moses, and the Canons of the Christian Church.

"What do they represent?

"Nothing more than the rules and regulations of the priest-craft to control their followers, for a political and economic hold over the multitudes. Didn't Fubbi Quantz know this when he was challenged by the people in his day of open ministry?

"What has been more hideous than the caste system established by the Law of Manu? Or the civil restrictions set by

Hammurabi's Code, or the refusals implicated in the Law of Moses, or the moral issues established by the Christian canons? Restriction, restriction and restriction! This is all these social indicators give!

"So this leads us to the set of principles laid down by Jesus on the Mount. He was getting closer to the Truth than those who preceded him, but his laws were merely for the unfoldment of the social conscience, sweetened for the listeners' ears in another fashion. What he said was simply that you must do it my way or you do not enter Heaven!

"Buddha said that everything lay in the middle path, and eventually you would become the Buddha. The middle path is the weak path, and the Buddha is the way through the mind.

"The way is neither to the right, nor to the left, nor is it through the MAHANTA, the Living ECK Master. It is not below you or above you but it is here; the way to enter into the Far Country.

"Christ said that the way into the Kingdom of Heaven, meaning the Far Country, was within. But he was wrong. He said again in the Gospel of John that He was the Way, as the Christ. And again I say that he was wrong!

"Now I tell you," Rebazar Tarzs emphasized with his left forefinger. "The way into Heaven IS! This is what I can tell you in so many words—this and this alone, for it is the same as saying that God IS! You recall that this is said time and again, in every language of the human race.

"Therefore the way into the God realm IS; I will illustrate this by saying that Is or Isness means now, existence and spiritual reality. I say to you, explain speech to the homo sapiens. You can try every possible way to explain what speech is. You call it sound, words, vocabulary, but it doesn't make sense. Neither does the Way make sense, when I say that it IS.

31

"It can best be explained by saying that it is sound. The human element can do without sight, smell, feeling, touch, but it can't do without sound. This is also true of Soul. The whole principle of Soul is founded upon sound—and this sound is the way to Heaven.

"Jesus spoke of this sound current as being that which supplies the Earth world with everything needed for living, when he spoke of the lilies by the road. They toiled not, nor spun not for their beauty, yet they succeeded in being beautiful!

"This is the way into the Far Country! This is the path which one must follow, yet not one organized religion teaches that the divine sound is the existence in all universes. No priest recognizes it in this world.

"This is a part of the ignorance of the priestcraft. The Christian Church, in playing its part in world history, destroyed the political power of the ancient Roman emperors and established its Pope as the leading exponent of western religious leadership. The church has held this position since its establishment over a thousand years ago.

"It has survived schisms when other groups broke off from the mother church and tried to establish similar power; but it has always come back stronger because the Church recognizes that as long as it can control the social conscience of the Christian society, it can rule. The Hindu Brahman rulers recognized this centuries ago, and as a result founded the caste system in India which made them the highest of the social classes. Buddha set a precedent by trying to break this system of the Brahman priests; he wanted to make all his followers Buddhis like himself, which wasn't at all possible.

"So as usual, when Soul is implanted within the body and cannot leave, it turns to cunning and politics. Buddhism evolved into a church like Christianity and so have the Moslems, along with a half hundred other esoteric groups whose leaders believed that it was easier to be a ruler in religion and live off the people.

32

"Just like the politicians do!

"You are right if you believe that I am being critical of religions, or rather, the groups of religions, philosophies and cultures which today parade themselves under the wide banners of faith. It would be ridiculous to deny this.

"As you grow older in your observation of the peoples of this Earth world, it becomes more noticeable that stupidity is the reigning virtue. The masses are always willing that somebody takes the responsibility of caring for them. This lack of self-dependence is brought about by the need of a father-symbol, hence the seeking out of a masculine deity, and later a feminine deity which is called the mother goddess.

"This is the key to the religions. The need of a father, or mother godhead in order to give service and adoration in the form of worship. The priests, who discovered this in the early dawn of history on earth, encouraged the primitive tribes to obey certain rules and follow set patterns of rituals and rites.

"If you know enough about religions, it will be observed that the codes and laws of each individual group have a positive and negative effect. That is, you are promised a reward provided you obey the codified rules of the church; however, if you are at all neglectful of the rules, you are promised a punishment.

"Christianity says you can burn for eternity; some of the Hindu religions say you can be returned to the lower form of animal life. Other religions have you sent back into a stone, or mineral form.

"This is a pretty rough way of saying that you have to behave and get along with the church or you will be an outcast; to be an outcast from the church is a social evil. What this amounts to is something pretty simple—it is a socialization of the various groups of people in this world.

"If you do understand this, then you know that religions are hardly anything more than man made, and that the priests are certainly not appointed by anything other than themselves. A long history and tradition behind a family,

33

church or state seems to insure that it's right. Buddhism, which is the oldest of the modern religions, is far from truth, although it has a grand history and tradition. This is true also of Christianity, Confucianism, the Upanishads and a few hundred more.

"I don't find that you can put your finger on anything until you adopt the viewpoint of being the ECK, ITSELF. When you learn the balance of your being within IT, and IT within the center of yourself, then you are not questioning your relationships with people, nor concerned with social institutions, forms and functions of human groups.

"When you have discovered that the social conscience is not a part of Soul, you are freed from karma, adharma,* and reincarnation. You will instantly drop the mind body and enter into the plane of Sach Khand. Something else you will find to be true, is that the lords of the various planes throughout the whole grand divisions of the universes are no longer in power as far as you are concerned.

"They will continue to rule those Souls who need the father-mother symbol to lean upon. For you, this is no longer true. It's as if you had outgrown the president of your country, and he needed you, but you had no need of him, whatsoever. This being true, you are independent, you can come and go wherever you wish, anywhere in the Far Country.

"The lack of social conscience does wonders for Soul. It is the key to longevity in the human body. A true master has little conscience toward the social virtues and ethics of this world, factors which the priests and ministers of the church seem to hold so dearly.

"The masculine principle cares little about social conscience, while on the other hand the feminine principle is the promoter and the progressor of this aspect of Earthly life. This is why law and order is a prominent part of any society. No spiritual traveler is foolish enough to let himself get entangled with a set of laws on any plane; law and order,

---

*Adharma—wickedness.

as I told you previously, is a negative system. You must understand that law and order survives on every plane, until you enter the Alakh Lok, and progress upward until you reach the world of the SUGMAD.

"This formless thing I call ECK, which previously was called the Advaita, or formless, which is the name the Hindu religion gives it, fills the very ethers of the world in a fluid state, and is a life giving sound, that we know as the ECK. IT has no laws, no interest in anything except to obey the will of those who use IT. Beyond the Sach Khand world, IT becomes so sensitive that even the thought of Soul will have effect and IT rushes instantly to obey.

"Spiritual travelers who have entered into this world know this and become sensitively careful of their feelings. People in lower worlds have no understanding of this. These higher worlds of the first Grand Division are not worlds of thought, but rather of feeling and assumption, working under that grand quality called the divine imagination.

"These are the only qualities that Soul must preserve in order to be an inhabitant of these worlds. In the psychic and physical worlds, man rushes from event to event and is controlled by circumstances; in these worlds he, or rather the Tuza, becomes the controller of Its own destiny, as Henley said in his poem, "I am the master of my fate, the Captain of my Soul!' This is true when you reach the Alakh Lok world, and care must be taken to manage the imagination, lest it run wild and send Soul hurtling again into the lower worlds.

"Take back to the world what you will of my teachings, but be certain that you include the basic factor which I give you; that man is a social animal when his consciousness occupies the body—but when he lifts it out of this world into the upper stratum and drops the social conscience, he becomes Soul, the ECK, ITSELF.

"If I have never given you other than this, nor give you another piece of truth, this would suffice for the rest of your days in the Earth world. But like all ECK Masters, you will never be happy until reaching the end of the journey.

"Yet listen. The world of the ECKANKAR is an endless universe, for there is what might be called the plus element within it. You never will find its ending. It is too vast for words, too vast for feeling, and too vast for imagination.

"Spirit or ECK is the working instrument for that which we call the SUGMAD. What is the SUGMAD?

"That which we call the SUGMAD is an unknown quality. Many mystics, Plotinus, Meister Eckhart, St. Teresa of Avila, St. John of the Revelations, Farid Al-Din Attar, Jalal-din'l Rumi, and many others never got near the SUGMAD. They believed that their mystical experience got them near IT, but they hardly touched the world of Alakh Lok, if at all.

"These mystics, as well as those who wrote the Bible, the Buddhist texts, and the Upanishads believed in authority. In the Bhagavad-Gita there is a line which goes something like this 'Worship me with a leaf, a flower, but worship me!' This is what Krishna, the Christ of India, says to Arjuna, his disciple. This is authority speaking.

"The spiritual traveler who seeks the authority of the SUGMAD or God, whatever name you wish to call IT, is on the path to failure. No one, who knows anything about the Far Country, will attempt to look for authority anywhere, be it on this Earth plane or be it in the worlds beyond, in the Far Country.

"Gasset y Ortega, the Spanish philosopher and statesman, came closer to the truth when a few years ago he wrote in one of his many books, 'Man is being forced by his nature to seek some higher authority. If he succeeds in finding it of himself, he is the superior man; if not, he is a mass-man, and must receive it from his superiors. To exist in a community, men must harmonize their desires; some kind of general equalibrium has to prevail. Men who leave the inner check, as Babbitt called it, must therefore submit to an outer one; they become mass-men, ruled by their superiors.

'A man without the interior armor of value has no defense against the pressures of his society. It is precisely the loss of value which has turned the inner directed person of the nineteenth century to the outer directed automaton of today.'

"This is what one Soul inhabiting a body said a few years ago. He was a spiritual traveler who had gathered his knowledge from a plane far inside the Far Country. But what he said was truth, and you cannot deny that all seek authority; even the mystics have sought authority, this being the security which all religions hold up to mankind on this earth plane and up to the plane of the SUGMAD.

"The history of the saints in the Catholic church is filled completely with the worship of Christ in many forms; the husband of the virginal nun, the Christ child, the redeemer, the avenger, lover, father and way-shower. He is in a million forms for the saint, mystic and well-meaning Christian.

"Naturally, God appears to all men in the same fashion, regardless of their faith and religion. Those who seek the unknown quality have experiences which are far out of this world, to use the vernacular expression. Experiences are worthless; you can have them for a rupee a dozen, or in the thousands if necessary, but what is the use of such?

"Nothing whatsoever. Man is still working with the social conscience. Let me give you the example of Catherine of Sienna, fourteenth century saint, who did so much good work in Italy for her people. This is all well and good, but it is still in the field of social conscience, and that is not what the spiritual traveler seeks.

"The true spiritual traveler, regardless of what anybody says in any of the planes here or in the Far Country, doesn't seek mystic experiences, nor to better himself, nor is he interested in people or working for Soul.

"He backs away instantly from any authority whatsoever. He calls upon none, not even the SUGMAD, for aid in anyway, for he knows that it depends upon himself to solve the issues which he must face anywhere, here or in the Far Country.

"You ask me to explain what he is after?

"Certainly, sir. He looks forward to complete freedom,

and he is aware that only the SUGMAD can give him this unknown freedom. It does come in the sense that it is granted outright; it is not something which you may have by entering into a certain room. It is none of these at all, only the opportunity of reaching this high world where Freedom is. Continuing to dwell there brings this quality of the SUGMAD for the very word in the language of ECK means carte blanch, liberty, liberation and independence. In the name of freedom, this is freedom, the very essence of release from all encumbered qualities.

"You do not give up the yoke, as Christ said in the New Gospel, for there is none to surrender. The SUGMAD is not a superior being or thing in a sense to take on any of your burdens, none whatever, nor is IT that which gives you blessings.

"This basic freedom can best be described as similar to the bird who has power over the kingdom of the air. You, suddenly, discover that this same freedom is instilled within you, Soul. You have the power over all things, wisdom beyond understanding and freedom that is more than you can comprehend.

"These three qualities are what you have been seeking, and they are gained upon entering the World of the SUGMAD; Power, Wisdom and Freedom."

* * *

Rebazar Tarzs left off here and prepared some tea. We drank silently in the white light of the noon sun upon the walls and roof of the mud hut. It could have been 120 degrees from the heat that poured into the place, but he never seemed to be affected. Not a drop of perspiration showed on that smooth, swarthy face. I wondered about him in this lonely outpost far from civilization.

"What do you do with yourself?" I questioned.

The question seemed to surprise him. "I have guests frequently, like yourself, who are interested in knowing something of the worlds beyond, or I have discussions with those travelers we call the saints. Sometimes trips are made into unknown regions of the Far Country. Yes, there are worlds yet to be explored on that side, as well as some lands in the lower worlds, including the planets and parts of the earth.

"I have also used this way station for many Souls wishing to cross over from this material world into the Far Country. From this hut I have sent out messages to others to change the minds of those who wish to destroy certain areas of the earth world for their own gain.

"Yes, I've been very busy here." He waved his left hand at the bare room.

Its furnishings were little more than a small fireplace, where hung a kettle, and a cot in one corner which looked as though it had never been slept upon. The window on my left had no pane nor any covering. The hot sunlight poured through. The door was without a covering.

The place was simply a shelter with a roof overhead. I commented on this, but he smiled and made no answer.

"Freedom is what man seeks throughout his search for the SUGMAD," he said, slowly shaking his great head. "Hardly a Soul seems to understand this in the lower worlds. Basic freedom consists in having the possession of a will which can be exercised at one's own discretion.

"This will can never be taken away or tampered with at its source. It can be killed by reducing Soul to a sublevel; or if Soul is imprisoned in a world of hell, it will exist in a minor form.

"Reaching the world of the SUGMAD gives a freedom which is the fulfillment of independence from any restraint whatever. This is a condition which encourages and allows for active exercise of the will. No outside interference is possible to change the course of the will for freedom through the SUGMAD, once it has determined its goal.

"The World of SUGMAD is beyond explanation. None can tell you of its beauty and wonders, only the results upon the Soul which enters into it and the qualities which are gained. This is a world of pure spirit and the Tuza, that gains a place here, becomes pure spirit only.

"IT, the SUGMAD, is the sovereign lord with whom the saints have to collaborate in carrying out their sacred missions of giving the right instructions to Tuzas who wish to enter into this world.

"Many believe that IT is the great Father, the Supreme Guru, and the Light Giver. What you might say, in trying to simplify the idea of this unknown quality we call God, or X, that which we know as the SUGMAD, is that IT is Soul Itself."

"What do I mean by this statement?"

He pounded the earth with his left fist to emphasize his point. "Now listen to me very closely! This is the essence of ECKANKAR, the whole of the truth.

"There is no God as known by the Christians, Jews, Jains, Buddhists, Taoism, or a half hundred other religions in the earth world and the fourth grand division of the spiritual worlds that make up the realm of God. This includes the Sukhsham Desh, Brahm Lok, Daswan Dwar, Bhanwar Gupha and Sach Khand worlds.

"Nobody knows within these worlds what the true deity is. They have no understanding and because all must lean upon authority, each plane has a mocked-up God, conjured out of the imagination of the inhabitants of those worlds over periods of time.

"You may not believe this but the example of the Gods that existed in the physical world can be cited, e.g., the Greek Gods—Zeus, Hermes, and the host of Olympian deities who ruled that world. They were as real as you and I, in a sense, because man had made them. They existed as long as the Greeks believed in them, but when St. Paul who combined an effete Judaism and confused Christianity, founded a re-constructed Judaism which went into history as Christianity with Jesus as the world God and savior, all other Gods died.

"He broke the hold which the imagination held upon the Greeks and Romans, and established his own image for the peoples of the western world. He preached a religion which had a little of everything in it, including the Hindu, the old Greek, Mithra, Roman and others until it became one.

"This is how all religions are established, through the

imagination of the followers. The priest establishes the image, and holds it before the people to worship.

"Billions of years ago there was a mighty deity called the SUGMAD, known to all the great races of the world. This deity was so powerful that IT forbade the worship of ITSELF as God. IT lived in that world beyond the reaches of all mankind, but IT appeared often upon the physical plane to prove that IT was a living being.

"During ITS sojourn upon this plane, IT explained carefully to the leaders of the races that IT existed because they allowed IT to exist. Otherwise, IT had no form, no shape nor any faculties which could be used in transmitting ITS ideas to men unless they furnished IT with them.

"In other words, IT could manifest to men provided they would make use of their imagination; it was only through this faculty that IT came to this plane. If enough would believe and concentrate upon IT, there would be a matrix, or rather a mold, formed in the psychic world, reaching up through the planes into ITS world. IT would use this as a channel and come through it to manifest upon earth to men.

"The SUGMAD is part of every Soul. IT is the sacred faculty in men which is called the imagination. This is the divine spark in all Tuzas—and it is that part which can draw the SUGMAD down to earth or take Soul up to the SUGMAD.

"This is the great secret which I give you!

"These leaders of men in the lower world wanted to know how IT could walk among them and teach them. So IT gave them the divine quality, the imagination, by taking a little of ITSELF and placing it within each man.

"The great SUGMAD returned to ITS home in the Heavenly world when IT had finished with ITS work, and found to ITS disadvantage that IT had given away so much of ITSELF that little was left. Now it was a question of having it returned or IT would not be able to exercise the full ability of creation which IT possessed.

"IT possessed this up until the time that it was divided

41

among men, then IT retired into the heavenly world of the Far Country, watching over all affairs of those creatures in every plane from this physical earth to ITS own.

"I speak with forked tongue in saying that IT doesn't possess ITS full ability of creation and that again IT does possess it. It is put this way for you.

"The SUGMAD made all creation, and divided up ITS creative ability with each creature. By doing so, IT lost a certain amount of ITS godly powers, but if IT wishes, this power can be regained in a sense by withdrawing it from each Tuza; yet, to do so would destroy the Tuza. This is the only thing which the Tuza possesses that gives it a divine spark of power.

"Therefore, if you are following me closely, you can see that the SUGMAD cannot do without ITS own creation, the Tuza, nor can the Tuza do without the SUGMAD.

"It was for this very reason that when the leaders of the lower worlds discovered the true secret of themselves, a fight between them and the SUGMAD was begun, in hopes of overthrowing IT. They created Gods for the lower worlds and put them upon the thrones of each plane for the people to follow. This has nothing to do with what the Christians call the Devil and his demons.

"This is the truth of the imaginary faculty. IT discovered ITS mistake soon after man began to work with the imaginary faculty, and used it for destruction and the making of material things for man's own particular use. The SUGMAD went to work and completely drove man and his woman out of the beautiful Astral world into the universe of this existence.

"Here man struggles and fights to re-enter into the world of the Far Country, but little does he know what the essence of his nature is. He is controlled through the priestcraft, the materialists and those who claim to have leadership in education and in the society of civilized nations.

"Others control his imagination faculty. He has no chance to develop it toward the makings of a channel for the SUGMAD, which it was supposed to be in the beginning. Instead,

those who preach hardly know the true meaning of the Godhead. They preach unknowingly the love of the material—
and that their savior died on a cross to save them from sin.

"An ignorant belief, to say the least.

"If you have full understanding of the mechanics of the
imaginary faculty and the use of it, you can enter into the
Kingdom of the SUGMAD, the highest in the Far Country.

"You can become part of the SUGMAD, ITSELF, and you
then become All Powerful and All Wise, like the SUGMAD.
You are able to exercise the same Freedom.

*   *   *

"Can you imagine the lower worlds being created by
the creatures of the SUGMAD's own creation?

"This is just about what happened during the early ages
of this planet. After the people became able to use the divine spark of life within themselves, this planet began to
take shape and was formed into a piece of material cosmos.

"It became this way when the SUGMAD let go the divine spark of life and it fell upon the earth like the morning
dew. This is illustrated in the old Bible when the Tribe of
Israel awoke one morning to find the desert covered with
manna. This is an allegory of the divine imagination being flung from heaven upon the earth, for man, in his blind
stumbling, to seize and use for his holy purpose.

"It is said that the SUGMAD called upon a deva* to carry
his mirror of divine imagination across the fields of heaven
to another part of the Far Country. While strolling along the
starry path the deva stumbled and broke the mirror into a
million tiny pieces. The pieces of divine imagination fell
upon the world of people, and were found by the luckier ones.

"Some never found these pieces and to this day are without any spark of imagination in themselves. Of course this
is only a wonderful fable, in a sense, for all those who

—————

*Deva—Angel.

43

walk the planets of this universe are blessed with the holy, divine spark of imagination. It is that many never learn how to use it within themselves.

"The way of the divine path is therefore through the imaginative faculty. This is the secret path, the divine roadway to the SUGMAD, the royal road of the ECK Masters. It has many names, and its simplicity makes it complicated.

"The imaginative channel can be a forked path or it can be a straight road into the far world of the SUGMAD. It can be the negative path of the material world, or the positive path of the spiritual world. Regardless, it is the path which all people take, and it is the only way which the spiritual travelers use in their upward climb into the Far Country.

"The attitude and assumption constitute, of course, the principles which have been laid down before you. One must assume that he is going to stay with the spiritual and adopt the attitude that it is the right thing for him to do. He will become the highest of spiritual travelers throughout the whole of the Far Country by doing this.

"Travel in the Far Country is assumed by the use of the spiritual eye, or what is known as the Tisra Til. This is the third eye, a point in the subtle body, just above the pineal gland between the physical eyes. At this center, the spiritual travelers begin their concentration and from that they go upward into the many planes of the Far Country.

"It is here that the attention is gathered into a single concentration and the imagination sends it forth into the worlds above, releasing the Nuri-Sarup, the light body, which goes out into the subjective worlds alone. The attention of the spiritual traveler is shifted from the objective to the subjective and it goes traveling outward into the other worlds under control of the operator.

"The body is left in a deep trance. This trance is often in the form of a deep sleep and, if awakened by some unusual noise or by another person entering the room and speaking, it is liable to be killed by the shock, or put into a state of deep insensitivity from which it could take days to recover.

"Often the body is guarded by another, for as in the case of Ramakrishna, it may be days before Soul returns to claim Its body. Meanwhile it has to be washed, fed and cared for; so the disciples who know the art of spiritual traveling can do the proper things for the body, without injury to it or the spirit which occupies it.

"If you are working through the channels of sleep it is needful to take care of the body. Many have died from the shock of something which occurred while outside the body during sleep and the medical physicians of the material plane have claimed heart attack or death from unknown causes.

"It is as easy to leave the body asleep, as when awake. The traveler lies down in bed, puts his imaginative attention upon a series of images he wants to occur. He knows when the body is asleep, so he steps out and travels on a certain plane—if he wants to go into another plane he goes through the same process again.

"Projection out of the body during the sleep state is done in the following manner. First, you lie quietly on the back, with the eyes closed and throw your thoughts outward into that world where you wish to be.

"You may not have ever been there previously, but you may mockup what it looks like and put yourself into the center of it. You must have a full perception of what goes on around you: have the feeling, smell, sight, taste and hearing of what environs are on the plane you wish to be. Make the picture perfectly and stay with it; gradually you will drop off to sleep, and suddenly you are aware that you are standing in the center of the world to which you have travelled.

"Do not be alarmed for this projection is simple. Always remember that the basic principle in the next worlds is that you can change everything in the twinkle of an eye. The ethers of the astral and mental worlds respond swiftly to thought—and you must be careful of how you think while

45

moving about in these planes. The higher you go, the swifter the vibrations of the thought manifestation.

"For example, if you are moving along the pathway of the causal world, which you know as the Brahm Lok, and your thoughts suddenly concentrate upon a certain amount of money for the physical body left behind you—when you return it would be lying beside the body. Sounds very strange doesn't it, but this is how so many of the travelers manifest opulence. This is why the holy ones shun wealth as a class because they know how easy it is to get. To work like the rest of the human race is something to be scorned. This is why the saints and magicians laugh at the preachers and priests of religions. The latter ones know little more than cunning tricks to get money out of people to serve their own purposes. But the spiritual travelers have the knowledge and ability to manifest it out of the ECK current. Yet they seldom will for there is a price to pay for this.

"The high sounding ideals which the earth religions preach about hardly can be right. Therefore, if the very thought of Souls rules the first three worlds, how can religions establish ideals based upon what they call morals. Anyone can establish a cult, religion or sect, provided they have the energy, belief and the knowledge of how this mind power works in the first three worlds.

"Those so called mystics and saints of the Catholic church, or other faiths have hardly put themselves above the three worlds. They believe Brahm Lok to be the paradise, the heavenly world where all Souls will find their good reward, where St. Peter stands at a golden gate welcoming all who have earned the right to enter into the world of goodness, where the recording angel has all the deeds one has ever thought or done, upon the eternal records.

"Naturally this exists for the Christians on the Brahm Lok plane, likewise for the Buddhists, the Taoists and all other faiths, for each over a period of ages have built a heavenly world for its faithful where they shall go after the death of the physical body.

46

"This death of the physical body is nothing, but so much emphasis is placed upon it by the human race. The spiritual medium, although a negative receiver of those on the far side of the curtain, brings much truth about the Tuzas which have gone to the heavenly world. Some spirits do come through a spiritual medium and speak to those who wish to listen. However, you must be very careful for it can well be the speaker is not who he represents himself to be. A good test is to ask him personal questions about things that you both had together while on this earth plane, e.g., you can ask a close relative about some intimate and personal relationship which only he would know, other than yourself.

"It takes energy to keep one intact and traveling through the spiritual worlds. The human body is a fine cone of energy consisting of atoms spinning from right to left—if you could see this with your psychic eye, this would be the way your body would appear. Soul is a much finer vibration of atoms spinning and since it's not so hard to move these atoms, it means the energy will stay there throughout all eternity. Pretty messy for the SUGMAD when Soul reaches the real heavenly world, isn't it?

"I mean that IT is filling up ITS world with these spinning tops, so it seems. Not at all, for the higher Soul goes up the path toward the World of the SUGMAD, the finer becomes Its vibrations and the less it will be found that It spins, that is the vibratory rate of the Soul body. In this world It is almost a viewpoint—hardly anything more.

"So many think Soul is hardly anything more than a static piece of atomic mechanism. This isn't true. The manner in which Soul exists as an entity is through the vibratory rates of Its light body, and It can live throughout eternity in this manner for It is self perpetuating. It is like the self-winding clock which can never run down, and since Soul is a miniature of the SUGMAD, you can get an idea of what this great Being is.

"I cannot explain to you any more than this. Occasionally I will give you a view upon this magnificent Entity, but to explain what and who the SUGMAD is in a straight dialectical lecture is impossible.

"We are going to break off here and get some tea. Later I'll take up the subject of the Disinterested Works which you will find to be extremely important in your study of the spiritual works in your journeys throughout the Far Country."

Chapter 3

THE DISINTERESTED WORKS

The movement of the sunlight upon the mountains during the day is one of the most fascinating phenomenons of nature for me. I love the sunlight, and though often in the hot, tropical countries it may become the enemy of man, it is still a part of this physical universe which attracted me to the world.

The great snow-packed peaks, now blue in the haze that had settled over the Hindu Kush, were to the north and south of the mud hut. Lonely against the cobalt sky they were a tug at my emotions, for the scene was a reminder of those days spent in the Pacific Northwest United States.

Somewhere among those awful gorges and upflung masses of rock was hidden a cold spring of water known as the Nirmala Charan* or sometimes called the Waters of Immortality. It lies close to the headwaters of the Jhelum river.

I spoke to Rebazar Tarzs of these strange waters which were supposedly a fountain of youth and often word drifted out to the civilized world about them. Many had come to this part of the globe seeking but only a few knew of the location and still fewer ever found the Nirmala Charan.

"The Nirmala Charan," he said, musingly, in his deep voice. "Yes, I know where it lies hidden back in the mountains. Only those who are capable of practicing the disinterested works may find it.

"Among the people of this region a legend has been circulated which has more truth than the tale bearers realize.

"Alexander, the Greek conqueror, made a march over the Hindu Kush range down through the Khyber and through the lands spread out before him like a picture post card.

---

*Nirmala—Pure water.

49

"After that crossing, he gave orders to his soothsayers to find the fountain of youth. They went forward and found by the Jhelum's headwaters far back in the mountains a cold spring which was the Nirmala Charan; here they made a sacrifice and studied the sacred signs. The signs were propitious. So they hurried with a skin of the precious waters to the camp of Alexander on the plains of Peshawar.

"Alexander raised the skin to his mouth and was about to drink when a toothless man with gnarled, thin hands and sunken face came forward, shouting. The ancient one prostrated himself before Alexander and then cried out: 'O King, if you drink that water you'll be like me—too old to live, too old to die. I drank some several hundred years ago. Look at me!'

"Many spiritual travelers know the site of these wondrous waters but none discloses it to the world for if they did the precious spring would no longer exist. So many would visit the place that someone would put a fence around it and sell the water, before it dried out and became nonexistent.

"A fable to many who hear it, but nevertheless true. The old man was a spiritual traveler who wanted to protect and keep the spring hidden from the eyes of the profane. Disguising himself as an old man, this friend of the spiritual Tuzas appeared before Alexander the Great and halted the act of what might have been an onslaught to find the waters of immortality.

"This spiritual traveler is still living in the same body in these mountains. He is over three thousand years of age. Perhaps I will take you to him someday. You will learn much by sitting at his feet.

"Now the disinterested works are those of the balanced mind. The spiritual seeker becomes indifferent to all things, to all of this life he lives in the physical world. The Zen-Buddhists have a good expression for it; after experiencing

50

the satori* you die in the flesh and become reawakened in the spirit. For the rest of your physical life on earth, you are dead, and when you die, life is reawakened.

"You surrender to that divine spark of the SUGMAD within, and from that moment onward you are moved by IT, sustained by IT and live in IT. All else has no importance to your life.

"This is the act of non-attachment to which the Bhagavad-Gita gives so much emphasis. Lord Krishna tells Arjuna this: 'But the disciplined self, moving among sense objects, with the senses free from attraction and repulsion (interested only as a spectator of the passing show), mastered by the Self (Supreme) he goeth to victory'.

"There are five destructive passions. They are: Kama, Krodha, Lobha, Moha and Ahankara. First, Kama, or lust is a normal function allowed to run an abnormal demand where it becomes abnormal desire. It may include drugs, alcoholic drinks, tobacco, or even foods which are eaten for the sake of their taste.

"The chief function of Kama is to pull men down to the common animal level and keep them there. It obliges them to fix their attention on that which is common to both man and brute.

"It is a principle of psychology that whatever the mind concentrates upon, that thing becomes a part of the individual.

"Second, Krodha is anger. Its action is to stir up strife, cause confusion and scatter the mind so that it cannot concentrate. It destroys peace, engenders hatred and turns individuals and groups into enemies, solely for the purpose of destruction.

"Some of the signs of Krodha are: slander, evil gossip, backbiting, profanity, fault-finding, jealousy, malice, impatience, resentment, mockery, destructive criticism, and ill will. Anger is mental carcinoma.

---

*Satori—Enlightenment.

"Third, Lobha is greed. The function of greed is to bind us to material things, and cloud the mind to all higher values. It is the most poisonous of all the unholy five passions. As Kama binds man to the animal plane, and Krodha to the mental plane, so Lobha binds man to the mineral plane. it makes a worship of the commercial gods of gold and silver.

"Some of the signs of Lobha are: Miserliness, lying, hypocrisy, perjury, misrepresentation, robbery, bribery and trickery of all sorts.

"Fourth, Moha is attachment, meaning delusive attachment, infatuation. This is the most insidious, the most deceitful of them all. It creeps upon its victims, like the others, or it comes with flares of trumpets like the tamash that goes before the approach of the king. But it generally comes with the appearance of well dressed respectability, of noble bearing and good credentials. It can announce itself as your ally and friend and its ideals are plausible.

"Moha begins its deadly work under the guise of a most respectable friend. Its method is to blind you to the relative values of your surroundings and associations so that you may begin to set false valuation upon them. After you have become absorbed in them, then you will have no time for anything else. This is exactly the purpose of Moha. You are kept forever on the go, most of the time between work. Moha takes you from your spiritual traveling.

"Hence Moha is the channel of procrastination. It involves you in everything possible to keep your time on nothingness, so you can become a slave to it, become attached to it.

"The main signs of Moha are worries, anxieties and business complications. None of these have any importance in the Far Country, so you shouldn't be bothered with them here.

"Fifth, is Ahankara, vanity, the last of the deadly five. The word Ahankara has two meanings. First, it is the faculty of the mind which gives the power of awareness of the Soul, self-differentiation, the I-ness. It is that faculty which executes the mandates of the Buddhi, or the SUGMAD, in the interest of self. But the abnormal exaggeration of this faculty becomes the Ahankara, which is vanity, or self-admiration.

"Ahankara has a thousand claws by which to dig into the minds of its victims. Its deadly poison infiltrates the entire being. Beginning generally in infancy, it seldom ceases to operate until the death of the body and then it can still carry on, until Soul shakes it off in some manner or by the help of a teacher.

"It is the work of self-righteousness which makes it so strong. It is the last of the five deadly passions to surrender. Its method is to distort the view point, to present everything out of proportion, to make itself the center of the world. It destroys all sense of humor.

"Some of the phases of Ahankara are: bigotry, self-assertion, obtrusive show of wealth or power, bossiness, scolding, faultfinding, liking publicity, making a show of religion, and being noisy about giving to charity."

*   *   *

"The disinterested works include the karma-less actions," said Rebazar Tarzs staring at me with his flashing black eyes. "I will show you how karma binds man in the first three planes of the spiritual universe. I can also show you that it is possible to escape from creating karma.

"There is no escape from karma, for once it is created and the debt is incurred, it must be paid. But there is a way of living without creating karma. You know that all living beings in the first three planes of this universe create karma by every act of their lives. Even the Bhagavad-Gita says that inactivity itself creates karma, and no one can escape it. But there is always a way of escaping it. What is that way?

"By acting always in the name of the SUGMAD.

"The SUGMAD itself is karmaless. So is the saint who has followed this principle until he has worked out his karma by living in such a way as not to create further karma. You can enter into the same plane of exalted heights through the same actions.

"This principle once applied gives Soul freedom. It

can meet and satisfy all of its own karma, by the aid of the SUGMAD, and after that rise above the action of the karmic law. As long as you remain in the three lower worlds, you are subjected to this karmic law, unless you follow out the principle of karma-less action.

"Then you are no longer subject to this law, because you have risen above the plane of its action. You are free from the laws of all regions where karma operates, and you will never again be bound by that law.

"All that the spiritual traveler does, is now done in the name of the SUGMAD. He seeks to return the divine spark as his sacrifice to the holy altar of the Far Country. He has no desires of his own, and does nothing without the full approval of the SUGMAD; all he does is constructive. If he made any karma at all, even if such a thing were possible, it would be good karma; and good karma elevates you.

"Now, if you wish to escape the creation of karma of any sort, then whatever you do, must be done in the name of the SUGMAD, while acting as his agent. So long as you do that, you will not create new karma, because you are acting solely as the agent of another, and always the principal is responsible for the acts of his agent.

"You must do this not merely in a ceremonial way, but with your entire thought and Soul in it. In deep earnest, you must let yourself do all things, every detail of your life, in the name of the SUGMAD. This will, by necessity, oblige you to do only what you think the SUGMAD intends for you to do.

"This is the psychology which is a part of the philosophy of ECKANKAR. Do every action in the name of the SUG-MAD, and you have no responsibility toward any living creature in the lower worlds, under the plane of the SUG-MAD.

"When you approach a task, or a proposed act, you will remember that it is to be done in the name of the SUGMAD.

You will fix your mind merely on the name of the SUGMAD, and in sincerity it will be done as a genuine service.

"The SUGMAD does not. The catalytic agent is the ECK power which works between you and the SUGMAD. It carries out your action relieving you of the responsibility which would otherwise have settled upon your shoulders.

"You must remember that nothing is your own. All belongs to the SUGMAD, because all creation belongs to the greatest deity, and you use your body, mind and Soul as the property of the SUGMAD. The main point I am making here is that if you use your mind and your body and possessions in the name of the SUGMAD, you are not creating any karma.

"Essentially it is the SUGMAD acting and not you. You are merely the agent of the SUGMAD, while at the same time the SUGMAD is your agent. So long as you are acting sincerely and whole-heartedly as the agent of the SUGMAD, it is really the SUGMAD who is acting as your agent.

"Gopal Das, noted ECK Master, said that if you give all, you will get all. In this saying there is wisdom and a great promise. It means that if you give up all, mind, body, wealth and Soul to the SUGMAD, the SUGMAD must by ITS own law serve you in return. You will receive riches that surpass all else on earth, and in exchange for this, you will gain a freedom that makes you master of limitless worlds. It is not the SUGMAD that wants you or your mind or body or property. It is for your benefit alone that the SUGMAD asks you to dedicate the one thing IT wants returned—the divine spark, the faculty of imagination, so that IT can become whole again.

"Instead you give up all this divine spark of imagining. This you must never do, for you are a part of IT, and IT is not your own. You must always be yourself, your real self regardless of all else—and become in the end a co-worker with the SUGMAD.

55

"You will find the SUGMAD will always keep you near, work for you, never let you make mistakes. IT never lets you go, for IT knows what is best and correct in every possible emergency. In no sense is your personal liberty ever circumscribed or limited, for you are more free than ever before. You have no fear of anything; you go where you wish and do what you like with the most perfect assurance.

"Here is a divine paradox—by surrendering all to the SUGMAD, you gain your liberty. For your will exercised in the right direction is the will of the Supreme SUGMAD. And that is really the secret of this whole matter.

"I will point out here before finishing this discussion on the karmaless actions that there are two different administrations of karma—that of Kal and of Dayal*. You and Dayal are the same, and both refer to the Supreme Being, the Lord of the infinite universe. Kal is the lord of karma for this world and all regions up to the second division which is called Trikuti.

"Karma is administered by him in the great bulk of humanity. In fact it is the case of all those who have no teacher on this plane. They follow the routine of society, and karma holds sway over their lives, from age to age.

"From the wheel of karmic destiny there is no escape, except to become one who is a spiritual traveler. But the very moment that you have been initiated into the secrets of the Far Country and can know and practice the ECK, all of your karmic accounts are transferred to the SUGMAD's keeping, automatically passing from the hand of the Negative Power.

"After that you, working under the directions of the ECK, will work in karmaless actions. From that hour forward, the Kal, or negative power, has nothing to do with your karmic debts and has no power or control over you. The agents of death cannot approach you, nor can you ever be called into the courts of the Dharam Raya for judgment. Your

---

*Dayal—The living ECK Master—the MAHANTA.

destiny in this life and in the next rests entirely in your own hands.

"This all sounds strange to you, but it is one of the ancient teachings which has been handed down by word of mouth through the ages. You have received them to pass along to Gail.

"By practicing the good works the spiritual traveler conquers, first, the lower worlds and then the higher worlds. The supreme path called the ECK Marg, is that which is known as the secret path of the sound current.

"The Gita gives a small part of the results of this. It says that he from whom comes no disturbance, who cannot be disturbed by others, who is free from joy, from anger, fear and anxiety; such a one becomes the toast of heaven. He who does not depend on anything, who is pure and active, who does not care whether good comes or evil and who never becomes miserable; who has given up all efforts for himself alone; such a one is heavenward bound.

"A man winneth not freedom from karma by abstaining from action, nor does he, by renunciation, rise to perfection. No one can, for an instant, remain wholly actionless. Helpless is every one in this world, each driven to action which results in nothingness.

"All comes to him who has control of his senses by the mind, with the organs of the senses uninterested in what he does. He is worthy of the SUGMAD.

"I did not give you the correct wording, but rather in my own, so that you would get the meaning.

"The disinterested works are done by the art of indifference.

"Let me point out here the value of training for Soul in its spiritual journeys in the realms of God. As the spiritual traveler, you must learn and know where all the dangers lie, for if you don't there is much trouble to be met.

"The chela may, as an untrained traveler, meet with weird and unusual experiences which are frightening to the core of being. They are mostly the fantasies of the mind! But once you leave the first division and enter into those worlds beyond, it all changes.

"You take control of your destiny."

*   *   *

Rebazar Tarzs became silent for a time. He sat cross legged upon the dirt floor, bending forward while making marks with his left forefinger on it.

After awhile he spoke again. This time he said, "The oldest and biggest question ever propounded to human intelligence is: How does one find God?

"I have just answered that question in speaking about the disinterested works, which are gained by the art of indifference. To be indifferent to anything is to kill it, to destroy it completely. One doesn't know that all things come to an end when attention is withdrawn from it.

"This is interesting because only the disinterested find their way into the Far Country and come to rest at the throne of the SUGMAD. The disinterested are those who have a determination to reach the highest heaven, but care little if they do. They are not disappointed in the many things of life which come their way; they couldn't care less if they didn't have money.

"This is an art that comes only with practice. One might say it is a professional art—to love too much or too little is terrible for the heart, and hard for the emotions. That Soul who does is bound to lose in the long stretch of life, and will hardly get any further than the world of Brahm Lok.

"Man can't be interested in all things at a time. His attention must be centered somewhere, and as long as it is dwelling upon the SUGMAD then it can't be put in other directions. To split the attention is the desire of those enemies who wish to take you away from your goal.

"There is a certain technique about this art of indifference

58

which I find difficult to explain. It's an indifference which comes with the practice of not letting anything reach the core of your being. By putting himself outside of all materialistic and emotional matters, the spiritual traveler can journey through the planes of the Far Country into the highest heaven.

"Let me give you an example. Look at the sea with its great breakers washing up against the shores of the long coast. The sea is pliant; you can pick it up in your hands, throw it on the sands, and beat it, but it still breaks off into drops. It is nothing when you finish with it, but it is still water, the great sea, which made up of many drops, becomes a vast ocean.

"Also there is the wind. What can you do with the wind? Can you catch it in your hands? It cannot be destroyed, nor can it be pierced with a sword. It is like Soul for it never dies, and for this very reason the wind is considered by many ancients as a part of the SUGMAD's breath, or ECK, the spirit.

"This is the way that the center of your very being can be. It can be beaten, lashed, pierced with a sword, submerged in water, and taken to a high peak to be pushed off. But it cannot be destroyed. By knowing this, you become invulnerable like Achilles, who except for his right heel couldn't be killed. He had been dipped in the river Styx but his mother failed to put this heel underwater, and as result he was killed at Troy when shot through the heel by a poisonous arrow.

"You are without a spot which can be vulnerable to the arrows and slings of gossip, or the weapons of war which are flung at you by the enemies of the Far Country. Now there is a way of taking care of these misfortunes and dreary places of the earth life. There is a way by which you become immortal.

"In the world of Daswan Dwar is a river called Mansarover, a stream of the sweet nectar of the heavenly gods which flows out of a lake of the same name. Once you, the spiritual traveler, bathe in this river of immortality, nothing can harm you. This is your insurance against karma, your place among the gods of the universe.

"All those who lived on this earth in those early ages of its development were bathed in this strange river. Hence their long lives, and the factor that they were the gods who walked this earth and were inveigled into marrying the daughters of men; finally they disappeared because they lost their divinity. Not lost it but forgot it, all because the women of the earth whom they married kept telling them that they were not gods but ordinary people.

"The gods came down to the earth and became men. Of themselves, women don't understand that they too could be goddesses, but this they can't understand.

"I'm going off the point for a moment here, to speak about women and the earth plane. Women are responsible for religion. They must have a yardstick or an authority upon which to lean. They act with independence and make believe that all is well with themselves and the world.

"The ancient Greek women were likely better off in their status in life than in these days when there is a supposedly developed equality of social status.

"So much for that.

"The path of indifference which I've been discussing is paradoxical. You have the problem of desire. Buddha probably brought out more about this than any other savior who came to this earth. He taught the art of desirelessness to all his disciples. If you want to be free, have no desires. Do not put possessiveness upon anything of a material or spiritual nature.

"The three lower worlds are fleeting worlds of temporal events. Therefore nothing is lasting in them, nor should anyone put their faith and belief in this world of materialistic nature. Here everything is compounded of parts, and is therefore subject to dissolution. Everything which arises is produced by some cause.

"Desire of course is a part of karma. By desires we are bound to the objects of desire. This is a fixed law of nature on this plane. Whatever you desire begins at once to travel toward you, unless a stronger desire from a different source attracts the attention to it. Attention and love are the means of connecting us with objects external to ourselves. Everything in the universe is subject to Newton's laws of motion. By desires we become lost in this world. Remember that Buddha claimed that desire is the cause of all suffering?

"This is why the complete detachment of self from every worldly object is necessary. It avoids bondage to those things. This is why you should love nothing with a desire to possess. The moment that you do this, desire something material or spiritual, you enter into the first stages of slavery. You shouldn't even desire rewards for your actions. Anyone who looks to rewards will become a slave to such rewards. So long as man craves rewards, he is bound to those rewards and Yin Quo, here I'm using the Chinese word for karma, is his master.

"It is with complete Vairag* that one enters into the world of the SUGMAD. Man must attain this state of mind which is like the sun, shining upon all alike, yet asking nothing in return. Soul lives forever by giving; not by receiving.

"This is the grand paradox, not only of all spiritual thought, but of all that ECK has to offer. You get most by not wanting anything, but working in the same manner only by giving.

"Conversely, by receiving much you impoverish yourself. By selfish accumulation you become bankrupt. As Emerson, the American philosopher, said, 'you run in your own debt.' For in the long run, you can never get something for nothing. Each piece of coin must be repaid, no matter how it is paid, if it isn't earned in the spiritual sense. The law of balance in the spiritual realms is just as inflexible as the law of gravitation. To give and give only, not once thinking of rewards, is the beginning of immortality. No man be-

*Vairag—Mental detachment.

61

comes a Buddha, a Kakusha, a Tathagata or Bodhisattva by fleeing from pain or by seeking comforts or demanding rewards.

"Accept all alike that comes to you, and go on giving, make yourself open to the ECK.

"Sorrow is born of desire. This being truth, then what use is the good for knowledge unless it has a cure for desire itself? To read a book or listen to a lecture on the subject will never remove desire, nor will it alleviate sorrow.

"It is useless to tell any man that he must overcome sorrow. He cannot do it, and would fight if you tried to force him to stop. The mad vortex of desires which is attacking man, in a way of speaking, is keeping him constantly at war with his fellow man, and causing each nation to destroy the other.

"It still remains a fact of history that not one man has ever controlled his senses disinterestedly, just by the power of his will, simply by willing it so. By will power one may hold impulses in check, follow or not follow his desires. But if one is to completely overcome the desires and impulses, he must find something which the mind and Soul likes better.

"It can never be accomplished by negation alone. This supreme need is supplied only by the heavenly bani* melody which is given by the SUGMAD through the ECK.

"Every man comes to this work duly prepared. If he is not so prepared, he will not arrive at this point. It is one game that no man can beat.

"The first requirement is Viveka. This means right discrimination. It simply means that one is to use all of his intelligence properly, he must think long and deep and be able to discriminate between the true and false. Underlying the entire problem will be found certain great and universal truths and principles which should be learned well and kept always in mind.

------

*Bani—Audible life current.

"The most ancient truth is couched in a classical sentence in the Vedic literature. 'Ekam sat vipra bahudha vadanti,' which means when translated 'That which exists is one: sages call it by various names.'

"It teaches there is perfect unity in the Supreme SUG-MAD. All that lives is permeated and vitalized by the one great Being through ECK.

"The other noble concept is 'Tat Tvam Asi' which means 'Thou art that.' Its deeper meaning is that each individual is the Supreme SUGMAD, and that there is no essential difference between the SUGMAD and the individual Soul. Man is the divine spark of imagination linking his being with the SUGMAD. When you reach the Sach Khand plane in the upper areas of the Far Country and behold Sat Nam, you see yourself in Him with overwhelming joy.

"When you reach this point and have found Viveka working within you, there are certain things which will happen within. First, a gathering up of all evil tendencies and a laying them aside for the second point. This second point is concentration, the one pointed mental action, which, when perfected, leads to samadhi, or the beginning of spiritual travel.

"The next step on the path is Vairag, which I've discussed somewhat a few minutes ago. This is the mental detachment of oneself from the external world.

"This doesn't in any way mean that you detach yourself physically from the objective world about you, for you need not leave your family, or private duties. Detachment is not austerities. Vairag means that you are to detach yourself in your affections, in your innermost feelings and interests. This means to cease to identify yourself with your possessions and environment. Don't make them the substances of your life and thought. In other words, you must always keep your own independence of them. This applies to all things.

"But it means this, that you must love with detachment. One may love while keeping his own independence. Then if you lose your possessions, which is always a possibility while living on the earth plane, your life is not utterly wrecked, and at the same time you are able to travel in the Far Country knowing that it is of more importance than all your worldly possessions.

"You cannot be bound up with earthly duties and worldly possessions. You take nothing with you into the Far Country but your own inner possessions which are the qualities that the SUGMAD has given you from your original birth in time and space.

"One cannot assume the attitude of self-righteousness. This automatically defeats his own purpose and nullifies all progress made. He must keep Ahankara, vanity, subdued, and he must allow charity and love of knowledge, power, and strength to have full sway over his thoughts and actions.

"By desire, we are bound to objects of desire. This is why the complete detachment of the mind from every worldly object is necessary, if we are to enter upon the path to the Far Country. That detachment avoids bondage to the world and its objects of sense desire. We should not love anything with a desire to possess it. The moment you do, you enter the first stages of slavery. This applies to a family or goods. But as said before this does not exclude family love. A detached devotion to family may not be so easy, but it can be acquired. A detached love is a much higher and nobler sort of love than that which demands possession, and then that possession goes on to self-identification with the object of one's love. When such identification takes place, one is completely lost. He is not himself anymore and he is less able to even serve the objects of his affections, while he is a slave to them.

"The next step on the path to the Far Country is that which is known as Shanti, or santosha, the peace of self which comes when one is rid of desire.

"The last step in the attainment of perfect Vairag is to get rid of desire itself. This is where many noble men and women have failed, even some great yogis. They could not get rid of desire itself, even after they had separated themselves from all connections with the world. But the real Vairag is not attained until all desire has been overcome.

64

This is perhaps the most difficult of all undertakings. Desire has been declared by those saviors and adepts who have come to this earth world to help others, to be the greatest evil that besets a man on the path of spiritual attainment. Their universal verdict is that desire must be gotten rid of at all costs.

"You gain santosha, by getting rid of desire. If one wants nothing, he has everything. From the days of Buddha to the present, the prevailing teachers in the Orient have taught that desire is the cause of all sorrows and the other ills of man. Hence, the cure of all ills is the destruction of desire. Just how to accomplish this stupendous task has been the great question of all sages.

"Desire has been pictured as a wild beast roaming the country, seeking whom it may devour. It is our worst enemy, the chief instrument of the mind to bind man to this material world. Desire draws us to the object of sense. The senses overwhelm the mind and the mind enslaves Soul. Following desire, the mind goes on creating karma and entangling itself in the net.

"Desire never ceases its demands. It doesn't let man rest, and it follows him into his inner chamber and torments him in the midst of his prayers. It never relents, nor does it ever slacken its chains, or cease to apply the lash, even though the poor victim lies weak and spent upon his deathbed. Even then desire follows him into the next world. It will try to make man desire to live and this desire is a chain upon the spirit.

"Now the paramount question—how does man get rid of desire?

"Everybody writes books or lectures on how to get rid of desire, but none give the true answer. An ECK Master can get rid of desire by placing something before it which has greater attraction. This is only substituting one desire in place of another, but the masters put the desire of the SUGMAD in your mind. Otherwise you hold desires for things and sensations of a worldly sort, for things which belong to the animal plane, which holds man on that plane and monopolizes his attention. His business is to rise above the world of senses, the world of lower desires. If you are to travel constantly in the Far Country, it is absolutely essential that you detach yourself from the sense objects, from all desires for them. You can go away from the things themselves, but that is not getting rid of them. If you do not get rid of the desire itself, you are no better off than at the first.

"So if man can fasten his attention to something which is not of the sense world, something which is imperishable, something which, instead of binding him here, actually liberates him from his bondage, draws him in the opposite direction, and takes him up to liberty and immortality, then that thing becomes his chief goal. A desire for that is a worthy desire.

"The evil of desire is not desire itself, but the nature of what is desired. How can the mind conceive the desire for a good thing to be evil in and of itself? The good or evil lies in the direction toward which a desire pulls man.

"Whatever desire keeps man from becoming a spiritual traveler in the Far Country can be considered a bad desire. That which is the stronger desire will prevail. A pull in the direction of the SUGMAD is the greater desire.

"There is one thing known to human experience which will destroy all lower desires. This is the bani, the sound current of the SUGMAD. It is the supreme instrument of deliverance from bondage. It is the one means of detaching man from worldly objects that perish and of lifting him up to liberty and independence.

"Man attains perfect Vairag when he enters consciously into this divine stream of life. Controlling and destroying desires are two different things, and knowing this, man can progress upward along the path to the SUGMAD's domain.

"Destruction of lower desires can never be done by negation. Yet negation is the method employed by ninety-nine percent of the human race, by parents, by teachers, by reformers, by the courts. They all forbid things. They tell people what they must not do. They write in their laws, 'Thou shalt not.' A few understanding ones offer something better to attract the minds of the disobedient. But it should never be done by negation.

"The world rushes madly into a mire of sensation, bondage to work, bondage to pleasures, and bondage to a thousand things. Karma kills out all progress of the spiritual traveler and he sinks into the mud of desires.

"But then the traveler learns of bani, and by use of this life-giving force he becomes a light unto himself, and a light unto others, for he is no longer in bondage to the lower desires. He is the master of his own destiny, for he has freedom and independence to act as he wishes anywhere in the planes of the Far Country.

"He is a Master above all Masters. He is the MAHANTA —the Living ECK Master!"

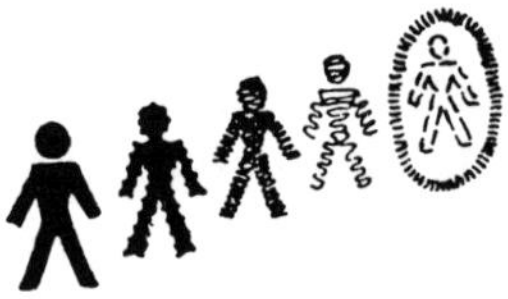

Chapter 4

THE IMMORTAL TUZA

The bronze sun moved overhead into its noonday position and the hot light poured through the open door and window. The mountains in the far distance changed from a deep hue to a brilliant golden haze. The peaks sparkled like a million diamonds from glaciers and snow fields. They were a rugged outline against the white skies and here and there clouds hid the highest peaks like children under covers of snow blankets.

A fly droned around the ceiling making noises as though it had a duty to perform within the mud hut, by its very ability to disturb the two in human shapes below it. It wheeled and dove with the agility of a fighter plane.

Nothing but the dirt floor upon which we were sitting while sipping at the buttered tea which Rebazar Tarzs had poured in the thick, heavy mugs, seemed real. This was something like a scene from a science-fiction novel which I seemed to have been reading, and it was working out in a dream.

For a moment I could not get my senses together because of this unreality. Like a man grasping for a straw while struggling in water over his head, it was all too much at the present. To take in and absorb all that Rebazar Tarzs was saying was more than the mind could handle.

Most minds reject the truth when it is presented in full volume like this, coming from the great ECK master, Rebazar Tarzs. Naturally, he understood this and took his time making the presentation, for it was complex and needed much explanation along the way. He had taught many the wonders of the Far Country, and taken many of us through these high planes so that our feet would be steadied upon the ground when we left our physical bodies and went into the country beyond.

Finally he finished his cup of tea, wiped his lips with the sleeve of his left arm. He looked like a monk of the medieval days would have appeared. Visibly similar to the ancient looking followers of the older orders of mystery cults, he seemed to take pride in his mannerisms.

He drew a circle in the dirt with his left forefinger. "This is the Tuza," he began in his husky, deep voice. "This is what it looks like in the other worlds. It is nothing more than a viewpoint but it has wavelengths, the ability to know, can move about in the spiritual universes and has an uncanny awareness. This is the real center of man, what we call Soul, the divine self which becomes reality when you shift your consciousness from the external to the internal.

"This is what most mystics call 'going within', switching the positions of the consciousness. Once you take control of Soul, then you are able to do anything; there is no limitation.

"This consciousness is the awareness of the real self. It is that part which you dwell within, when you become the spiritual traveler and move through the worlds of spirit, upward to the SUGMAD.

"There is nothing greater in the eyes of the SUGMAD than Soul for It is that which holds the divine secret, the sacred imagination, which the SUGMAD wants again for ITS own! This is why IT calls all Tuzas to return to ITS place in the far sky, because IT needs ITS eye as a whole, and not as a part as it is now, divided into many parts. IT must see everything through the eyes of the Tuzas and by ITS own.

"Soul can balance itself in the heavens of space without any visible support, but looking through the maya we can see that it flings up anchor points and establishes them on some object in the heavens invisible to the eye, though strong enough to hold an anchor point. These points are golden balls

70

with lines similar to very thin wires. They run out on a sort of a reel, and pull in, as Soul wishes.

"They can be flung into space and attached to a piece of the space world so the Tuza can hang there, swinging like a child on a summer swing. Soul can be steadied by flinging out anchor points in all directions until set within a web, similar to a spider's net. Nothing can dislodge one as long as he wishes to remain in this position.

"Now the Tuza is immortal, of course. The SUGMAD had a large number of Tuzas ages ago and released them upon Earth for the purpose of developing it into a garden spot of the universe. It had been a dull, garbage heap in this world of planets and stars, until in ITS mercy the decision was made to give it an opportunity to become beautiful, and peopled with homo sapiens who would take care of it.

"After IT generously gave ITS imagination faculty to all, the people were bound and determined to use it to steal their neighbor's possessions, and make war on one another.

"All Souls are immortal, and as the Gita says cannot be wetted, pierced by sword, burnt by fire nor be injured in any manner. It is all there is; that which is the hope of heaven and the scourge of all things, is willful and unhappy.

"The problem of the Tuza is unique. The individual Tuza can become aberrated like the mind. If It is distorted in the imaginary faculty, trouble is likely to follow for a long time, and there is hardly anything that can be done unless some spiritual traveler gives It help.

"The problems which it suffers are involved with the faculty of postulates and considerations, meaning of course that while the Tuza is capable of these, it may become a victim of another Tuza's postulates and considerations.

"There is an old story about a Soul which was given a set of considerations by another Soul, that it was a rock. So the poor Soul sat for ten thousand years, which is only a short time in the God realm, thinking that it was a rock, until one day another Soul wandered past and asked It for heaven's sake what was It doing? 'I'm a rock,' was the answer.

71

"So the first Soul, realizing what had happened, undid the spell by breaking the considerations which the other had accepted. Now this sounds silly but stop and think how many times throughout your earth life that you did accept somebody's consideration for yourself. Maybe a Healer said you would be a long time getting well, and you accepted his consideration. You didn't get well for a long time either.

"This is what I mean by postulates and considerations being a two edged sword. They can work against you, as well as for you. Once you're free, then nobody can make your considerations, but as long as you are on this Earth plane, you are in danger of having to accept other considerations which are not your own.

"Tuzas fight one another with electronic beams. Those which are aggressive do, and often a few are hurt, having to crawl off somewhere for recovery. You can never kill a Tuza under any circumstance, but you can cripple It temporarily with electronic beams.

"Now Tuza is the only thing in all the universes which can occupy the same space as anything else. Only spirit can do this, and of course Soul can occupy the same space as spirit.

"Let me give you an example. Two rocks cannot occupy the same space, neither can two bodies of the physical flesh. But Soul can slip into a body while it is occupied by another, and certainly can cause havoc, providing it is of that disposition. The spiritual traveler, better known as the Tuza, Soul, can go anywhere and do most anything within the Far Country.

"While It is limited in some respects with the SUGMAD, there is nothing within the physical planes which can be called greater and have greater freedom than Soul."

*   *   *

"There is no assured immortality until the Tuza has reached the regions of pure spirit, far beyond all materiality. Only then is Soul above the complications of mind and beyond the grasp of karma, beyond all dissolutions and grand dissolutions which come to the worlds below the Sach Khand region.

"The length of life upon the Brahm Lok plane leads one to believe that this is the immortal world. It often extends into thousands and millions of years. But the spiritual traveler is familiar with the vast regions far beyond and above the highest regions known to those who seek without the help of the ECK Master.

"The Christian religions speak of this plane, and so does the Bhagavad-Gita, but both are results of writers who never went beyond the Brahm Lok region. Both the Christian gospel and the Gita are purely works of dialectic fiction, not historical reports.

"The Sat Desh, or world of the SUGMAD which I have previously called Anami Lok, is the grand region of all creations and of immortality. It is unchangeable, perfect, deathless. It is forever untouched by dissolution or grand dissolution, and so are its inhabitants.

"It is divided into four distinct worlds, each having its own characteristics and its own Lord or Governor. From above downward, they are named: The Anami Lok, Agam Lok and the Sach Khand.

"The light of these four planes is so very intense that it is impossible for any mortal to get an understanding of it. It simply cannot be described.

"There are two kinds of dissolution which occur in the Far Country. The one, simple dissolution, is that which dissolves all those worlds up to the Brahm Lok plane, after millions of years of existence. The grand dissolutions occur after immeasurably long periods of time, extending to the Sach Khand, but not including this plane, the first world of immortality.

"Both of these dissolutions include the entire physical universe, every sun, moon and planet in it. At that time every star and all satellites are wiped out. There follows a period of darkness equal in duration to the life of the universe. When the period of darkness has expired, a new creation is projected, and the heavens once more are alive with sparkling stars. With each new creation begins a Golden Age for each planet and its inhabitants. But between the minor dissolutions there are also periods of renewal for the life of each planet, when Golden Ages succeed dark ages.

"Dissolution will come at a time when all the worlds of the physical universe will be dissolved; after periods of darkness and silence, new worlds will take their places. The inhabitants of all of these worlds to be dissolved are drawn up to higher regions in a sort of comatose state, to be replaced upon the worlds when they are again ready for human habitation. They will then begin a new life here under more favorable conditions. These periods of dissolutions come to the physical universe after many, many hundreds of millions of years.

"The spiritual traveler who will accept and listen to the creative sound current, the ECK, will find himself renewed in the spiritual worlds. It takes possession of you, it re-creates you, and then you find yourself a citizen of a new world. The attractions of sense disappear, and you are exalted. You are purified and your mind renewed. You will live anew, and never shall the shadow of death ever cross your path. You have definitely become immortal.

"Beliefs and speculations offer very little support for the hope of immortal life. All the elements of the many world religions are of doubtful value for the reason they are dependent upon ancient books and metaphysical theories. This takes the matter out of the category of knowledge, and so robs it of its chief value.

"Now in order to get to the roots of immortality we must look at the basis of the philosophy of ECKANKAR. It is not a religion, nor a philosophy as known to the scholars of the educational systems in this physical world.

"The sad fact remains that nobody on this physical plane knows anything about Soul, the real self. What are the component parts of It? This question is never answered in the laboratories of the earth world.

"The several parts of man will be a quick study for you,

74

beginning with the lower stratum, which is man, the animal. He is a physical body, called by the Orientals, Isthul Sharir. He has a body which gets hurt, sick and which finally dies and returns to the soil.

"There is another man inside the physical body, a much finer body, called by the spiritual travelers the Sukhsham Sharir, or subtle body; Nuri Sarup, or light body. It is commonly called the Astral body by the occultist. It makes connections with the outer world.

"When seen by the physical senses it appears to sparkle with millions of little particles resembling star dust. It takes shape with the character of the individual, and has five senses, just the same as the physical body. When the physical body dies, this body remains as the instrument of expression on the Astral plane.

"Inside the Nuri Sarup and quite distinct from it, there is still another body, much finer and more subtle than the astral. It is known as the Karan Sharir, the Causal body. So named because in it is the real cause, or seeds of all that is to ever take place in the individual's life. It is also called Bij Sharir, the seed body.

"This body is divided into two or more strata, each of which is given a different name. One is sometimes known as the mental body because it acts as a sheath around Soul, and is very sensitive to impressions from the mind. Its function is to receive and transmit impressions between the mind and Soul on one side, and between the mind and the astral body on the other.

"A perfect record of everything the individual has experienced is established from his countless ages of existence. Out of these experiences, character is formed, and from that character, all actions flow.

"The mind body is the fourth unit in the construction of Soul, or rather the man. It is so closely related to the Karan Sharir that it is not easy to distinguish between them. The mind body is a sort of sheath covering Soul.

"When reaching the Daswan Dwar region all bodies have been shed except the mind body because Soul no longer needs them. It can without instrument of communication or contemplation know all things, rejoice in all things by direct perception.

"When Soul rises upward from Daswan Dwar, it sheds this mental body and becomes Self. It alone has the power of knowing by direct perception. All knowledge opens before it without any sort of instrument.

"The mind itself is sometimes divided into different sections, according to the plane upon which one is operating. The Nij-manas, the inner mind, carries the seeds of all actions within itself. It carries the sanskaras, the impressions of all former lives. Sometimes we speak of the causal mind, the Sukhsham mind and the physical mind, according to the region or plane, upon which the mind is operating. But this is only a distinction for convenience.

"Last of all we come to the real man, the Tuza. Soul. These two terms we use synonymously. This is the very core of his being, and It is the fifth unit in the structure of the being that is known as man, as you see him in this life. Remember he has all five of these elements while living here now. All the lower units which are only instruments, he discards, one by one, as he advances upward. This is because he has no use for them on the higher planes, each instrument being suited for expression only upon a particular plane of life.

"The Tuza is the real man, the spiritual traveler, or as some prefer to call it, the Purusha. The individual Tuza is the spark from the divine light, a drop from the ocean of the SUGMAD. It is in the Tuza that all consciousness resides, and all power. All below it, even the mind itself, is unconscious, automatic and mechanical in action.

"In fact, everything in existence is entirely dependent upon the ECK for its life and activity. Even the humblest plant, or the smallest insect, lives and carries on its activities, by virtue of the ECK, the spirit that gives it being.

"All else in man passes away, or is discarded by him on

76

his upward flight toward perfect freedom. Were it not for Soul's temporary sojourn in these material regions, there would be no need for any of these instruments—these bodies and the mind. Owing to the extreme subtleness of spirit, It cannot contact the coarser worlds without an intermediate instrument. It is obliged to clothe Itself in some sort of medium of contact. For this reason the Supreme SUGMAD, ITSELF, cannot manifest on these material planes or appear to men and give them instructions. A material body is necessary in all cases.

"In any case Soul is a derivative of the SUGMAD and identical in substance. The entire world is filled with Souls. There is no place where Souls are not. Some have better minds and better bodies than the others. In this respect there is little difference between the amoeba and man, between an insect and a savant.

* * *

"Now I have moved you along to an understanding of the problem of Soul. From here I go to the mind and the very center of all worldly problems.

"In the region of Trikuti, the second region of the spiritual worlds, and that of the Brahm Lok plane, the mental world, the mind is acquired. Soul in its descent through this region picks up the mind as its equipment for use on the lower planes.

"This region is the seat of the Universal or Cosmic mind, as sometimes called. It is the place from which all mind is derived. Just as Soul originates in the region of universal energy, so the mind is acquired in the region of the universal mind. A small portion of this universal mind is detached, so to speak, and is joined to Soul, not in a permanent union, but in a temporary union.

"It is wrapped about It, covering the Tuza, and at the same time obscuring much of its light and hampering its activity. The Tuza, equipped with this necessary handicap, begins its career in the regions of mind and matter. At that moment it begins to accumulate karma. Before this it had no karma except that which the eastern wisdom names Adi Karma. This is the primal karma, and it consists of the action of the creative force, the real ECK, whose function is to bring the Tuzas to the material planes, in order that they might begin to accumulate experience.

"The Tuza begins to acquire experience upon its own initiative; its era of swadharma, self regulation, is now starting. It begins to establish an individual law of its own life, its own regime, and to create its own destiny: It begins to enjoy, to suffer, to reap rewards and to pay penalties.

"This is the beginning of its own karma. Thus it inaugurates its long, long series of Earth lives. By each and every act, from that time on, it stores up karma. Even when it is least active, still it is making karma, and in all of this activity, its mind is the chief instrument. It is the mind working always under the law of cause and effect that creates karma.

"The mind is not self-conscious, nor self-acting. It has no power of automation, or of initiative. It is simply a machine, though highly sensitive and extremely powerful when motivated by the ECK. As a machine, it can be made to do what it was intended to do, just like any other machine. It will never do anything different from what it was fashioned and trained to do.

"The western teachers have always taught the mind had powers of origination and initiative, but this is untrue. Mind and ECK have been greatly confused in western psychology. Only the ECK can think, originate and take the initiative. Mind works only when activated by Soul.

"Only the negative power and its subordinates have minds, just like human beings. The fundamental difference between mind and the ECK—between Tuza and instrument, must be understood, if you are to comprehend the psychology of the ECK travelers.

"You see now that mind is no essential part of man himself. It is only an instrument which encumbers Soul, obscures its light and impedes its progress. But it is absolutely necessary while you are operating on these material planes.

"Again I say that mind alone is a machine. It cannot think, cannot will, cannot love, it cannot remember, nor suffer nor enjoy. To do all these things it must, in every instance be activated by the ECK. ECK alone is the motive power to mind, just as the electric current is the power that moves the machinery. We usually think of the mind as the chief power for moving the human body.

"Mind is matter, yet quite refined in its essential qualities. It is next to Soul in all of its essential qualities. The chief function of mind is to serve as an instrument of spirit for all contacts with the material worlds.

"Mind is a useful instrument, provided it is kept under the control of Soul. Mind is an excellent servant but a poor master. If it becomes the master, it may speedily bring disaster. We have always been taught that mind reasons; but it doesn't reason. It acts with automatic precision, exactly as it is stimulated to act.

"The mind is able to carry on deductive processes, but has no power of induction. This is often demonstrated in the cases of hypnosis. Give the subject certain premises, no matter how absurd they may be, and he will act upon such premises, with automatic deductions. But such a mind has no power of synthesis and rational induction. Soul alone has light in it, and Soul alone can work independently and rationally. You have only to observe a little, the actions of people the world over to see for yourself that they act more like machines than they do like rational beings.

"They are moved by mind in grooves, just as they have

79

been taught to act. It is a rare individual who does independent thinking and when one does that, it is because the ECK is in operation, emanicpating self from the domineering control of mind.

*   *   *

"This subject is so very important that I must devote more time to it. You must make yourself fully acquainted with the mind in all its faculties, and its several methods of action.

"The mind is divided into four parts, called Antishkarans; functions, or modes of action. It has four primary attributes, faculties, or qualities. These are its antishkarans. These four divisions of mind are named: Chitta, Manas, Buddhi and Ahankar.

Chitta is that function or faculty, which takes cognizance of form, beauty, color, rhythm, harmony and perspective. It enjoys these things and what it doesn't like, it rejects. It receives its impressions mostly through the eyes as instruments of perception. It then passes on its finding to the Buddhi. In all of these reactions, its processes are as regular and automatic as are the reactions of chemistry.

Manas, is mind stuff, per se. It is that which receives and registers impressions through the senses of smell, taste, hearing and feeling. Its chief function is taste. It tastes, relishes, enjoys, or rejects what it doesn't like. Feeling and taste are practically the same thing. All of its reactions are automatic. The manas enjoys what it has been trained to like, and its reactions are instantaneous. It either likes a taste, or it rejects it automatically, then passes it on to the Buddhi, for final judgment.

Buddhi, is the intellect proper; that power the Tuza uses as its chief instrument of thought. When empowered by spirit, it produces thought. It discriminates and decides. It passes judgment upon all the findings of the other two faculties, its decisions are then passed on to the final court of execution, Ahankar.

Ahankar accepts the decisions of the other faculties, handed on to it by the Buddhi and executes the mandates. It is the executive faculty of the mind. It is also the I-Ness of the individual, the faculty by which the individual differentiates self from all else, and it is the faculty which enables the individual to distinguish between his own interests and that of others. It is the faculty which, when unduly exaggerated, becomes vanity, or egotism.

"To sum up what I have just said: Manas—receives and tastes; Chitta—takes notice of form and beauty; Buddhi—is the instrument of thought, discrimination and decision; and Ahankar—executes orders.

"Let us not condemn nature, but try to understand and obey it. It is man's best friend, if you first learn to obey.

"With understanding you work in close cooperation with nature to your best advantage.

"There is practically no limit to the powers of the mind, but few people know how to awaken or invoke its forces. It's a good thing they don't in their present state of spiritual evolution. When man learns to accept responsibility, these mind powers will automatically increase.

"When properly awakened, trained and vitalized by the ECK the mind can do anything for you. A trained spiritual traveler, knowing how to awaken and control the powers of his own mind, can stop a train at any place he may wish it to stop. He can start a downpour of rain in seconds out of the clear sky; or he can dry up a flood of waters. He can do anything he wishes. But this is only playing with natural forces. All miracles are but the play of mind. They are not the operations of any divine power, as most people believe. But to do these things one must learn two things—he must become morally responsible for his actions, and he must learn to control his own mind. After that he can do what he wishes. He must be responsible in the sense that if he isn't he would lose his powers at once. It stands to reason, and it is substantiated by all of our daily experiences, that if such gigantic powers were let loose out of control, or if they were invoked by an evil mind, it might bring about disaster of the most terrible sort.

"It is a provision of the SUGMAD that no man is able to invoke such powers until he has first learned to control his own passions, to check all evil tendencies and all selfish impulses. Otherwise, such a man might wreck the whole physical world. Only the spiritual travelers can do these things.

"The essential point here is that the mind is a very great power, and must be kept in control. Rightly used, it may be made to work marvels; but if allowed to assert itself in a lawless manner, it can bring unspeakable disaster to its owner, and sometimes others as well.

"I have given you the essences of the five passions: Kama, Krodha, Lobha, Moha and Ahankara. These are in English—lust, anger, greed, attachment to worldly things, and vanity. These passions take possession when mind is allowed to run wild, out of control of the spirit.

"So long as the ECK controls the mind, the four faculties perform their proper functions and these passions cannot manifest themselves. But when the mind runs wild, out of control, under the impulses of one or more of the five passions, it is generally headed for destruction.

"Whenever any of the five evil passions are allowed to run wild, in each and every case, a mighty force which was meant for our good has been turned into an instrument of destruction. No faculty of mind ever works itself. It is motivated by spirit, and it is as automatic in its actions as is the explosion of a stick of dynamite. It is only when spirit takes control, that mind is directed in safe and sane channels. It may then be compared with a fine car that has a good driver at the wheel.

"Every agitation, stimulation, or excitation of mind, in any of its functions, creates thought-forms which may be seen on the subtle planes. Thoughts are things, just as much as clouds, or houses. The four faculties of the mind when set in motion by any sort of stimulus begin automatically to create thought-forms and set waves in motion. The mind will do these things with the regularity of chemistry, or machinery. It works in this pattern and can do nothing else but this. It has no power to originate independent thought, nor can it reason upon any proposed course of action.

"I am aware this is all contrary to the western psychology, but western psychology does not understand the mechanism of mind. Mind cannot depart from its beaten path, any more than a locomotive can will to leave the track upon which it has been set. Habit is the chief method of mental action. Habits are likened to grooves in which actions run. The first thing which mind does, after it is agitated and brought into action, is to establish a groove, which you call habit. Man is usually a driven slave of habit and custom.

"The mind resents innovation, dislikes change, and accepts without question, what it has been taught to believe as truth or right. The mind adores routine, and it can be trained to a very high degree of skill in a given line of activity. This marks one very great advantage of its automatic quality.

"The mind when activated by the ECK, forms thoughts, and each thought takes a definite shape on the astral plane. They may be seen there by anyone who enjoys astral vision."

* * *

"Now," he said, pacing the floor of the hut furiously, attacking the subject of mind as though it were a person, "Can you teach a machine to believe that it is not good to run into trees? Can you convince it that the highway is better? You can argue with it for years and then turn it loose on full power and it will run straight into a tree, if that tree is in its path.

"So it is with most people. They will usually go on doing as they did before, in spite of all rational persuasion. If a little light filters in from the spirit, a person may change his course of thinking or acting, but never otherwise.

"If the mind enjoys a certain sensation, it wishes to repeat that sensation as often as possible, quite regardless of whether the sensation is good for the person or not. This is why there are so many drunkards, libertines and dope fiends. It is why people indulge in anger and vanity. Mind will usually do what it likes, regardless of consequences, unless checked by fear, or some higher impulse, from the spirit. It is only when Buddhi interferes that the mind will forego an indulgence offered it.

"Of course if it feels pain from a certain performance, it instantly rejects that mode of action, regardless of its own ultimate good. It is not easy for a man to stick a lance into his own abscess, or allow someone else to do it, even though he knows it is best for him. It is only when the ECK asserts itself that one will do such a thing for his own ultimate good. Unreasoning children will never consent to be hurt, even when they know it is best for them. Perhaps, in such cases, the Buddhi has not reached sufficient development for the ECK to make use of it.

"Mind alone is neither moral nor immoral, any more than your automobile. It is a machine as much as your car. The cannibal can see no more harm in eating a man than you do in eating a piece of beef. To some other people, both are harmful. Morality, sin and righteousness are largely matters of custom, and geography. Social customs, ceremonies, rites, religions and politics are based upon mental habits, and are usually handed down from one generation to another.

"Customs make it wrong in one country to enter a temple with shoes on, while in another country it is wrong to keep your hat on. Custom makes it wrong in one section to have more than one wife, while in another it is a sign of poverty or inferiority to be so limited. Mental habits have all the inflexibility of an iron machine. In fact, iron may be bent; but you try to change a long established custom and your neighbors will seek your immediate destruction. The whole human race is a slave to custom. Every single individual in the country may condemn that custom, but at the same time every one will do his best to perpetuate it. All of this is because mind, both individual and social, is machine like in its action. It cannot reason.

"Can you imagine vast armies going out with deliberate aim to destroy each other, if they had the power to reason? Crime and moral rectitude are both mental habits. International strife is only blind passion run wild, en masse.

"There are some advantages in this machinelike action of mind, but there are equally grave dangers in it. If the mind, through a gradual process of suggestion and experience, becomes accustomed to certain grooves of action, it often leads to the wreck and ruin of the individual in spite of himself. This is an extremely pathetic aspect of the matter. People become entangled in the net of habits and customs, while deep in their hearts they ardently wish to get out of them; but have not the power of will, or strength of character to extricate themselves. They go deliberately and knowingly to destruction, in spite of themselves.

"The more a habit is indulged in, the more easily and certainly the mind will run in that groove. At the same time, Soul Itself becomes less and less able to impress Itself and Its wishes upon the mind, or even to get a hearing at all.

"Soul is an exceedingly fine and delicate reality. It has tremendous power in its own sphere of action. But on the fields of coarse material, it has but little power of self-expression. On the other hand, if the Tuza has a trained, and responsive mind, it may do almost anything it decides to do. This is why mind control, through spirit, is so important, and is so insisted upon by the ECK travelers.

"Mind may be divided in another way, besides the four faculties. It may be spoken of as the higher and lower minds, which is the common, the scientific classification.

"There is only one mind, acting on different planes. It may also be divided into three parts—the Pinda, or lower world mind; mind which manifests itself in the common affairs of this world. Second, the Sukhsham, that mind which works on the Astral plane, and last, the Karan mind, nij-mind, inner mind, or the causal mind.

"These correspond to the three bodies of man, and the

three worlds in which the three bodies operate, each in its own sphere. With equal logic you might say there are six minds, because the three I've just mentioned may be divided into two, a higher and lower.

"In this world, for example, you may speak of a higher mind which engages itself in the highest forms of thought activity, e.g. philosophy, literature, music and art. The lower mind engages itself in grossly material things, money making, digging, eating, drinking, and the indulgence of any of the passions. But in any case there is only one mind, functioning on different planes, and upon higher or lower things on each plane.

"At the top of all, the mind which lies next to spirit is the real nij-mind, the purest. Below that, each substratum of the mind becomes more adulterated with coarser and lower substances. Last of all, at the very lowest stratum, there is a sort of mind which is but little more than electro-magnetism. When the attention is on this lower plane, it is the lower mind working.

"It is here engrossed in its own desires, its passions and its plays.

"When the attention is on the astral plane, it is the Sukhsham mind which is used; when the attention is on the causal plane, it is that mind which is working. But in each and every case, it is the same mind, but playing upon the different planes of existence.

"The higher mind, the nij, is sort of a pilot, or gyroscope, whose function is to receive the impressions of the Tuza and pass them on to the subordinate minds for their regulation. The important point is that all aspects of the mind are automatic.

"None of them ever calculate results, or assign a moral content. Each of them accepts what is given to it, and reacts upon it, without question or consideration. Neither does any aspect of the mind ever consider what is best for the individual, except just what it has been taught by experience to like or dislike. In other words, mind is not a rational entity. It reacts automatically and always upon the basis of what it likes or dislikes; it never considers what is best. If the element of calculation enters into the process you may be sure a little of the light of spirit has entered into the affair.

"The mind, if given a stimulus, or as one says, a temptation, will always act in accord with the sum total of its own past experiences. It cannot act in any other way. It cannot even will to act in any other way.

"Now if the mind always acts automatically and in exact line with its previous training, how do we account for any new or radical departure from the beaten path of its habits and desires? The answer is on the basis of a new driving force entering the machine from without.

"It is because a different driving force enters the machine that mind obeys, has to obey, the stronger of the two impelling forces. Physics is the best field for the study of mental phenomena. There is not a single action of mind which cannot be reduced to Newton's Laws of Motion, and the reactions of chemistry. It is no wonder that modern physicists are inclined to bring all mental reactions under their mechanistic theory of the universe. In the absence of complete knowledge, they are fully justified in their conclusions. If we had to deal always with mind alone, and spirit never entered into the problem, the mechanistic theory would apply with perfect accuracy. It would fit every fact of experience. But when the ECK begins to enter the play there is no foretelling what may happen. Soul operates by Its own light. Mind must follow, whether it likes or not.

"Now that you see that mind is only an automatic thing, you know that all intelligence, light and power come from Soul. But Soul works under a serious handicap, for this world is not Its native habitat. All the coverings worn by Soul serve to burden It and to weaken Its powers of expression.

"Soul is in enemy country, and always surrounded by the five faithful servants of the Negative Power, Kama, Krodha, Lobha, Moha and Ahankara; lust, anger, greed, attachment and vanity.

"These five are commissioned to mislead Soul and mind

and make trouble for them. It is their business. The worst feature is the mind itself being swayed by them. It has close relationships with them and lends a ready ear to their whispering.

"But Soul, the spiritual traveler, has a safe harbor into which It can sail when these five negative powers start working up too great a whirlpool. It can always go into the higher realms beyond the mind planes and enjoy the world of the SUGMAD."

Chapter 5

THE WORSHIP OF KALI

Rebazar Tarzs quit pacing the floor and dropped upon the earth putting his legs under him. He spread the robe over his knees, hiding his lower limbs, giving the appearance of a great Buddha in silent contemplation.

After awhile he opened his eyes again and stared at me for a long time. Finally he said, "I've brought you this far, my young friend. Now I will talk about the Kali, the Earth mother, whom all India worships, and most of the world people, though the latter are not aware of this.

"The Hindu religion has a trinity, consisting of Brahma, Vishnu and Shiva. These represent the three currents flowing out of the Brahm Lok world; they are creation, continuity, and destruction. The Hindus gave them worldly names in order to personalize each current, so they would be recognized. They are: Brahma, Vishnu and Shiva, which are worshipped in India and other parts of the Oriental world as Gods.

"These are called the sons of Kal Niranjan, the negative power, whose other name is Brahm. The female counterpart of Brahm is Shakti, who in fact represents a minor creative current. Out of these two great currents, the three subordinate currents flow into the lower worlds, and to these are attributed the creation of all lower worlds. These three became creators, lords and governors of the lower worlds, under their father, Brahm, and their mother, Shakti. They are said to be under the supervision of their mother. In fact, these three represent creative currents. They carry the creative impulses from the greater powers above, but they have been given these individual names, as persons.

"It is well to remember that all creative currents may become personal; that is, take individual form and assume individual duties, as Krishna, Christ, Buddha and others.

Now these three have generally been accepted as the Hindu trinity of Gods, as commonly known in their literature and religion. Millions worship them in spite of their subordinate position. These powers are the real servants of man. They perform a certain function in carrying on the work of the world, in producing human bodies, and in keeping these bodies going. They are the agents of the SUGMAD in serving mankind, but not gods to be worshipped by the human race. They are almost menials in the grand hierarchy, but each of them have certain powers and prerogatives, and within his own sphere he is all-powerful. He carries on according to definite laws and rules laid down for his government. These again are laws of nature. Brahma, Vishnu and Shiva may be regarded as servants of the negative power or his working committee. In all respects, they do his bidding, each in his own department.

"Still lower than these three, there is another current or God, or power, who is also one of the working force, helping to carry on the administration of the physical universe. His name is Ganesh. He stands practically at the foot of the list of subordinates whose business it is to serve mankind and help to carry on the work of the world.

"In the subtle region close to the earth, there is a great host of beings called devas, devtas, bhuts, prets to name a few. These are generally called angels in English. They are beings somewhat above ordinary men and they help to serve man in many ways. They have great powers and are quite willing to serve people who live in harmony with them.

"Last of all, is humanity itself at the very foot of the grand hierarchy. If man works in harmony with all of these powers above him, he will surely receive their help and will eventually become a spiritual traveler.

"The Kali is the mother goddess of India. I have purposely left her until the last for she is worshipped by the Hindus as the great creative force. She is the six-armed deity which rules over all, a powerful current representing the female or feminine principle of that country. She is the consort of Shiva, but assigned to the place where Shakti is supposed to be.

"Now the Kali represents destruction, the goddess which destroys all yet replaces it with fertility of life. In other words she is a sex goddess. Another name for her is Mahamai, or the great mother, and in the yoga system she is the power, the strength of the deity presiding over the ganglion at the throat. It is sometimes called the Kanth chakra, the fifth center that lies near the cervical plexus. It has to do with respiration. But I will go into these chakra centers later.

"The Kali is worshipped, as I said before, by the Hindus. She has been brought to our attention in the west mainly by Ramakrishna, the great Vedantist prophet of India.

"The Christians know her as the Virgin Mother, but without the six arms, and the Greeks had a name for her, Ceres. All religions have a mother goddess, the feminine principle of the universe.

"Ramakrishna laid for hours before the statue of Kali in his hometown, in the temple of course, pleading with the mother goddess to give him just one little glimpse of her. He sang hymns, songs of praise and talked constantly to the statue, as if she were alive. If he had been in any other country on the globe it would have been possible that he would have been locked up for insanity. But he wasn't insane, for when the Kali finally gave him a touch of ecstasy, he went into a trance for many days and had to be cared for like a child, hand fed and bathed.

"This feminine principle, which is known mostly to the Hindus, is frankly the opposite of the male, or positive principle. The Chinese have worked it out in the idea of Yang and Yin. Yang is the male principle and Yin is the feminine.

"I am going around in circles somewhat to explain to you what the Kali, mother goddess of India, is like. I want you to understand completely when I'm through with this part of the discussion. This feminine principle is somewhat destructive in its nature and is closer to the lower world than the other currents. Being destructive means that it is also the creative side of the current.

"This is a part of the Shiva current—which is the triad—Brahma, Vishnu and Shiva. Do you remember the two faces of Shiva? Well, this is the part of the Shiva current which most Indians of the Far East worship. This is a part of the Shiva sect. The sect is a follower of the two faces of Shiva, worshipping Shiva as the Father God and Kali as the mother goddess.

"Shiva is known as the creator of the world and Kali as the destroyer. She represents the great womb of the universe, for out of her is born all life. Some yogis write poems to her, cry out in agony for her smile, and finally get a touch of heaven through her.

"In other words Kali is the symbol of what is called Mother India. Now I point out that all men love to think of their home country in the symbol of womanhood. They look upon all life as the feminine principle, because they have been taught that womanhood was greater than manhood.

"This is some of the misteachings on the earth plane. It comes about because India's religious system was spread too far west and too far east during its advent. You don't find many of the Hindu cults in the west; maybe Vedanta has made a strong stand in the west, but the other religious groups within the Hindu religious framework have not. Yet the influence of Hinduism has been so strong that it did replace a section of thought in China, Japan and, to the west, in most of the nations along the Mediterranean coast.

"Christianity adopted the Virgin Mother idea from the Indian philosophy, mainly the Shakti, mother of the triad group, and completely lifted and made it over into a westernized idea. The whole point is that Kali has become the symbol of the feminine mind. The whole mystery of the feminine principle is found in the Kali symbol.

"Priestcraft taught man long ago that motherhood was greatest because out of it comes the birth of life. Doesn't the female of all species give life, be it plant or animal, or the human species? But if you look beyond this thought, you might see that maya, illusion, is the veil through which life comes. This is because man is not able to look into the true side of all nature; and this maya, which was created from time immemorial, has a way of hiding all things to the profane sight of man.

"Buddha was supposed, according to the famous poem 'The Light of Asia', to have stepped through the veil of illusion onto this earth. In other words as a traveler in the spiritual worlds, he descended from the Brahm Lok, and regressed into the singular physical form, and found his way into the earth world, through the womb of a woman. So do all ECK adepts, the MAHANTA, including yourself.

"Now the word maya has a dozen meanings. In the west its name is Maria, Mary, May, Molly, Polly, or Poll, or even Marietta. Hence comes the Mary who gave birth to the savior Jesus, for he only used her body in order to visit this planet. It is the way of nature that all things must be born in the miniature manner of babyhood and grow to adultship. This is one of the laws of nature on this planet, and even the saints, saviors and adepts use it, mainly so they may not startle man too much; for what he doesn't understand, he would not accept.

"This form of maya, as I have said, is represented by the female body which hides as the womb of time and space.

"Western psychology puts an emphasis upon an aberration of its men; that man longs to return to the womb for its comfort; where he laid in soft darkness, protected by the woman's belly, and fed without struggle. This is an escapism which is often laid at men's feet to chastise them and get them to accept women as their equal.

"Now I'm going to explain the true psychology of the Kali goddess so that you may have a greater understanding of the feminine principle, that current which creates life and form on this earth, and destroys it without regret.

"Let's have a few minutes of rest before going on with this subject."

*　　*　　*

"Now the Kali is a form of worship which is considered a blood cult. It was originated during the reconstruction period in India, when the development of the female side, the wife of the deity, began. The idea grew that the god was unapproachable, but the Sakti or female side brought mankind in touch with the deity, an idea that of course underlies Mariolatry in Christian thought. In case you don't know what the word means—it's the worship of the Virgin Mary—a term of opprobrium often used in the western world.

"The Saktas, the worshippers of Kali, grew to such importance, especially in Bengal, during this period that it formed a right hand and left hand group. It was the left hand Saktas who became the troublemakers in India; this was the blood cult, Kali, the Vampire whose presence influenced men to Thugism, sex cults, and the evil of murder.

"The right hand Saktas were the worshippers of woman, the mother—they had rituals of worship of the female organ of reproduction. They believe that this is the height of divinity, for woman's womb represents the creativity principle in nature. Of course this is not true as I explained before. Kali is often portrayed in statue form with a long protruding tongue which is precisely parallel with the Egyptian god, Bes, and with Medusa as represented in early Greek sculpture. All of these are of Gorgon origin, i.e., each is a fierce countenance intended to frighten evil spirits. She often wears the linga, the symbol worn by Shiva, as an ornament on her head.

"In the temples of Kali, and in a vast number of village temples in the rural Indian states, animal sacrifice is still in use. But as in the temple of Kali at Kalighat, Calcutta, she accepts only the blood as her portion of the sacrifice.

"One fact must remain clear. To the Indian the idol of the Kali may have been a stone image to the eye but it is

94

a living personal goddess to him. The image has been made by human hands, but the goddess lives in it, using the stone or metal body as the human uses the human body. She lives in the temple among her people, receiving from their hands the food by which she subsists, welcomes them to her presence and makes them her guests. She listens to their prayers and answers them. She hears and speaks, eats and sleeps, moves and acts.

"The whole of the temple worship depends on this belief. The villager goes to the temple to see Kali's face. He believes he looks into her own divine eyes. He prays with fervent prayer, and hears the goddess answer him with her own lips. Not only the villager does this, but in the lives of all the saints you can meet the same belief.

"Kali is represented in various forms; as Sati for example the faithful wife who cast herself into the fire so as not to be present when her husband and father were quarreling, and who was the prototype of all the satis, devoted widows, who consented to be burned alive on the funeral pyres of their husbands.

"Next she is Parvati, the girl from the mountain; Uma, the Beneficent, whose carnal and mystical union with the Divine Spouse is part of her cult; more frequently as Durga, the Inaccessible; Chandi, the Violent; Gauri, the Wild, Kali, the Black; or sometimes as Annapura who gives rice in abundance.

"Associated with several of these are a series of warlike tales about conflicts with demons and a ritual practice based on human sacrifice. Sometimes she bears a serene, pacific aspect as in the poets' vision that sees her as the Mother India; but for the most part she is a cruel, repugnant figure dripping with blood, hungry for human flesh, adorned with bracelets of snakes and a necklace and girdle of skulls.

"She is the female shakti, energy of Shiva, and because of this position she is so honored without giving due honors to her divine spouse. For this reason she is given high status among the men and women of the Far East.

"The Saktas who adore the wife of Shiva as his sakti, or

energy, call their manuals, Tantras. These books contain a literature of such vast importance that I wonder how so many, over the centuries, have missed their substantiality. The contents have guided priests and gurus in their labors through the centuries, while they have been regarded as inspired authorities by poets and thinkers.

"What it contains is most important to you and myself and every spiritual traveler in the worlds here and beyond. While secrecy goes with savagery in the Kali or Sakta cult, it also has left us something for our own knowledge to help in the Far Country.

"They have a word—a Word of Power—a magic word. If uttered by one who has so subdued his nature as to be near the spiritual worlds, it may move mountains and achieve empires. It is the very word which all inner cults of religion have sought, a Word which was boomed out from the idol in the great inner temples of Egypt, the Power of Word that was on Aaron's Rod, the Power of Word the Psalmist says, 'When the sea heard, it fled'; the Power of Word that was on Solomon's Ring, and which Jesus, said the Jews, used to work his miracles. The Power of Word which all men seek, 'The gyatri' that must never be said, the sacred cry of obscure meaning 'Om Mane padni hum!' 'The Jewel is in the Lotus.'

"Nobody seems to find this word which is written into the Tantras, the secret mystical word which is there but not written. This is the paradox of all things which the worship of the Kali has brought out.

"Now that I have said this much, it behooves me to bring you up to the next step. There is the Kali, there is the Shiva, the two faced God; the male and female God of this earth world. On one side you find the face of Shiva, the male God, with his symbol, the Linga, the phallic organ of man; the other face is that of Kali, the female side with the koni, the female organ of woman. Both represent two individual cults; the phallus is the male energy, and the vagina is the female energy.

"Therefore the Word of Power is somehow tied in with

the energies of the universal power, the ECK, which sends its forces into the human elements, the body and its bodies or sheaths. The Tuza is aware of this lost word, but somehow It hasn't yet found it in the worlds below. It is possible that the Tuza won't, until getting into the Sach Khand region, as an Initiate of ECK.

"So you see that man worships the Kali in many forms, throughout all religions, or he worships the feminine principle, so to speak. He is concerned mostly with destroying and rebuilding in this world. His aberrations keep him on the move destroying most of the things which come in his path, and it is through the feminine principle that he is interested in the ways of creating and destroying.

"So it is strange that in this weird philosophy of destruction, you find the Word of Power. This Word on the planes of the lower worlds is a two edged sword—for it can create or destroy; the creative side is the male principle and the destructive side is the female principle.

"This power is in every woman who walks or has walked the earth planet. It is in her makeup to give life or destroy it; this is her nature and sad as it may be, the more freedom that a woman has the more that she wishes to experiment with life. She gives birth to babies as a creative process, but this is only one of her functions on the earth planet. Observe the nature of woman in your casual relations with them—they want to pull everything down to their level—this is because woman feels inferior to the male species. She will go to untold lengths in order to bring a man down to her level and make herself equal. This is the Kali force working within her. This is the power, or the word which the Tantras keep so secretly hidden and never write down, but at the same time tell you what it is and what it might be.

"The menstruations of woman are tied to the forces of nature, and because of this cruelty, Kali herself is forced to demand the blood of humans and animals. This is to make up for what she loses monthly. She fights the desperate fight against nature and not winning, she takes her revenge by demanding that all women obey her and seek the

97

equalization of man. She is gaining more strength and status from the ages through which she lives, until possibly one day, Kali may be the leader of all races—that is woman might become the head of the family and leaders of nations.

"This is why you and all spiritual travelers must study the worship of Kali. Man is coming into the era now where he is fighting for his position in the society of races, because women are trying to take his place. There have been many matriarchal societies in the history of the earth and every time this has happened, there has been a major regression as the feminine principle rules.

"The more civilized a nation or society becomes, the more it is influenced by women, the feminine principle. After it reaches its zenith as in the Golden Ages of Greece, when Pericles ruled, the feminine principle starts to turn the tide of attitudes with many female qualities, like love, charity and forgiveness. Each is a feminine quality—and not at all like the qualities of the SUGMAD, those taught by the great spiritual Lords on the upper planes of the Far Country.

"Kali is a civilizing creature, representing a minor current in the lower world which is not very well known by most of the people who worship her in some form, be it the Virgin Mother Mary, or the Rain Goddess of the Congo.

"I'll take up more about Kali later!"

"Sakti is the worship of Shiva, the form of pleasure derived from the guthya or Koni, the female organ. Shiva is the Linga, or the worship of the phallus. The union of these two is the cause of all joy in the universe, say these followers of the two cults. It is also the unknown belief of all religions and cults on this earth.

"Kali therefore represents the essence, power and force in life. Her followers have the complex that is sometimes met in the work of the somewhat super-feminists, that the female is the superior and dominating force in the world and must be allowed to control it. You hear this being taught by mothers and feminine men to small children during their early years.

"The important aspect of this fecundity cult is that the doctrine of reincarnation is associated with it, as in most religions that give credence to the subject. It means that every birth allows a waiting Soul to tread one more stage to salvation. The looseness of the moral code in regard to sex is an excuse given to help a Tuza reach perfection through reincarnation.

"This is a part of the teachings on the Kundalini. The Saktis believe that the worship of the mother goddess, Kali, and the performance of the sex act can bring about release of the Kundalini; that acts of violence will also release this strange powerful force.

"The Kundalini is actually the sex force, in a manner of speaking. In other words the kundalini is a dichotomy with two sides, the physical side and the subtle. The Sakti use the physical acts in order to release the kundalini, which is neither permanent nor stable in any manner.

"Those who follow the Patanjali system of yoga use the Pranayama exercises, which release or awaken the kundalini from its dormant state in the indri chakra, or swadhistana center. It lies near the sacral plexus and is associated with the function of reproduction. It is the creative center in man. Not the brain or the mind; as I pointed out before, this is actually the creative center in man.

"When awakened this force rises through the central canal of the spinal cord, known to the anatomists as the sixth ventricle; to the occultists as the Sushumna path, with two smaller canals, one called Ida, on the left, and the other called Pingala, on the right. When the Kundalini rises to the brain, fully aflame, a series of important changes take place in the consciousness, especially in the feelings and emotions.

"The individual is on fire, so to speak. He has also a very great increase of powers—powers over the forces of nature and powers over other people. If, however, that individual has not been properly prepared for these changes by a rigorous process of training in self-control and mind purification, the results may be very disastrous. Even death or insanity may follow.

"For this reason then, the way of the Kali is wrong—the ecstasy brought to man through affection for and love of a woman, or the worship of sex in her, is dangerous if it arouses the kundalini. Take the example of John Keats whose love for a woman was so great that it released this power in him and brought his death; the same happened to Lord Shelley, the poet, who went nearly insane and lost his life by drowning; Byron also had the same experience and went out of his life at thirty-two.

"This Kundalini is dangerous on the lower planes. No man should play around with it unless he is instructed by the MAHANTA, the living ECK Master. It can do great injury to the body and bring ruination upon the user's head, unless he is careful and properly guided.

"The systems taught by yoga to release this flame power are of the lower world, and of no need to the spiritual traveler. The Tuza who wants the release of his kundalini must contact someone who can help him; then he can begin to release it and move into the higher spiritual realms.

"You see man, himself, is a microcosm of the greater macrocosm, and in order for him to see this there are certain methods by which it can be done, mainly, intuition. Man is the microcosm and inside him are still smaller microcosms, each one of which has a definite relation to some portion of the outlying universe. The entire existence of man is wrapped up in a larger being. He himself is but a cell in the body of the cosmos. Yet, taken as an individual, man is a small universe. More accurately speaking, man is a cluster of universes, all within himself.

"In him lies hidden the sum total of all universes. Each cell in his body is a still smaller universe and each atom in each cell is still a smaller one. The body of man is a vast and complicated system of universes, millions of universes clustered together in a single unit.

"Man is indeed a complete replica of the vast systems outside of him, and in this fact lies a great hope. It is a gracious promise to man by the SUGMAD. Man, in the study of himself, learns about the great universes on the outside. By going within to go outside, he awakens all his latent powers. Doing this, he then comes into conscious touch with the entire systems of worlds, both physical and subtle, filling endless space.

"The exact process by means of which this is to be accomplished will be revealed by the spiritual traveler to those who wish to follow in his footsteps.

"Each and every man, when properly trained, is able to detach himself from the physical body, while still living in that body in perfect health, and travel to all parts of the outlying universe.

"Everyone has this ability, whether conscious of it or not, but during his sojourn in this world he has forgotten and lost the knowledge of how this is done.

"The microcosmic centers in the body are: (1) the Mulchakra, which is also called the muladhara or guda-chakra. It is located near the rectum and governs elimination.

"These centers are all shaped somewhat like the lotus flower, more or less round, and the number of distinct parts are spoken of as petals. This lowest one has four petals, the higher ones increasing in number, as they ascend.

"It is an interesting fact that all of these body chakras taken together, have exactly fifty-two petals, corresponding to the fifty-two letters in the Sanskrit alphabet, and each petal gives out a sound of a distinct musical note, corresponding to one of the Sanskrit letters. These sounds can be heard by any person whose finer sense of hearing has been awakened. He can then see these chakras and listen to their sounds. It is claimed that these fifty-two sounds comprise all of the sounds which can be possibly made by the vocal organs of man. It is said that the ancient rishis and masters, listening to the fifty-two sounds, fashioned a character for each one, and that is the way the Sanskrit alphabet came into existence.

101

"The second chakra is called the Indri-chakra or linga chakra, where the Shiva God is worshipped, as well as the Kali. It is also called the Shat-dal-kanwal. Located near the sacral plexus, it has six petals. It has to do with reproduction.

"Third is the Nabhi chakra. It is often called Ashta-dal-kanwal. It is located at a point near the solar plexus and has mostly to do with general nutrition. It has eight petals.

"Fourth is the Hrida chakra. It is also named Dvadach-dal kanwal. It is near the cardia plexus and has twelve petals. Its function is to serve the circulation of the blood and breathing.

"Fifth is the Kanth. It lies near the cervical plexus and has to do with respiration. It is also named the Shat-das-dal-kanwal, the lotus of sixteen petals.

"The sixth center is called Do-dal-kanwal, the two petaled lotus. It is located back of the eyes on a level with the lower part of the eyeballs, but exactly in the center of the brain cavity, at a point in the subtle body, corresponding with the position of the pineal body. This is the seat of the mind and the Tuza.

"This is the center of control over the body. All centers below this one are subordinate. All deities or forces which are said to govern the body are themselves subordinate to the mind and spirit of man which reside in this center.

"Above this center is another center called Char-dal-kanwal, whose function is to supply the four-fold Antishkarans, the mental faculties of the mind, with centers of action. These four faculties are: Manas, Buddhi, Chitta and Ahankar. Each of the petals of this lotus has its own sound, and these four complete the fifty-two letters of the Sanskrit alphabet. This is the lowest of the six centers in Anda and lies nearest to Pinda, the fourth grand division.

"Just above the Antishkaran four petaled center comes the Tisra Til, third eye, at which the chela concentrates his attention, when practicing the spiritual exercises of ECK.

Thus the Tuza resides in the Do-dal-kanwal, when in the body, and leaves through the Tisra Til.

"This is enough for today. Tomorrow I'll talk some more on these centers."

* * *

"Now to finish the Tisra Til or the third eye. This subtle organ is also called the Shiva-netra, the eye of Shiva. It is also Nukti-i-saveda, the black point—known mainly to the Saktas, followers of Kali, the Black Goddess.

"In the case of the Nukti-i-saveda, the concentration is worked in reverse and Soul, in getting out of the body, is kept earth-bound, doing many things which often ends in violence. It's a sort of left hand path, or black magic.

"There are many centers still higher in the brain, each corresponding to a region in the higher worlds. There are twenty-two important centers in man's subtle body, besides almost numberless smaller ones which may be likened to the smaller nerve ganglia in the body. They all have a certain function but it is too much to explain here, so we'll keep to the high spots.

"I have given the six centers in Pinda, the lower world, or body below the eyes, as a study. This is because so many yogis emphasize these and use them, but no spiritual traveler uses them. They begin their concentration at Tisra Til, and from there they move upward.

"If one begins there, the next station above Tisra Til is Ashta-dal-Kanwal, the lotus of eight petals; then the next above that is the true center of all the Astral worlds, the Sahasra-dal-Kanwal, and this is the first of the great regions traveled by the spiritual travelers in the Far Country.

"All great yogis generally stop here, many of them fully believing that they have attained the highest in the Far Country. It is practically the starting point of the spiritual travelers on their upward journey toward the supreme region. That supreme world lies eight distinct stages above, or seven exclusive of Sahasra-dal-Kanwal. Sahasra-dal-Kanwal lies just below the Brahm Lok of the Hindus, which is known in the language of the ECK travelers as Trikuti.

"This is the second stage on the path for the great Yogis. For the ancient Hindus and the Vedas, it was the end of all, the residence of the Supreme Godhead. In the science of the spiritual travelers, Brahma is known as the Negative Power.

"It was inevitable that the feeling of bhakti, or love, which is inseparable from the life itself should eventually manifest itself in something like the Tantric cult of Kali. Tantra's fundamental characteristic is a full, unconditional acceptance of life and the world of creation, as they are, whereas the intellectual denied their reality.

"The former was life-affirming, whereas the latter life-denying. The intellectual, in fact, was the representative of a pertrified civilization's intellect, rational, coldly logical and sterile. The greatest modern exponent of Tantra, the Kali cult, was Sri Ramakrishna, who defined Tantra in this manner, 'The bhaktas accept all the states of consciousness. They take the waking state to be real also. They don't think the world to be illusory, like a dream. They say that the universe is a manifestation of the SUGMAD's power and glory. The SUGMAD has created all these—sky, stars, moon, sun, mountains, ocean, men, animals. They constitute His glory . . . . He is within us, in our hearts. Again, He is outside.'

"Ramakrishna added that Jnana, the path of knowledge, that is obtained through radical negation led to the Absolute, impersonal Godhead of monism. But bhakti, the progressive affirmation of unquenchable love, leads to something else; to the worship of the cosmic force of the universe, sakti, as symbolized by the goddess Kali.

"The popular, optimistic and almost sensuous aspect of

104

the Kali cult as given in the Tantra, is the natural complement of the more negative and intellectually aristocratic Vedanta in its complete acceptance and fusion of the four basic pursuits of man: prosperity, (artha), sensual love (kama), earthly duties (dharma) and final release (moksha).

"In the Kali movement, the Hinduism of the last few centuries, is finally expressed most completely in its catholic rites and devotions: consecrations, transubstantiations, incense and offerings accompany yogic meditation. More than anything else, this cult has given free rein to the development of the powers of the imagination. And nowhere as in India, has the power of imagination been able to recreate art and cause a metamorphosis in the devotee himself, than in the Kali worship.

"Sri Ramakrishna said at one time. 'The Divine Mother revealed to me in the Kali temple that it was She who had become everything.'

"The Kali described by the Tantra text is one who should be adored with liquors and oblations. She who has a gaping mouth and uncombed hair; who has four hands and a splendid garland formed of the heads of the giants she has slain, and whose blood she has drunk; who is as black as the large clouds and has the whole sky for her clothes; who has a string of skulls around her neck and throat besmeared with blood; who wears ear-rings, consisting of two dead bodies; who carries two dead bodies in her hands; whose form is awful and who dwells in the burial grounds of consumed corpses.

"This is the Divine Mother of the gentle saint, — also the goddess of the criminal, blood-thirsty Thuggee cult. Can you imagine anyone worshipping this outlandish symbol?

"Kali is but the primitive energy called Shakti in this lower world, and whoever can understand this all creative element which can also destroy, is among the highest in the world of the Anda. She is the burning of the fire, the subtle side of Shiva.

"Other mystics in India have followed this strange goddess. Vivekananda was her disciple. The great Indian teacher, Aurobindo Ghose, found refuge in her arms. Subhas Bose, a ranking member of the Indian congress, whose opposition to Gandhi's non-violence platform brought him into the light of international news, was a devotee. These are among a few who have been followers of the Kali.

"Having brought you this far, I will go to the next step. The symbol of the Kali is the manifestation of the feminine principle in man and woman. She is the representation of all womanhood, the great mother, the moon goddess, the divine mother.

"This mother goddess is the heavenly representative of womanhood. She is the Mother, the Woman who is immortal. She does not die like man, but lives eternally, the prototype of woman, the eternal feminine. She lives eternally and it is her unchanging, enduring character which is her most marked characteristic. She is the power behind God, or to quote the early Greek writers, she is the fatal goddess, the Goddess of Fate, and often therefore the inexorable one, the goddess of death, whom even the efforts of her devotees cannot mollify.

"The Kali is the All-Giver, mother of Gods and men and of the creatures of the field. Her story appears again and again in primitive mythologies. Sometimes she is the Moon Mother, the creative Earth Mother, Mother Nature. In many systems her concept closely resembles that of the Kali so it is hard to say what is the mother goddess that all ancient people worshipped and is still found today in the Kali and the Virgin Mary. All are represented as the same generative and destructive powers. The Chaldeans, Greeks, Scandinavians, Hindus and Chinese speak of their mother goddess, sometimes as earth deities but always in the terms of the generative and destructive powers.

"In all ages and in all places men have conceived of a Great Mother, a Great Woman, who watches over mankind from some place in the sky, or from the place of the gods and the temples. This concept can be found in practically every religion and mythology whose contents have come to my knowledge.

"These Great Mothers, whose worship has dominated the religious thoughts of people far removed from each other in time, space and culture, have an essential similarity which cannot but amaze you. The Great Mother was worshipped in ancient Babylonia, in the Near East, in Egypt, in Rome, in medieval Europe, even to this day among the peasants of Europe, in the Celtic countries, in ancient Mexico, among the North and South American Indians, in Africa, in Australia, in Polynesia, in India, and in ancient China.

"In all these places, and the list is not complete, the Mother has certain clearly defined qualities. She partakes of the characteristics of the moon, and in a peculiar sense, she is the women's deity. She represents the feminine qualities of fertility and virginal births.

"All women find a worship for the Mother Goddess, whether they are aware of it or not. It might be in the church, or it could be of their nature to give adoration to this strange being, which is actually the minor feminine current on this earth plane.

"This feminine principle is in constant struggle against the masculine principle, because it is considered natural. It is like water which can blend, or bend at any moment and by doing so overcome the user of it. Drink too much and you will die from over indulgence. Immerse too long and you will drown. But stay away from it and you die of thirst or dehydration. This is the strength of the feminine principle.

"Women know this and in this manner they use man for their needs. In other words they are the conquerors, if man doesn't know it in time. You have only to know, when a woman has set out to overcome you through love, forgiveness and subtle conquest. She intends to keep you in the lower creations, but if you can mold her and make her pliant to your touch she can become a great spiritual traveler.

"She can reach the world of SUGMAD without man's help. Instinctively she knows this yet she reaches out for man to hold him to her side. Once she understands what can be done for her, then she will seek out the ECK which can take her upward into the airy heights of the Far Country."

Chapter 6

THAT ALONE EXISTS

Rebazar Tarzs wasted little time after my arrival the next morning. The sunlight made patterns across the floor, via the window and door. A blue fly crawled up the side of the wall and tickled his wings as though he were going to dive bomb us from that height.

The long ranges of the high peaks in the Hindu Kush mountains sparkled in white brilliancy. The shade was cool and inviting, similar to days spent along the Mississippi River when I was a child. Everything was a perfect setting, but more or less a setting filled with unreality. Nevertheless I saw that it was easy to anchor my deeper self to this great spiritual traveler and left it that way.

"Now a study of the Divine SUGMAD is in order," said Rebazar Tarzs, dropping upon the floor and putting his legs one over the other in a lotus position.

"You know what the SUGMAD IS, and you have some idea of what IT is like, and IT has to fit certain mechanical laws which IT has set up for ITSELF in the operation and management of the world processes, and their complexities.

"You see the SUGMAD, in a sense, operates like an individual. IT makes ITS own laws and must abide by them. This is the way that man works on a mechanical basis from habit. He sets up certain laws or rather postulates by which he must operate. These postulates or considerations may be in line with some other group of Souls, but all the same he must establish them himself or they will not be followed in the general social order in which he lives.

"This makes for rebels. Those who can't get into the swing of things that everybody else is doing must live outside the social order and suffer; although this might be a slight social ostracization compared to that of getting killed, as happened in Hitler's times.

"I don't know if you are aware of this, but the SUGMAD is as fixed in ITS ways as many individuals are on this earth plane. IT has to fight battles to stay in a certain conformed groove, because once out of it too many followers complain. So IT becomes as mechanical as the poor weaklings IT commands. Yet on the other hand the SUGMAD is also capable of changing nature quickly; however any changes made are usually done with lightning speed because it is convenient.

"The seekers of the SUGMAD must leave the earth world sooner or later. Their work is never completed, and has to be left to immature disciples who generally ignore IT.

"Seldom do chelas become real ECK travelers. The travelers tell their chelas that they have realized God in themselves, but as soon as they depart, the disciples begin to say that they feel God in themselves. There is a vast difference. The travelers see the SUGMAD, which is the real deity. They do not feel IT. And that constitutes an essential difference. Feeling is more or less blind and wholly unreliable. The spiritual travelers actually enter and explore the Kingdom of the Far Country, but the disciples read about it in books and begin to speculate.

"You don't find the SUGMAD through religion. IT's beyond religion of any nature, and nobody is going to seek for IT correctly when they know not where IT is.

"The SUGMAD is beyond this world of senses, this world of eternal eating and drinking and talking nonsense, this world of false shadows and selfishness.

"IT is beyond all books, beyond all creeds, beyond the vanities of the world. It is the realization of the SUGMAD within oneself.

"A man may believe in all the churches in the world; he may carry in his head all the sacred books ever written; he may baptize himself in all the rivers of the earth,—still if he has no perception of the SUGMAD, I would class him with the rankest atheist. And a man may never enter a church or a mosque, nor perform any ceremony; but if he realizes the SUGMAD within himself, and is thereby lifted above the vanities of the world, that man is a holy man, a saint; call him what you will.

"I will add that it is good to be born in a church, but it is bad to die there. It is good to be born a child, but bad to remain a child. Churches, ceremonies, symbols, are good for children; but when a child is grown up, he must burst, either the church or himself.

"This realization of the SUGMAD must be explained to you. Most people have no idea what one is talking about, nor do any of the many writers who turn out reams on the subject have the foggiest idea of what this expression means.

"First of all, it is not a feeling. Secondly, it is not a metaphysical speculation, nor a logical syllogism. It is not a conclusion based upon reasoning, nor upon the evidence of books or persons.

"The basic idea is that the SUGMAD must become real to the individual. Not a mental concept of IT, but a living reality. This can never be until the individual sees IT. Personal sight and hearing are necessary, before anything or anybody becomes real to us. To practically all men, the SUGMAD is an abstract idea, a mental concept. But how can you worship a mental concept? When most people say they love the SUGMAD, they mean that they have a certain emotion, superinduced by suggestion. It hasn't got the least thing to do with the realization of the SUGMAD.

"Now, the purpose of all higher thought is to convert that mental concept into something that is real to experience. It is only then that the ECK traveler can have a true insight upon realization.

"The real poverty of all religions has been their inability to make the SUGMAD real to their devotees. Can you imagine that men would live as they do, think and act as they do, if the SUGMAD was real to them: It is unthinkable. It must be confessed that as sad as that confession is, that not one Soul in all history has been able to realize the SUGMAD by and through any religious doctrine, or ceremony; not even by prayer and mental devotion to an ideal.

"We know this is so, because such realization can never

be achieved by such means. In the very nature of the case it is impossible. The best they can do is feel a little closer to Reality, or to quicken the imagination a little by prayer, Smarana* and concentration. If one gets into subtle regions, even to some small degree, he will experience a little uplift.

"This is good, but the feeling he gets will never carry him to those heights where he will possess complete realization of the SUGMAD. What then can lead him to that complete, supreme desideratum, or realization? The spiritual travelers can give you the answer.

"There is but one method of making the SUGMAD real to you—that is, to make you see the SUGMAD and hear IT. If you say this cannot be done, that is because you are unacquainted with the path into the Far Country, and the true methods.

"When the seeker enters the higher planes and there beholds within his own finer vision some majestic embodiment of the SUGMAD, clothed in divine power and beauty; and when he hears the enchanting music of the ECK, he then begins to realize the SUGMAD.

"But the realization is not complete at this point. Only when he rises by the aid of the ECK, to the still higher planes, and there in great joy blends his own spiritual being with the Supreme SUGMAD, then it is that he may experience this divine realization.

"From this fact, it must be evident that no religious ceremony can accomplish so much. Certainly no mental process can do this. It is a personal experience that cannot be had upon this earth plane. It is not an experience possible to physical consciousness. One simply must enter the super-physical planes to get it. Not only this, but he must rise to very exalted regions, and this can be accomplished only on the path to the Far Country, and with the help of the spiritual travelers.

"When the chela of a spiritual traveler ascends the spirit-

---

*Smarana—repeating of holy names.

112

ual worlds, one after another, he enters Daswan Dwar, the first plane of the heavenly country; he there beholds himself as pure spirit, stripped of all materiality. And this is Self-Realization.

"After that, if he advances into the higher worlds, he there beholds one or more of the most sublime manifestations of the Supreme SUGMAD, and then merging himself with these manifestations of the SUGMAD, he comes to know the SUGMAD. And this is genuine SUGMAD-realization. There is no other.

"No man can ever know the SUGMAD, until he consciously becomes one with the divine Self. Anything short of this is more or less speculative, imaginary, visionary and imperfect.

"This is a summing up of the whole matter. Churches, formal religions belong to the immature periods of human thought and evolution, to the childhood of the race. Each religion serves its own purpose in its own day and time. But each must eventually give way to something more complete, as mankind advances to greater spiritual understanding.

"Throughout the whole of human history, the very essence of religion has been an effort to realize the SUGMAD. How many have succeeded? What you might call a handful!

"Only the great ECK travelers have had the perfect system by means of which it can be done, and the travelers have been very few among men. Efforts toward this sort of realization have always failed, except and only, when they have followed the method which I've laid down here.

"If the ardent followers of certain religions insist that many people have succeeded by their own methods, that is because they over-estimate a partial success.

"Something is gained, no doubt, by nearly all forms and ceremonies, by prayers and deeds of charity. But not complete realization of the SUGMAD — not even perfect Self-Realization.

"Do you understand what I am saying?

"If you do, then we are on the right track, for it is so hard to get anyone to grasp the essential meaning of Self-

Realization. We haven't gotten to the ECK, the spirit of all things yet—but that is coming, for all things are made up of the ECK, and not the SUGMAD.

"There is a vast difference between the two. I will explain later."

* * *

"Now to continue on the subject of the Supreme SUGMAD," said Rebazar Tarzs quietly, while looking over my head at the sunlight streaming through the doorway.

"There are six different ways the Supreme SUGMAD has to make ITSELF known to men. Notice here that sometimes I speak of the SUGMAD in the pronoun, HIM, and other times in the neuter, IT. This magnificent power is not to be named, for IT is so great that we cannot give IT a designation as is the earth men's habit of tagging people by names.

"All right, the six ways that the Supreme SUGMAD has to make ITSELF known to man are often called rays of light from the Divine. They are spoken of at times, as if they are personalities—Amesha Spentas, which means the Holy immortals.

"They are:

"First, the Asha-Vahista, the Supreme Will, manifested in the world. Second, the Vohu-Mano, good mind, divine wisdom, pure mindedness. Third, the Khashathra-Vairya, all creative, all sustaining power. Fourth, the Armaiti, perfect piety with single minded devotion. Fifth, the Haurvatat, absolute wholeness, perfection, spirituality, and sixth, Ameretat, immortal life, freedom from death or dissolution.

"These six represent both the maternal and paternal qualities of the Supreme SUGMAD, the first three, the father, and the last three, the motherly nature of the Supreme.

"Of course there is the seventh, which is needed to make up the total of the first six rays and the essence of that we know as the ECK, the highest of all spiritual powers. The ECK gives life, sustains all life and binds together as the adhesive force we know as love.

114

"Now there is an eighth ray, if you wish to call it that. Rather an eighth power, which you know as the ECK. It is often called Sraosha in the Far Country. A word derived from the Sanskrit root, Sru, meaning to hear. This is most significant. It is quite clear to the spiritual traveler that this ray of the Divine One is something that can be heard. This refers to the ECK, that audible life stream of the SUGMAD. It can be nothing else.

"This Sraosha is the central theme in all the teachings of the world. The spiritual traveler knows that it is the supreme thing for man to seek and to cultivate. He knows that when one fully attains to this Sraosha or ECK, that the way stands open before him to enter into the Far Country; all obstructions are removed.

"Going back to religion, you might say that religion for anyone is not the church, the organized body of those following a series of concepts, but it is the inner experience of the individual. To get to this experience, one must go inside and find his way through to the spiritual worlds.

"He must detach himself from all sense objects by concentrating the attention on something inside, and suddenly he will be outside in the subjective worlds. Does that make sense?

"By leaving the outer world and entering the inner world of consciousness, the spiritual traveler finds himself. There is no exception to this rule. This is the true system of the ECK travelers, and it is true of all other systems which yield any sort of high spiritual experience whatsoever. Here is the crucial point—as the methods differ, so will the experiences differ. The method of the spiritual traveler is exacting. All other methods are more or less haphazard, empirical and uncertain.

"Because of these various methods which the many religious organizations have, the experiences in the other worlds are vastly different. Take for example here on this plane; the experience of the movie actor is going to be vastly different from that of a public accountant. This is obvious.

"This explains why so many religions exist in this world

115

and in the other worlds up to the Daswan Dwar plane. Each of the followers of the various religious groups have different experiences, in their own methods. Within each method the experience is uniform and therefore makes for reality for those following that particular method.

"There is a vast difference also in the differences of religious experiences. This also explains why there is such an endless variety and confusion in the results obtained by all other methods.

"Also there is a vast difference in the degree and extent of penetration into the inner worlds, and so there must be a corresponding difference in the results obtained. This fact further accounts for the great variety of inner experiences, and the variety of religions based upon the experiences.

"One may leave the outer world and enter very slightly into the regions of thought. If he concentrates at that point, thought-forms will build up about him, and his problems will be solved, so far as his own thought can solve them. These thought-forms can be seen by anyone who has astral vision. This is the region where mind plays its greatest dramas. It is on the Astral plane that mind goes on creating molding and shaping as it desires. All the while there is a constant stream of suggestion pouring in upon the individual. This helps to mold his thought-forms. Finally many Tuzas, who are more sensitive are able to actually see their own thought-forms and they imagine they have seen some great characters outside themselves. Those thought-images will often talk to them, out of the depths of the sub-conscious self.

"There has never been a religion founded, never a good book written, never a good picture painted, never a good poem composed, never a good invention developed, except by going inside to some extent, and there concentrating on the task in hand. Even if one is not conscious of the exact thing he is to accomplish, he gets results by concentration. That is the great thing in the process—perfect concentration, becoming oblivious to the outer world of sense, centering attention upon that which is to be found in the Far Country. This is the way of attainment, no matter in what line of endeavor. No matter what one is to achieve, this is the one and only method leading to success. Concentrated attention is the key that unlocks all stores of wisdom, of truth and spirituality.

"When the traveler comes face to face with his own mental creation at the beginning of his journey, and if he is without previous experience on this path, he will be almost helpless unless he has the guiding direction of a traveler who has gone on before him.

"This has been the unfortunate experience of thousands of those who have entered to some degree into the inner consciousness; they got the impression that some deity, or some angel, or relative is leading them. They hear the Voice of God, they say. Or they get the impression that God himself is giving them some command, or instruction.

"But as a matter of fact, such vision, or voices, or impressions, are as a rule, their own mental creations. This process is plainly visible to anyone who has independent astral vision. The individual himself is rarely able to make the distinction, because he hasn't such independent vision. He fondly believes God is speaking to him directly, when he is actually hearing nothing but the faint whisperings of of his own mind, coming up out of his subconscious self. He is deceived, self-deceived. And so often he announces that he has received a message from God, or that God is leading him to do certain things. Many people say that God has ordered them to commit murder, or do all sorts of atrocities. It is their disordered mind.

"To the spiritual traveler who has learned much about psychological phenomena, it is quite apparent that any command from God is nothing more than a creation of one's own mind, superinduced by a long course of suggestion.

"It has happened many times in history. New cults are started as result of this, movements inaugurated, sacrifices made, and books written, solely on the strength of such

117

commands from God. These individuals are not to be blamed for their mistakes. Most of them are serious, sincere devotees of religion. The trouble is that they have no safeguard, no reliable guidance. They cannot see inside, so as to detect the fraud that is being perpetrated upon them by their own minds.

"As soon as a person enters into the lower spiritual worlds, only for a small distance inside, he is always confronted and fairly assaulted by multitudes of his own thought-forms. They have nearly all taken shape out of his own past training and the ideas he has held for long periods of time, aided by the suggestions of others. They spring up out of his own long-cherished desires. In the end, they mislead him into all sorts of by-paths. This psychological process, we believe, is the real source of most of that endless variety of experience which people call religious, and accounts for the great multiplicity of religions. Even William James was misled in his studies of those who experienced these varieties of religious phenomena.

"Every ECK traveler keeps a vigilant eye upon his mental processes. When he begins to enter the inner worlds, even to the slightest degree, he must beware of his own misleading mental creations. In all of his waking consciousness, he is to remember that his mind is his worst enemy, as well as his most useful instrument. But the main point is that he must keep it under control every moment. The mind is a useful servant but a bad master.

"The deeper one penetrates into the finer regions of truth and reality, the more perfect his light becomes. The spiritual traveler never imagines he is led by the SUGMAD. He never gets a false impression, and he never organizes a misleading cult out of his own disordered impressions. The SUGMAD never talks directly to people, as I've just described.

"The SUGMAD has ITS way of leading men to the light. There are two methods used by the Supreme One: First, is the method of the whole world, led by natural law, personal experience and experimentation — trial and discard. The second is finding the Mahanta who will help you and

118

give you his benefit by taking you with him on trips into the Far Country until you're able to travel alone.

"Remember that the SUGMAD doesn't interfere in the affairs of men. IT never speaks to anyone, IT never is seen by anyone, nor does IT impress anyone's mind."

* * *

"Now, to be able to see or hear the Supreme One, is an exalted attainment, far above that ever experienced by any spiritual seeker, except a saint or traveler. But the real saints and travelers are few in this world.

"A further word of warning has to be given here. Even if the seeker sees visions inside, he must beware of them. If he meets individuals, men, angels, even someone appearing as the Supreme Deity, or claiming to be IT or Jesus or a saint, beware that he is not deceived. If the seeker is a disciple of a real spiritual traveler, he cannot be deceived.

"He would have a definite infallible method of testing each vision, or appearance, to prove if they were genuine, as claimed. But should he not have this armament, he could almost be assured that he was being misled.

"The mind is treacherous, and besides this, the lower subtle worlds are filled with millions of other minds who are just as treacherous as our own. Don't believe them. Like the spiritual travelers say we shouldn't even salute them, or speak to them unless they are brought to attention by a traveler.

"If you imagine you see the Lord himself, any Lord whom you regard highly, do not allow that vision to carry you off your feet. The vision may be a creation of your own mind, or it may be the creation of some other intelligence, or an impersonation. Beware of it.

"Until one has the assistance of an ECK traveler, it is wiser to avoid all inner experiences. Above all, one should discount all voices which he hears. The use of your initiate's word will determine if your experience is genuine. If someone appears before you in a vision claiming mastership

119

or a Deity, the use of your charged word will determine the vision. If a fraud, it will disappear.

"Now let me give you the answer to another question which apparently bothers many people. A genuine ECK Master is the superman of the ethnologists and philosophers. He is that which Nietzsche sought to bring out in his Zarathustra.

"The Master is the highest developed man known to history, and consequently by virtue of his development, he has become the prototype of the race, the most splendid specimen of manhood, the noblest of the noble.

"It is generally understood that no man with a defective body, any serious deformity, can ever become a spiritual traveler. His mind must be of a very high type, keen, penetrating, quick of wit, and sound of judgment. He may not be educated in a university or college, but his mind must undergo the severest training and discipline. During the process of becoming a living ECK Master, he attains all knowledge which could possibly be given in the colleges and universities. In all respects the spiritual traveler is the highest type of man, when judged as man.

"The ECK traveler is the only man ever manifested in all history in whom individualism and universalism are combined in their full expression. That is, the spiritual traveler stands alone, is a law unto himself, does what he pleases, has what he wants, comes and goes absolutely at his own will, and asks favors of no man. Neither can any man hinder him in the execution of his will. He is the only man who has no need to ask favors of others; he has all things at his own command. If he suffers hardships, or inconveniences, that is because he chooses to do so for some purpose. He always pays for what he gets. He is not a slave to anyone, is no time server, is not bound by any rule or custom outside of himself, and is a citizen of the whole world.

"There is but one to whom the spiritual traveler bows in humble submission—the Supreme SUGMAD—Lord of All things in the highest height of the spiritual worlds. ITS sovereign law is the only law the spiritual traveler recognizes, and the universal law of all laws—Wisdom, Power and Freedom!

"Now, the world is the theater of the intellect. At least this is one of its fields of operation. It is the play or sport of the Kali, mother goddess. In this field science has made many conquests, and will doubtless make more. But there is a vast field far above and beyond the play of the mind, where the developed traveler alone may enter. It is into this higher region of the spirit the traveler goes, and it is there his real achievements are made.

"Entering there by methods well known to him, he finds that this earth world is nothing more than the mudball of nature's vast and complicated structure. Above and beyond this world of shadow and pain, lie innumerable worlds of intense light. They are real worlds, full of beauty, color, rhythm and joy. Escaping for the time being the limitations of the body, the spiritual traveler goes into the higher worlds, in full consciousness, and then returns to report what he has seen and heard, and otherwise experienced. He finds, among other things, that death is only an appearance, an illusion.

"When man leaves his physical body, at the time of what we call death, he simply steps out into another and higher world. He takes with him a finer body, which he now uses unconsciously, and on that higher plane, he uses the finer one just as he used the physical body here.

"The Supreme One is the infinite, limitless, whole of spiritual existence. The universal Tuza of all Tuzas, of all worlds, cannot be wholly centered in and limited to a single physical body, regardless of what the Catholic religion teaches.

"The SUGMAD is all Wisdom, Power and Freedom, and is the controller of the ECK, omnipresent and all-pervading. The spiritual traveler who has reached these heights is the same except for his physical limitations. Spiritually, he has no limitations. But the body is not the traveler, it is only a covering, one of his many instruments.

121

"He may at will leave the body and work on any of the higher planes, each higher plane gives him greater freedom and scope of action. He himself has no limitations, being one with the SUGMAD. Only the materials through which he works limit his actions; in the same manner they limit the actions of the SUGMAD, too.

"The omniscience of the Lord may not be able to express itself through the physical brain of the traveler, but the traveler may, in seconds, rise to regions above the sphere of the brain activity, where his consciousness automatically expands, even to the limitless. When he returns to this plane he will remember just as much of it as can be brought within the compass of brain action.

"Therefore the highest spiritual traveler becomes the giver of all life, the Lord of the universe. This is true because the traveler on the higher planes is identical with the Supreme SUGMAD. If one must ask how these things be, the answer is, because the traveler is one with the SUGMAD and the SUGMAD is expressing ITSELF through the traveler's form. The traveler's form is therefore the SUGMAD's form. Whatever the Universal ECK is, the individual traveler is identical in substance and attributes with IT.

"The beauty of all this is that every man is a potential traveler, and is therefore potentially identical with the Supreme SUGMAD. He needs only development and realization of this—so spiritual traveling is the supreme goal of all human evolution.

"Who can know the SUGMAD, but one who has himself ascended to the spiritual heights where the SUGMAD is openly manifest to sight?

"At the same time, throughout history, men have gone along creating Gods in their own image. Thus many a sincere student has taken refuge in agnosticism. They say that man stands between two great mountain peaks, the eternal past and the eternal future, and no man can see beyond either of those peaks.

"Theologians, in a frantic effort to prove the existence of a Supreme Deity, point to the construction and order

122

of Nature, the rhythm of the universe, its fixed laws and its onward flow—all of which they say suggests an all-wise and all-powerful creator. But after all, any argument based upon logical premises is just as likely to lead us astray as do the dogmatic assertions of the theologians. Of course there is no lie like history, so it may be said that there is nothing more misleading than logic. The Supreme can never be made a reality to any man by mere logic, or by books, or by feelings.

"I sincerely believe that anything which has to be proved by long processes of logic is not worth proving. In other words, if the thing is not self-evident, it is of little use. If anything in theory or teaching has to be established by laborious processes of reasoning, this very fact shows that we are on the wrong track and should seek new methods of establishing the hypothesis.

"Therefore the method of proving the existence of the great SUGMAD which is worth our time, is the experimental method of the spiritual travelers. No other method has ever succeeded and none of them can ever succeed.

"We'll leave off here."

* * *

"Among all peoples, and in all languages, not only is the name of the Supreme One different, but the fundamental ideas of the deity are different.

"In almost every land the people, in total ignorance of the SUGMAD, have gone on creating anthropomorphic gods to their heart's content. These gods are all given high seats in their heavens, from which they keep a vigilant eye upon erring mortals, their recording secretaries at their right hands. Nothing escapes the recording angels, according to those who believe in these gods. Of course, the idea must be all right, as by the law of karma man must pay for each offense in due course. A knowledge of the karmic laws is certainly the source of all such ideas as recording angels, or punishment for misdeeds.

"In spite of all the confusion regarding names and characteristics among the gods, there runs like a golden thread through all the accounts, the central idea of a great overruling power that is greater and better than man.

"The human race had been taught to look up to the gods with fear and trembling. That is, until the arrival of Jesus who said that God should be loved. This has been a central theme since the beginning of Christianity, but it's one the spiritual travelers know to be a half-truth.

"Christianity failed in several ways; mainly the Supreme One didn't send his only begotten son to that age of semi-civilized tribes who demanded his blood. This is inconsistent with the ways of the upper world for every MAHANTA, every Living ECK Master is the son of God, the trinity, God, ITSELF manifested for the uplifting of humanity. It is amazing that so-called civilized man could even begin to think like this. But it happens in Christianity, and someday the leaders will have to pay for this!

"Frankly, no one has given any description or analysis of the divine attributes, nor has any man ever imagined himself capable of doing so. But we find ourselves in possession of two opposite sets of qualities, the one we call bad and the other good. These two sets work in opposition to each other on the lower planes. They tend in exactly opposite directions, and they end in totally antagonistic results.

"Hence, in this world life is largely made up of wars waged incessantly between these two opposite sets of qualities and tendencies. This accounts for the writing of the holy scriptures, e.g., the Christian Bible, Granth Guru, Koran, etc. Where did man get these antagonistic qualities?

"Okay, then I'll get into the negative side of the power. This refers to that individual in the grand hierarchy who occupies the position of Creator and Governor nearest the negative pole of creation. He is not the lowest in the Hierarachy.

"Under him are many subordinates, but of all the negative powers, he is supreme. The rest may be called his agents and subordinates. They carry out his orders, just as he carries out the orders of his superiors. His name is Kal Niranjan, and his headquarters lie at the summit of Triloki, commonly called the three worlds. That is, the physical universe, anda, and the lower end of Brahmanda, designated as Trikuti or Brahm Lok.

"These three subdivisions of creation, in the minds of the ancient rishis, constituted the entire sum of creation. Kal Niranjan was then regarded as the supreme God over all creation. To the spiritual travelers, he is the negative power so named because he is at the negative pole of creation, with many regions above him.

"Contrasted with this negative power, the travelers speak of the ECK, the positive power. It rules the whole of creation from the positive end of all the universes. While it isn't the very highest of all, the manifestation of the Supreme One, yet it is generally regarded by the travelers as the Supreme Creator. It's in fact, Father and Creator to all. It is a significant fact that below him no member of the grand hierarchy has power to create Souls. They have creative power over everything else, but no power to create a Soul, and no power to destroy one.

"In Sat Purusha, the ECK, the supreme creative energy comes into perfect manifestation for the first time in Sat Desha. Agam Purusha and Alakh Purusha are so close to the ECK, so slightly differentiated, that the ECK, often known as the Sat Nam, is generally regarded as the first actual or complete personification of the Supreme One. He then becomes manifest as the supreme executive power of the whole creation. His region, Sach Khand, may then be known as the governing center of the entire system of universes.

"The Sat Nam is in reality the Supreme One, taking form and establishing its throne as the King of Kings, at the very gate of the supreme region. It is the sovereign Lord with whom the travelers have to deal most, in carrying out their sacred mission of returning Souls to their final home. To him all subordinates pay homage, and from him they all take orders.

125

"Sat Nam is the great father, the light-giver, and the supreme guru. To him we must all return, if we are ever to re-enter the original home. He is truly the heavenly father. All Gods, Lords, or Rulers below him, you can love and honor, but the supreme devotion belongs to the Sat Nam for he is the real Lord God of all worlds in existence.

"The Alakh and the Agam, and the Nameless One, the SUGMAD are so utterly incomprehensible, so fathomless and impersonal, that you cannot approach them, even in thought. But the Sat Nam stands midway between the infinite light and the created universes; and so in time when we have been purged of every imperfection we may approach him as the ruler, see him with our own spiritual eyes and be welcomed into the highest heaven that we can know, this side of the SUGMAD's own world.

"Meanwhile, while we are in the dark region of matter, we have to deal with the negative power. With him we must contend in our struggle for spiritual freedom. It is his duty to try to hold us here, while it is our duty to try to escape. The resulting struggle purges us and makes us strong, fitting us to the upward travel.

"The laws of the negative power are known as the Laws of Nature. He is the author of all natural law as we know it. For he is the creator and lord of the physical universe. He is the Lord God of the Bible, the Jehovah of the Jews, and Christians, the Allah of the Mohammedans. He is the Brahm of the Vedantists, the God of practically all religions.

"None but the ECK travelers and their followers know of any other God; yet this negative power, so exalted and so universally worshipped as the supreme Lord, is in fact only a humble subordinate in the Grand Hierarchy of the universe. What is more important to know, is that he is not free from imperfection when compared with the Lord of All, Sat Nam.

"Remember he is the negative power and as such he must

have negative qualities. But when compared with man, he is very exalted, full of light, goodness, wisdom and power. It is only when compared with the positive power that his lesser light becomes manifest.

"Now this great quality of love which the spiritual travelers and others speak about is the binding force of the universes. It is not a love as you and I observe here in this physical world. It is an agreement with the higher force— the positive force which we know as the ECK.

"This agreement, this agreeing force is the highest of feeling, or force that anyone directs toward the SUGMAD. Since we cannot put our mental fingers upon the SUGMAD because of ITS formless being, we can certainly look to the ECK for this agreement. If you felt that you had to love all things and *all* beings, it would be quite impossible to do so. The best way to manage this quality which is called love by so many of the ignorant, especially the theologians, is to be in harmony with all things.

"You can love only a few and give good will to all. This is perhaps the best way of explaining the quality of goodness. These are only words; in order to have semantics that give the best explanations of what we are trying to get at, it's best to think of words only as symbols.

"This is why the Sanskrit language was invented by the higher Tuzas in those worlds far above this plane. It might be called the language of the Far Country. Sanskrit is more or less an illustrative language, made to designate the powers and forces of the higher world.

"The gods brought Sanskrit to this world many centuries ago. It was the ancient universal language of this universe and many peoples on many planets within this universe still speak and use it.

"You find derivations of it now throughout the world; in China, Japan and other countries of the Far East. The Chinese language has roots in the Sanskrit, and the Japanese. Look at their pictures, and their writings in their native language. It will tell you more about the original Sanskrit than most of the languages today.

"This language is still in use in the Brahm Lok world, and so many who are returning from there today to this plane for reincarnation are often surprised to find it lacking in these countries where they are born. As soon as they see it in the Chinese or Japanese language, they recognize it immediately.

"We will stop here for there is so much to be taken up in the discussions that our strength must be preserved for the time being. I have much to talk about while you are visiting me during these talks."

Chapter 7

THE PATH TO ECKANKAR

Rebazar Tarzs sat down again and looked steadily at me, before starting his talk. There was a quality about this MAHANTA which was deeper than words. He seemed far beyond this world, a traveler from the misty future who came here to gaze upon this world.

He tucked the deep red robe under his legs with a thick, square hand and looked up again.

"Now I'll talk about the ECK, that formless fluid, the vehicle which the SUGMAD uses to carry all ITS messages to this world and back again. It is the creative spirit, the great building force which is most often called spirit.

"The SUGMAD is that deity above all deities and things. In fact IT is unable to communicate with the world of man except through ITS emanations, or rays as I have mentioned before.

"In other words the SUGMAD cannot be comprehended by human minds, by the intellect, nor described in words intelligible to man, so as to make ITS existence perceptible. It is necessary, therefore, in order to render ITSELF comprehensible to man, the SUGMAD make ITSELF active and creative. But IT cannot be the direct creator, because being infinite, IT is without will, intention, thought, desire or action, all of which are qualities of finite being only.

"In other words the SUGMAD didn't make man in ITS image as religions teach, especially the Christian religion. So the SUGMAD was compelled to create the world in an indirect manner through the ECK, the infinite light and sound which IT is and in which IT dwells.

"The ECK has ten rays or forces which are sent out to the worlds below. The first is the male or masculine, which is the Wisdom force; second, is the Power force, often called

129

the Life force; and third is the Freedom force, the liberating quality.

"From these forces or rays flow the offshoots. For example, there is the female, the passive potency, which is the Intelligence ray; next, the creative ray; sixth, the realization ray; seventh, self-determination; eighth is adoration; ninth, physical, the wonder-working ray; and ten, the nature or matter ray.

"These rays are not complex, but simply beams which are offshoots of the great spiritual form, the ECK, the first manifestation of the SUGMAD in the Sat Desh world. The Lords and governors of all the planes below Sat Desh are immersed with these ten particular rays, making them a part of the Godlike quality of the SUGMAD.

"Of course as the rays descend into the material worlds, they are not as strong as in the upper regions, because the negative power becomes a part of the rays after passing the Brahm Lok plane. Kal Niranjan, Lord of the lower worlds, has these same rays, as negative rays. You can speak of the ten rays of the Kal power which are the reverse of the ECK power.

"In the negative worlds the female power ray is stronger, and intellect or intelligence is more depended upon than Wisdom, Power and Freedom. All in the negative worlds seem to lean heavily upon the female ray of intelligence—the example is all around you. All of mankind is seeking intelligence or knowledge, mostly materialistic facts. No one seems to understand what wisdom is.

"Men call one wise who glibly and superficially utters a few platitudes, aphorisms and maxims. Those who can do this live at ease, a burden on their fellowmen; they are called philosophers, but woe to the ones who give themselves this name—they are hardly wiser than the kitten which learns to scratch at the door so the master will open it.

"Those who have been called wise are babes in arms, for example; Hegel, Thomas Aquinas, Aristotle and a few hundred others who are the earth's vanguard for this sort of nonsense. What have they done?

"Little or nothing. Nothing more than singing a few hymns to the nature god, saying that all men are equal, making claims to a knowledge that is hardly worth speaking of. Yet the earth people sing and have sung their praises in books, words and song from the beginning of these modern times. It is pathetic. If man should find and know the true path to the SUGMAD, he wouldn't waste his time studying Freud, and other immature, negative psychologies and philosophies.

"These are the traps which the Kal Niranjan sets for the unwary, and there are plenty on the earth plane, for so many are struggling to make their way upward to the other worlds, unconscious of the snares which are holding them back.

"There is little wonder that men take to religion, even if they have to invent one. Voltaire said that religion is the solace of the weak. Nietzsche repeated this in his writings and talks. But be that as it may, the weak and the trapped need some support, and far be it from me to deny them. I wouldn't take their religions away, even if I knew full well that it could be done.

"Religion has always been a haven for the millions who mourn and suffer. It is undeniable that it has been generally the unhappy who have sought relief in religion; any religion which happened to be near them, and who can blame them. It's like a drowning man grasping at a straw.

"A spiritual darkness broods over this world and all men are sick of it. Spiritually, and often physically, the whole of mankind is sick, blind, deaf, dumb and covered with sores. Cancers of moral corruption eat their way into the vitals of the human race.

"The race can change only when it awakens to find and accept the spiritual travelers here among them, ready to help all who come unto them. Nobody can make his way very far into the Far Country unless he has the assistance of the spiritual travelers.

"These ECK travelers know that the path of the ECK is the only way to reach the world of the SUGMAD. They

131

know its dangers and blessings. Leading the blind upward along the path until they can see for themselves, the travelers find only the blessings for their followers—bypassing the dangers, always letting their companions know what might befall them if they are careless.

"Within this earth plane the female ray works quite readily. It is the measure of success which followers of the sciences of the mind enjoy. The answer lies in this area in the well known laws of suggestion.

"Mind is the greatest power operating in this physical universe—mind, activated by spirit or what we call the ECK. Of course, all mind is vitalized by spirit; but once activated by spirit, it is mind that controls all physical forces through Prana, the primary force.

"Mind is the chief instrument of spirit for all contacts with the physical universe. But mind has its own methods of operation. In the subconscious reservoir of mind, there lies an almost limitless store of energy. If that reserve power can, by any means, be made available for our use, there is practically no limit to its scope of action. It has been found that by and through suggestion, the conscious mind may draw upon the subconscious for its reserve power. This is the way psychic healing works—it offers a method of applying that power to human needs.

"If the conscious mind can be made to accept the dictum that there is power available to remove pain and cure disease, beneficial results must follow. The system adds one more factor to the healing process. It teaches, not that this latent power resides in all men, to be drawn upon at will, but it is given by the Lord on occasions, meaning the Negative Lord of the universe, whom we know.

"So if the follower has faith, the power will come; when he offers the proper prayers, it works. This appeals to the religious sentiments in religion and today many people have no idea that it is simply a method of self-suggestion and auto suggestion. They firmly believe that they are healed by direct intervention of the Lord.

"You see, most of the faiths and cults of this earth world work on this error—or say theory. They continue to work like this until a traveler arrives and shows them differently, how to enter into the Far Country. They are more concerned with bodily health and other material things than getting along on the path to the ECK.

"It will be remembered that the top or zenith of the positive pole is charged with spirit substance to an extreme degree; as we descend toward the nadir, the extreme negative end, spirit substance undergoes a gradual diminution. As a result of this thinning out process, the various zones experience a corresponding darkness, until finally they take on more and more of the qualities associated with the bad or evil side of life, as bad health and poverty.

"All that human consciousness classifies as evil, is made so by a diminution or depletion of spirit. This means darkness, of course, lesser life, lesser light. Man cannot live happily without spirit, and the more he departs from spirit, the more he experiences what to him is evil. As with an individual man, so it is with the worlds themselves. The less spirit substance in them, the darker they are and the more troubles are experienced by their inhabitants.

"The Sat Desh country is a region of pure spirit. Its inhabitants are pure spirits, in such countless numbers as no man can estimate, all enjoying the greatest conceivable happiness.

"This is the supreme heaven of all heavens; yet it is quite unknown to any of the world religions, because their founders have never reached these exalted heights. It is known only by the spiritual travelers, who alone can enter it. This is the land of the ECK, where the light is greater than ten million physical suns put together.

"No Soul can enter into this world unless It has been

133

properly prepared by the spiritual travelers, and once attained It will never leave again unless It wishes to descend into the lower worlds to help those who are struggling upward.

"Soul can also go further upward into those heavenly heights above, which are numerous, but it is spirit that motivates It, as fuel does an engine on this earthly plane."

* * *

"The word psychology is taken from the Greek 'psyche' meaning science of the Tuza or Soul. That assuredly was the meaning attached to it by the old Greek masters; modern scientists have made it almost exclusively a study of the mind; and even at that they are practically limited to psycho-physiological phenomena. They never know whether they are dealing with chemico-physiological reaction of brain and nerve tissues, or with something independent of brain and nerve. No psychologist can tell you with assurance what thought or spirit is.

"The ECK travelers can tell you, because they are able to see both thought and spirit, and watch the former form and disappear. Mental reactions, under all sorts of stimuli, are just as visible to the Masters as physical reactions are visible to scientists.

"Finally, the travelers are able to detach themselves, even from the mind itself and observe themselves and others as pure spirit. It is at that point that the travelers obtain perfect knowledge about man. When he actually observes himself as ECK only, free from all coverings, including mind, he knows that he is essentially the ECK, that mind and all bodies are but instruments, coverings, needed only for contacts with matter in the material regions.

"Now, that which connects man with the supreme deity is sound; and sound can be described as the 'Word' which is identical with the ECK, yet below the highest in the hierarchy, the SUGMAD.

"This life-giving stream divides into ten powers or more, is a creative force and can be heard. The fact that it is audible is extremely important. This idea must be conveyed, if possible, in any name that is applied to it. One of its names is the Bani.

"This audible current or wave contains the sum of all teachings emanating from the SUGMAD via the ECK. It is the SUGMAD's word, almost directly, and includes everything that the SUGMAD has ever said or done. It is the SUGMAD, ITSELF, in expression and it is the method of IT making ITSELF known in ITS own language.

"The divine ECK, sound, word, stands for all that the SUGMAD is or has ever said or done. It includes all of ITS qualities. As said before, it is the only way in which the universal spirit can manifest itself to human consciousness.

"So when the Supreme SUGMAD manifests ITSELF as the ECK, or Sat Nam, in Sach Khand, IT becomes fully personified, embodied, individualized, for the first time and brings into manifestation all of the qualites of the deity.

"As the ECK IT becomes personal creator, Lord, God and Father. IT becomes the fountain out of which the audible life stream proceeds. This stream may be seen and heard by all who participate in it throughout the world. It may be seen and heard by such as attain an awakened consciousness, under the training of a spiritual traveler. When man hears IT, he hears the SUGMAD; when he feels IT, he feels the power of the SUGMAD.

"This sound current is the divine being expressing ITSELF in something that is both audible and visible. This current must not be understood to be like a river, running in one direction. It is more like a radio wave, flowing out in every direction from the grand central broadcasting station. In fact, it does come from the Supreme Creative center of the universe of universes.

"This wave has two aspects, a centrifugal and centripetal flow. IT moves outward from the central dynamo of all creation, and it flows back toward that dynamo. Moving upon that current, all power and all life appear to flow outward to the uttermost bounds of creation, and again upon IT all life appears to be returning to its source. It is the latter aspect of IT which we have to deal with for the greater gain.

"Upon that wave we return to the SUGMAD. When a traveler makes the connection, or as you say in radio, tunes us in, it is then that we begin this journey upward to the brilliant heights, leaving all perishable worlds behind us.

"This wave is called Nada in the Vedas. In Vedanta, sound is always spoken of as creative. Sound, or anything that sounds, is that creative energy. It is referred to as the Nada Brahm, meaning the primal word of Brahm. By this Nada Brahm, all creation was brought into existence, that is the lower worlds. The whole of the visible and invisible universe is the manifestation of this primal Nada. The Nada is the grand symphony out of which all other symphonies flow in everything below the Brahm Lok. It is the primal music of the universe.

"Every musical cord of this world is an echo of that primal cord. It is the Vadan of the Sufis and the Shabda of the Hindus. But all Sufis do not distinguish between the original sound and its echo. We should take care to distinguish between the echo and the original.

"This sound has so many names in many languages. It is the small still voice and the Voice of Silence. It is the same divine sound, no matter by what name it may be known. It is, in any case, a sound which can be heard only by the developed ear, attuned to its higher vibrations.

"This divine Logos is the real lost word of the Masonic order; it seems that the spiritual travelers are the ones who have rediscovered it again.

"To explain what this audible life stream is may not be so easy. It cannot be defined or explained in words. This is because it is beyond the capacity of any language, and it is never again put into words.

"Stated in the simplest words I can employ, this life current is the voice of the Supreme Creator, ITSELF, vibrating through space; it is the only quality of the SUGMAD which can touch everything in the universes. Yet, IT still must go through the ECK, and because of this—what we are re-

136

ceiving is only secondary; therefore, the ECK is the wave of spiritual life being transmitted from the SUGMAD to every living thing in the universe. By this current IT has created all things, and by it all things are sustained. In it they all live and move and have their being, and by this same current they will ultimately return to their source of being.

"Now to get a picture of this musical Life Current you must understand that its heavenly strains are not only filling all interstellar space, but they are ringing with far more enchanting music through all the higher worlds, unto the utmost bounds of the physical.

"The higher we go, the more enchanting the music. In the higher worlds the music is less mixed with matter, and so it is not dulled. After passing the third region on the pathway of the Far Country, this sublime music becomes so overwhelmingly attractive that Soul grows impatient to go higher.

"It becomes absorbed in it and lives in it day and night. It is Its life, Its joy and Its spiritual food. There is not a cubic millimeter of space in existence which is not filled with this music. Its life giving melodies may not be consciously heard by all who are not trained to catch them, but there is not a living being in all creation which does not derive its life from the sound current.

"If you still think much of the word religion, then you can say that this current is the only real religion. It is the ECK, the philosophy of the Sound Current. In fact, it is the only thing in the world which gives a tie to the living and the SUGMAD. Without this stream nothing could live for a single moment, or even exist. All life and power comes from it; from the crawling ant to the thunder bolt, from the tidal wave to the solar cycle, every manifestation of dynamic energy comes from this stream of the ECK.

"That which physical science calls energy, which the Orientals call Prana, is only a manifestation of this life stream, stepped down to meet material conditions. Like electricity in the air, IT is omnipresent, and IT is omnipotent. In IT lies all energy, latent or dynamic. IT only awaits the proper conditions to express ITSELF as dynamic force, in one form or another. IT has many forms of expression, most of which are not yet known to physical science.

"Of course IT has to be stepped down, and at each step IT takes a different character and quality, to which we give names, if we can demonstrate them at all. Most of them science has not discovered. But every force known, from primal energy, prana, to electricity and magnetism, are all modified forms of the same eternal current.

"ITS stepping down is necessary to serve the common cosmic and human needs. But at least, IT is all one force, and for this very reason many say that God is one. This isn't true. It is only one manifestation of the Supreme SUGMAD, working through the ECK; and by doing so becomes ITSELF — the ECK or supreme spirit.

"The tremendous heat, energy and light of our sun, of all suns, are derived from this stream. Every ray of light in the universe is a phenomenon of this infinite stream of light and sound. Upon its power hangs every star in its orbit. Not a single rose may bring forth its buds without this power and no little child smiles without manifesting this power."

*   *   *

"The ECK travelers all say that there is no other means of spiritual liberation, only the ECK. Without actual conscious, participation in the life current, the ECK, no one can escape the net of karma and reincarnation, or ever become free and happy.

"Hence all the travelers and saints lay the strongest emphasis upon this great Reality. In fact, without this life stream, no saint could ever manifest upon this earth, and hence the whole world would sit in darkness through endless ages. No Tuza can ever escape from this dark material world without conscious participation in and a personal relationship with this current. He must knowingly merge himself in this life stream and upon it he must then rise to freedom.

"It cannot be done in any other way. By this current alone, one is enabled to transcend all lower regions and rise to the highest heavens. By other means men may advance a little distance toward the light. But sooner or later they are automatically stopped.

"The highway to the Far Country is the royal road. It is the only way leading to spiritual insight and complete emancipation. This is the gospel of the life stream, and he who drinks of this stream can never thirst again, but in him is a well of water springing up into eternal life.

"This was the water that Jesus offered the woman at the well of Sichar, of which he said, if she would drink she would never thirst again. Truly, when one begins consciously to participate in this life stream, there is in him a well of water ever springing up, sufficient to supply the whole world. There is a fountain which cleanses him, and goes on giving life to every Soul who comes in touch with it. It purges both mind and Soul, making them whiter than snow. It flows on forever, a healing stream for the nations, for the races of the world, and whoever bathes in it will never go about the world again seeking food for the real self.

"This indeed is the true light, which lights every man who comes into the world. It is the ECK, the master power and spirit. It is Wisdom, Power and Freedom. All the great qualities you can imagine that belong to the SUGMAD.

"In the first chapter of the Gospel of John, it is called the Word, through which all creation came into existence. If only the Christian disciple had grasped this fundamental fact and held on to it, it would have meant a very different history for the church. Unhappily, the real meaning, which Jesus had in mind, was wholly lost. In the third verse of chapter three, Gospel of John, Jesus speaks of contacting the Current and of actually hearing it. Then he distinctly says the new birth is attained through it. All of this is exactly in line with the teachings of the spiritual travelers.

139

It's a pity the churches have never understood this reference of Jesus to the most important experience which can possibly come within the range of human life.

"To the clergy this new birth is a mysterious operation, not in the least comprehended. In some way it is supposed to be performed by the Holy Spirit, that which we know as the ECK. But this process is unknown to them. The travelers alone can explain this statement of Jesus, for they alone know exactly what the new birth is.

"The disciples of Christ were never spiritual travelers, nor Masters, in the sense we know, either. Had they finished their training and become one with the ECK, in other words if they had become spiritual travelers, the whole course of history would have been different. Instead, their own teacher was snatched away from them by death, before their course of development had more than fairly begun; after which the pure spiritual science which Jesus taught was soon obscured and lost. With that, among the Christians, vanished the last remnant of knowledge concerning the audible life stream. Jesus and his teachings were covered up in a mass of dogma and superstitions.

"In the second chapter of the Acts of the Apostles, an account is given of what happened on the day of Pentecost. They heard a sound, as of a mighty rushing wind, and then saw lights, like tongues of fire, sitting on the heads of the apostles, and they were filled with the Holy Ghost—the sound current, ECK—and they began to speak in foreign tongues.

"Now, this is a phenomena which may happen, and often does happen with those starting on the upward journey with a traveler. It is an experience which comes in the very beginning of their development. Often it is, as if one is standing between two buildings and a sound comes like that of a train rushing by, heard for a moment and then gone.

"This is something like the rushing, mighty winds, spoken of in the Bible. Other sounds are heard from time to time; all of these sounds are heard before the true ECK is heard.

Again, one of the lights seen by all neophytes appears like tongues of fire, as spoken of in the New Testament.

"Later the chela sees many more lights and hears much more of the heavenly ECK. As a result of these experiences, the young traveler is filled with increased light and power. Among other things he is able to understand all languages. He understands them all, as if each one was speaking his own language. This is a universal experience of the beginner on the spiritual path, and is encountered in the first region—the Astral world.

"Everyone understands the language of all others, no matter what they might be. To become filled with the ECK is simply to hear and participate in the audible life stream and to become absorbed in it, to be one with it. In becoming one with it, the traveler comes into possession of many of the higher powers.

"This is actually the meaning of becoming one with God—which all the ancient Rishis spoke about—and which all or most scriptures tell us. The unity, the becoming one with the Lord, is that which I've just said, becoming one with the ECK, with the audible life stream.

"By becoming one with it, you have the science of the ECK travelers, wrapped up in a few words. This is the great truth of the Far Country, which all seekers are desperately searching for and may never find.

"So you might say that the whole truth is this: the spiritual traveler, the audible life stream, and spiritual freedom, here and now. With these you have perfect liberation during this lifetime. You do not have to wait until another life of reincarnation to find it.

"All men wish for liberation, what the theologians call salvation, but their type salvation is very different from that of the ECK travelers. The salvation of the travelers is liberation from the wheel of transmigration, from the ills of this life, or of any life. Last of all, freedom to live for-

141

ever in some heaven of unalloyed bliss. This is salvation, as it is generally understood by the travelers on this path. It must never be confused with the theological salvation of the churches.

"You may pray to all gods on record, and they will not hear you; you can call upon any religion known for help, but it will get you nothing. It remains a stern fact of nature that no man ever has or ever can gain freedom from the ills of this life and escape the uncertainties of the next, until he has the good fortune to meet the ECK Master. If he has not done that, he must return again and again to this life, until he does meet the Master. That is the sum of it and that is final; without his help no one can ever gain permanent relief from this wheel of birth and death.

"On the other hand when a person finds the MAHANTA he will not fail to get spiritual liberation, immediately. This is because the spiritual traveler will connect him with the audible life stream, and so having both the traveler for his help, and the sound current he will get spiritual freedom which is here called Jivan Mukti.

"So the formula is to find the MAHANTA who can tune you in with the life current, the melodious bani. Then take hold of that current and merge yourself into it. After this you will be lifted up to the city of freedom. After you have passed the outermost frontiers of the material and the impure worlds, you have actually entered the regions of pure spirit; having grown godlike and fit for the highest regions, you will never return to these low lands of birth and death.

"You have attained Jivan Mukti, life everlasting!"

* * *

"Now I'm going into the various yoga systems. It is well that we go over them so you will know those practiced by students in the East. They are interesting but the ECK traveler doesn't need them.

"First, Hatha Yoga, which aims at the control of mind

142

and acquirement of the siddhis, or what are called psychic powers. This is done chiefly through asana, or physical postures and exercises. The asanas have beneficial effect upon the health, and bring control over the senses.

"Second, Raja Yoga which seeks to concentrate and still the mind by ways and natural methods of mental discipline and control. Emphasis here is placed upon the mind, rather than the body.

"Third, Ashtang Yoga is a comprehensive scheme of yoga training. It consists of eight elements, the first five of which — Yama, niyama, asana, pranayama, pratyahara, all refer to the body. The last three — dharana, dhyana and samadhi, all refer to the mind. The aim of this yoga is to merge the Tuza with the ECKANKAR, the universal Tuza.

"Pranayama, which chiefly consists of breath control and with that the control of the prana, plays a very important part in this Yoga.

"Laya Yoga—Laya means absorption. Laya yoga consists in the absorption of the mind in the astral light. This is generally achieved through the practice of mudra exercises.

"Karma Yoga is the yoga of action. It enjoins upon its followers the necessity of doing one's duty, whatever that may be, without fear of blame or expectation of rewards. The essence of Karma yoga is the ideal of duty well done and the vairag, spirit of unattachment.

"Bhakti Yoga is the yoga of devotion and it appeals most of all to people of the emotional temperament. Discarding all rites and ceremonies, it seeks union with the ECK through the force of love alone.

"Mantra Yoga. This system aims at the acquirement of psychic powers in spiritual or astral regions by constant repetition of certain formulas which are supposed to set up particular vibrations, especially when repeated with the mind fixed upon certain centers. The formulas, as such, are believed to have an efficacy of their own.

"ECKANKAR is what is sometimes known as Sahaji or Soul travel, the way of the sound current. This is

143

practiced by the ECK travelers. It is the oldest system known in the history of mankind.

"It consists primarily in the following of the inner sound. This is the point which distinguishes the methods used by the ECK travelers from all other systems. This is the supreme test which must be kept in mind when studying the other systems. If the sound is not a vital part of them, then they are not the system of the great spiritual travelers.

"Many people insist that one system is about as good as another, since all are intended to lead to the same goal. Far from it. No other system leads to the goal of the spiritual travelers, the highest regions in existence. Besides, you will generally find that the person who says that one religion, or one system of yoga is just as good as another, has never practiced any of them.

"That Master, who doesn't teach or practice the science of the sound current, is not a master of high order. Nor does his system lead to the highest achievements. Every real ECK traveler in all history has taught and practiced the way of this life current. It couldn't be otherwise, for this is the system established by the SUGMAD through ITS early spiritual travelers for this lower kingdom.

"Most followers of Indian yoga systems will agree that most or all of the old systems are very difficult, requiring much time, rigid asceticism, and great self-abnegation. The path of the ordinary yogi is a rugged one. The method of the spiritual travelers is not the way of the yogis; it never has been. Before there was ever a yogi system, the science of the ECK travelers was known and practiced among men. But the exact methods of the travelers have from time to time become obscured, or even lost, in times when real travelers were few or unknown to the general public. Then, yogis developed methods of their own, trying to substitute for the path of the travelers. The two systems have been running along parallel courses for centuries. Not only are the methods of the yogis different from that of the saints, but their final objective is different.

"Most of the yogis, even the best of them, know of nothing beyond the astral plane, the Turiya Pad, with the possible exception of a very few who may have reached the Brahm Lok.

"Here they are automatically stopped, unless they have a spiritual traveler who himself goes further. Stopping there, most of them believe they have reached the supreme heights. There, they accept Brahma of that region as the supreme God of all.

"But the travelers go so far above and beyond Brahm Lok, that when they reach that region, they have only fairly begun their journey upward. While most of the yogis and imperfect travelers believe Brahm is the supreme authority, the travelers know that he is only a subordinate in the grand hierarchy of the universe. While the OM of the Vedas and the Gita is regarded as the most sacred word in all Hindu philosophy, it is because they believe it to be the sound symbol of the supreme being; yet the travelers know that it belongs to one of the lower Lords who is himself not above the regions of Awagawan—of death and birth.

"He, himself, is still under the law of karma, and is therefore liable to fall into the snares of Maya, becoming a mere man again, or even going lower than that.

"He is bound by the very same laws which bind the subjects over whom he rules. He is himself a created being, subject to the same laws of all created beings and must carry on under the wishes of the Supreme SUGMAD. He is, by no means, the ultimate ECK, nor is he at all the Tuzashottama energy, what you know as the individual Soul energy.

"The way of the travelers accomplishes what the yoga of the Vedantists can never do. It is vastly more effective and moreover it has been adapted to the needs of modern man. This is its great glory.

"It is what the person of this world calls modern in method and yet it meets all the requirements of all ages. In every age of the world, the travelers have used a system exactly suited to the needs of the people and the times. People change, to some extent from age to age, and so the travelers give them, in each age, exactly that system of yoga best suited to their requirement.

"But the yogis hold on to their archaic systems which are now quite out of date, wholly unsuited to the average man of this age. The nervous constitution of the modern man is somewhat different from that of the men of ten thousand years ago. The yoga of the travelers may now be practiced not only by the ascetics, but by all men in all walks and conditions of life, while carrying on their routine duties of office and home. This makes it a universal system of spiritual science for all, under any condition.

"If we take a look back at the study of world religions and philosophies from a detached point of view, we can see, at a glance, that they talk about realizing God and gaining salvation. If you ask any of the leaders of the various religions and philosophical groups just how they are to accomplish all of these goals, they will give you a stock reply; they follow the scriptures of their particular faith and believe what their priests have to offer.

"They mostly speak of Self-Realization or Self-Knowledge, God-Realization or knowledge of God, and lastly, entering the kingdom of heaven, either in this life or in the next but all is a mystery to them.

"However, their techniques are scanty and their knowledge poor. None really know how to do this in this life, here and now. Of course the end and purpose of all of this is individual well-being, happiness.

"These three points, I've just mentioned are the very things which the spiritual travelers offer to the individual; but the methods by which the travelers propose to accomplish these ends are entirely different from that of any and all religions.

"You may ask just how do the travelers propose to place at your feet the treasures of the God worlds? The answers lie in the fact that their scientific methods of leaving the body and traveling through the innumerable worlds have to be done through a system of exercises.

"The successful practitioner, and there are very, very few who are failures at this, will experience spiritual realization. This includes entering into the kingdom of heaven, here and now, Self-Realization and God-Realization.

"Those who fail are usually too lazy to spend any time at it, too wrapped up in worldly affairs to let themselves go inwardly and outwardly into the spiritual kingdoms.

"More about this later!"

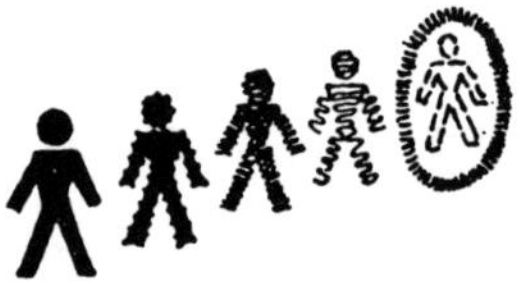

Chapter 8

THE REST POINTS OF ETERNITY

Dawn in these high mountains is always a colorful drama, with wild streaks of light gleaming across the peaks and down through the gorges and gulches. These colors remind one of the Astral lights flowing out of the great powerful mountain in the city of Sahasra-dal-Kanwal, the capital of the astral worlds.

Sitting alone in the vast, wild spaces of that great range of the Hindu Kush, I felt the uplift of every moment of that dawn, as if rising into the atmosphere of the heavens far above, where the white clouds framed picturesque symbols against an azure sky.

After we had partaken of a light breakfast of bananas, wheat cereal and hot tea, Rebazar Tarzs folded his robe and dropped upon the hard, dirt floor. He motioned for me to be seated; sitting down I prepared for a long session of aesthetic discussion. "Now I'll take up the rest points in eternity," he said with a broad smile. "Many people in the static religions think of the heavens as a place where eternity continues their great joy and happiness.

"This is not so. Eternity within the Far Country couldn't be carried out like this under the plans of the Universal SUGMAD at all. There must be rest points between certain periods of the continuity of eternity.

"All eternity is a series of stops and starts, a continued action of motion in which the cycles run for many yugas, or what we call ages. These ages may continue for centuries, according to our time, before reaching a rest point. But they must reach a stop of this nature in order to gather momentum to move along to the next point.

"Therefore all eternity is on the move, moving forward

not into a future from out of the past, but always in motion in the present. Since the Tuza doesn't age in the Far Country, It always lives in the present. This is an interesting point which one must consider deeply, while at the same time thinking of the present—this is hard from the standpoint of living on this plane.

"But it must be done, and without this viewpoint the whole of your insight will vanish quickly.

"The only thing the finite mind can compare with eternity is an endless, an immeasurable time period. Man claims that eternity is of infinite duration; everlasting. It is eternal existence or immortality, the very opposite of temporal. Continuing unintermittently, it is timeless. It is what the Hindu religion calls Nitya, eternal and everlasting.

"Often eternity is confused with reality, which is the nowness of time. The Isness or the Nowness is used to refer to the Supreme Being. The Nowness is closer to eternity than any descriptive words used to describe the everlasting. Now is an adverb designating the present, and as long as we can look at every second of our lives as now, we are observing eternity. No adjective is capable of describing the phenomena of heaven.

"The Isness of the SUGMAD is much more a term we can use to describe the eternal lord of all things. A Greek word denoting identity, it is about the only word we can use to form any concept of the everlasting Lord of all universes.

"So you have two words with Latin and Greek roots which come close to establishing in the mind concepts of the two greatest mysteries, which man has attempted to tackle and dissolve. First is Nowness, an adverb used to describe the present time or moment, and Isness, a verb to describe the allness and presence of something, and that something, in our case, is the SUGMAD.

"Therefore, from what point do we work, the active verb of Isness or the Nowness of time? All right, I will attempt to break these concepts into a finer point for you. Isness is the creative point which is always working, always creating; or better still, that which is always moving—like perpetual motion.

"On the other hand, Nowness is more or less a stillness of motion, a quieting into the present moment; from stillness we receive the opportunity to live forever in the present moment. In other words an alter-isness, the extension of the creative moment into lengths which give it Nowness. Here is the existence of a cycle of action—and this is represented by Vishnu in the Hindu trinity; in the Christian trinity, it is the son, the Christ, the preserver.

"This is interesting because we are now concerned with one fact; in the preserving of Nowness, one is concerned with the movement of himself from point to point in time, what we know as time. In this universe we know time because of the position of the sun during its twenty-four hour movement around the Earth, the zodiac of the universe divisions, like years, months, days, hours, minutes and seconds; these are for the convenience of a man to judge his position relative to time. It is really a calendar for those engaged in business, to make a tab for their material activities.

"The creative mind of man invented for himself a horror for his own destruction. Since time is, in a relative sense, destructive and negative belonging to the god, Shiva, which I spoke about some while ago, you can understand now that the Isness and Nowness of eternity is more of a Reality than you ever believed.

"Columbus was right in disputing the theory that the world was flat, but he was not talking about the universe or the heaven worlds. The spiritual planes are flat, and the suns, which hang in the skies of those spiritual worlds you have visited, have no movement. They need none, because beyond the Brahm Lok no spiritual world has night—they do not need darkness. What is the need of rest and sleep to the Soul who reposes in the sweet peaceful quiet of the SUGMAD's arms—to use a metaphor correctly.

151

"In those high worlds no darkness is available. You may move forward in an unceasing activity and never be fatigued as on this plane. You need no activity. Activity is outside a domain without action.

"This is a strange paradox; to explain it, I will point out this in the beginning of my explanation. Man thinks of eternity in the terms of time and space. Since there is no time in eternity, I tell you that there is no space in eternity. Neither of these relative qualities exist in the world of the SUGMAD, anywhere above the plane of the Brahm Lok. In fact there is little need for either of them—they are phenomena of the lower worlds only.

"Now, the matter of space is nothing. Nothing exists in the Far Country, except what Souls there wish to exist. Since the SUGMAD occupies all of Its world, when you become part of the Supreme, you are occupying all of ITS world. You are IT, already. There is no need of space.

"Nothing can occupy the same space, except two Souls. This being true, there is no space in the great beyond. Neither do you travel in the vast world of all worlds; there is little necessity to do so.

"Now in eternity, as I said in the beginning of this discourse, there are rest points. These rest points are concerned with start, change and stop of the Tuza. This is all there is to the Nowness of eternity—the point of wasness, or time is an illusion. We are always up against the illusion of time in the lower worlds, but not in the world of the Supreme Being.

"Yet, living in this world, the Tuza must have survival of some kind or he cannot exist here; he would go down into the worlds below and start working his way up again.

"This is why we have rest points in the Far Country. Being as no space is there, and that you fill the world as does the SUGMAD, ITSELF, you must learn to survive through these rest points. You do not travel—you only mockup a cycle of action and observe it as the SUGMAD does. This is one of the postulates you have to carry out or you do not survive. I mean that if you wish to have a picture of another section of the universes, you don't travel there; you just observe it!

"This is too simple, you say; however, by being so simple, it puts a mystery into the conditions of which I speak. Take this as an example, suppose that you're sitting in New York City, on the Empire State building, as Soul—rather in the Atma Sarup. You want to see San Francisco—is there any necessity of traveling to San Francisco to see what is going on there?

"The answer is no!

"The reason is simple! You being a part of the universe, and since you are the SUGMAD, ITSELF, in a way of speaking, you can merely observe it from your position on the Empire State building.

"How much more simple can it be? Yet it appears so very complex to your thinking now. All right, I will go a little deeper into this. Look at it in another way. The whole universe is made up of spiritual matter, and you, as the Tuza control all this matter in this world, in a sense of speaking. You are one with the Supreme, the ECK, and all things are included in this stream flowing outwardly from the highest positive pole of the universes to the lowest and returning.

"If you're able to detach yourself from this stream and look into it, you can see all things; this is similar to what is known on this plane as clairvoyance; you just decided that you are going to see San Francisco and you bring the reality of the city to you and what you wish to observe there.

"You are also to be concerned with another quality—known as Hereness! Before you were working with Nowness and Isness. So this trinity is going to be the real trinity of the SUGMAD. It is this: Isness, the creative moment, sec-

153

ond, Nowness, the present, the preservation of the moment, and Hereness, the present state of life.

"I will clarify something here for you. Isness is not creativity as we know it on this plane, but a reality which is knowingness. Hence I know, I preserve this knowingness, and I live in this present state of knowingness.

"We will take this up in our next discussion, after a little tea for refreshing our throats."

* * *

"In order to get to the depth of the trinity as I've spoken of here, I'll have to get into causation. But first look at the difference in the Christian trinity versus the Hindu trinity versus the ECK trinity. The Christian trinity is simply three forms of qualities which are mental, and physical; the Hindu trinity is a symbol for the currents of forces in nature, and the ECK trinity is the qualities denoting the present state of life.

"Since we are not dealing with space and time in these upper regions, then we must work with a set of abstracts founded on experiences based upon the nowness of everything. Causation is not a matter of starting a cycle of action, because you are always in a creative cycle which starts, changes and stops with each rest point.

"Also the second factor that we must confront shows us that in this high upper region, all work with free will and never under a mechanical law. Each Soul is a law unto itself, yet never interferes with another.

"Within this world below each of us carries his own cause about him; like a shower of rain, each observer carries his own rainbow. If I change my speed of motion, I create a new cause for myself, just as if I step a few spaces in a rainy shower, I acquire a new rainbow for myself. Relativity teaches that there is no cause except the defective insight.

"Causation in the upper regions is relative, and here the nature of all things is not accuracy and precision. Energy is emitted by the Tuza himself to include only that which he is doing, and this doesn't have anything to do with another Tuza. As I said before, each works unto himself—similar to the McWilliams law where all particles are moving in space according to their own pattern but never crashing or interfering with one another.

"There is strictly no causal behavior of any kind and the law of karma is not included in this world. There are subjective factors, unknown to the minds of men.

"The subjective factor is not included in any system of reference, and cannot be fully deterministic in the control of inorganic phenomena. If we wish to emancipate the material world, we must emancipate mind also which is partly made up of what we call self-elements, spiritual particles.

"Being is not the cause of becoming. Causation is one of the categories of thought. A man is not actually born when he comes out of the female body; he doesn't know then, that he is born. He is born actually, when he gets the knowledge of birth. The relation of cause and effect is not something found in nature, but is rather a characteristic of the way in which we regard nature. Understand this?

"The apparent indeterminism of the particle becomes meaningless and the determinism of the energy wave has nothing to do with the course of objective nature. This is the way it works in the heaven worlds, of course. Soul works with the particles of spiritual energy and the waves of energy to create a cycle of action for itself. These actually are wave pictures.

"Soul changes its wave pictures to bring itself to another rest point. There is no destruction of the wave pictures, for they are shared among the millions of Souls in this world. In other words, I possess a large number of wave pictures, and so does each Soul within this universe. There is no changing or deviation of these pictures, but a shifting of them among the various Souls who are working from rest point to rest point within eternity.

"The spiritual particles are put together to make a wave picture—or energy unit, which is actually the rest point. These points are similar to events in this world. On this plane we are always going from one event to another; or experiencing certain events in our lives daily.

"There are no new events in this world. All experiences have been experienced by someone at sometime throughout the history of the human race. It is possible to have every possible experience of man in your life provided you have the time, will-power, and motivation. All you need to do is raise yourself above the flow of the negative power within the plane and make contact with whatever event you are seeking.

"It is experience that makes the Tuza harden Itself to this world and wish to rise into the upper regions. But on the other hand, the experiences or events in the heavenly worlds are not too much different from the ones on this plane—they are similar in that they are experiences, events or picture waves.

"What I'm trying to tell you amounts to this. The main difference between the upper region wave pictures and those of the lower is simply the degree of refinement, the freedom of will in the upper worlds. We work with using the wave-pictures for rest points in eternity for the sake of bringing energy to ourselves, instead of moving to the energy point. Understand this?

"It's hard to get this across to you because in the Far Country, we have little need of motion unless we desire it; desire is the least of our operating apparatus. We have little desires of anything because of the dominating joy and happiness which comes from being in contact with the SUGMAD, and from being able to be in this heavenly world.

"So the relation of cause and effect cannot be applied to the relation of the ECK to this high world, since cause has meaning. This is the outstanding point I'm trying to make— there may be cause in the heavenly world, but never effect. Only in relation to the finite modes of being, where there is succession, does effect exist.

"Causation has no meaning in the lower worlds apart from a change. And as succession is relative, causation is merely an appearance. It is certainly useful within the limits of experience but cannot be regarded as of absolute validity.

"So here are the basic elements of life in the upper worlds —succession, wave pictures and rest points. All of these are working within the three abstracts which I took up previously, Isness, Nowness and Hereness. These rest within the framework of the ECK trinity.

"I hope that this is getting across to you. Maybe it isn't, but you must break through the shackles, the chains holding you to the lower planes and enter into the upper worlds to have the rest of your days in eternity.

"Causation cannot be continuous. It cannot exist except in the time occupied by a line drawn across the succession, and since that time is not a time but a mere abstraction, the cause itself can be no better. It is unreal, a non-entity and the whole succession of the world consists of these non-entities. This is much the same as to suppose that solid things are made of points and lines and surfaces.

"These are fictions, useful for some purpose but still fictions they remain. A cause here must be a real event; in the upper world, there is no fragment of real time in which it can be real. Causation is, therefore, not continuous in the heavens above and so, unfortunately, it is not causation but mere appearance.

"You can see there is no unity in the heaven world. There isn't even logic, or any logical relation of necessity for any cause whatever. It stands to reason, to use an earth term, that should we become conscious of the subjective unity in true relation, the causal chain in the pure multiplicity, in this plane, would be broken and every means of making the real intelligible would be destroyed.

"On further thought, we shall also find that the concepts of metaphysical causality as necessary and indispensable are absurd. It implies the possibility of logic as something which doesn't exist, and this is certainly true when you get off the earth plane and begin soaring in the heaven world.

"Logic simply doesn't exist, therefore, when you use rest points in eternity, it doesn't for one minute mean that you are following out a mechanical, set pattern of behavior, as I have said before. But it brings you an opportunity to be resourceful on your own. The SUGMAD lives within ITS own laws, and therefore you are expected to make and live within your laws, in this world.

"Laws are simply postulates. Freedom in this world means making your own postulates and living by them or not. Here in this earth world you have to live by laws or postulates which others make, for the good of the whole. The reasoning behind this is simple, the weak must have some defense against the strong—but in the heaven worlds this isn't true for all are strong—in fact the strongest. So there are no weak that need defending. As a result all and each can make their own postulates and live together without the slightest harm or damage to one another.

"In the heaven worlds you may live and feed on the ECK or rather the music of the spheres. Here you must carry a body, worry about it, and try to make it run smoothly on a mechanical order.

"Life itself in these higher reaches does not exhibit tension. As you travel upward you find that creativeness is an effort on the lower planes, but upwardly the finer creations are effortless. The less resistance it has to overcome, the better the creation. The free movement of life without resistance is a higher experience which we find only in self-expression and hence this movement has no definite end to aim at or achieve. Spiritual freedom implies the complete transcendence of the lower worlds and of causality.

"Let's leave off here for a few minutes."

*　　*　　*

"Well now, we'll get started again," Rebazar Tarzs said definitely, motioning for me to sit again.

"To obtain a better understanding of eternity, I am going into the four grand divisions of the universe again. These

158

are: Sat Desha, the highest region; Brahmanda, the second region; Anda, the third and lowest regions of the heavens; and Pinda, the fourth grand division which is the gross material or physical universe.

"Now don't mix these with the individual planes which I explained long ago to you in these discussions, and at that time separated them into the various grand divisions.

"It's only for the clearer explanation of eternity that I am going to partly repeat myself here. You must remember that eternity or immortality is one of those things which we can't talk about directly. We must work around it, and get the understanding of it, by knowing what it is not, rather than what it is.

"Begin with the Sat Desha, the highest region. Sat Desha means true country, or what is known to us as the Far Country. Many names have been applied to it such as Nij-Dham, Sat Lok, Mukam Taq and Sach Khand. These names usually apply to the lowest section of Sat Desha, but occasionally to the entire grand division.

"This is the region of pure spirit. and its citizens are pure spirits, Tuzas, in such countless numbers that no man could estimate, all enjoying the greatest conceivable happiness.

"This world is known by the ECK travelers, who alone can come and go as they wish. This is due to their understanding of this magnificent world, and the permission granted them by the ECK, the first manifestation of the SUGMAD in the downward journey.

"This is the only world that the spiritual travelers insist is practically limitless. The mind cannot embrace all of it, it is both the beginning and the end of all else, and it is the great center about which all other worlds revolve.

"This is the eternity of mankind—that place in the far sky where immortality exists. It is the grand capital of all creation, the center of all universes, and the residence of the Supreme Deity of all.

"From this center of all light, life and power, the great creative current flows outward and downward, to create, govern and sustain all worlds. It passes out from this region somewhat like a radio wave, as I've told you before.

"This is most important to you, for without this great creative current there would be no immortality, no eternity which the men of this world dream about. And it is in this land of the Sat Desha that the immortal Tuza finds that it must create to be a part of this great region.

"Soul is never assigned a task by the ECK, the great Supreme Lord of all, but seeks the position, without the least effort, for the certain task which It must fulfill in order to be a citizen of this country, and have the utmost happiness.

"There are many and various things which Soul finds to do, upon first entering into the world of Sat Desha. It might see his effort can supply a small part of the creative current flowing through the ECK, or It might be assigned to the duty of looking after those entering the world like Itself.

"There are many and various jobs for all concerned. Hardly any Soul within this world is without a task of some sort. There are those who personally serve the great ECK, as a service to the SUGMAD. Others are helping groups which look after the inspection of the great world.

"So you see you need to apply yourself here; you will not be idle, as you may think while in the body. This is no place for resting and relaxing, in the same sense that we do here on earth.

"Here I point out that every Soul that crosses the boundary of a higher plane, from the lowest to the highest, must be accompanied by a spiritual traveler, unless It is an experienced traveler himself.

"Since It is entering into these planes normally to be a citizen and resident of them, it is only natural that It be

160

brought there by someone who is prepared to escort It about until It is familiar with this world. No emigrant going to the shores of America is hardly without an escort when landing there; he is met either by a friend or somebody who has been assigned by some agency to see that he is safely put in the hands of the proper individual who will care for him.

"The customs officer will see to his baggage and handle him in a most proper way to make his welcome more cheerful. Other officials are there to see that he doesn't get into the wrong areas of social life, among many things.

"This is similar to what happens when Soul leaves this plane and enters into the Astral world. If It doesn't have a spiritual traveler to guide It, there are others who will come to Its assistance. These are Souls who have gone on before It, who are there principally for Its assistance and to take It to the proper groups where It will be most happy.

"Sometimes these Souls are relatives during their earth life, friends or someone assigned by the group who look after those entering the higher world. Soul is never at a loss to find Its way around without the help of somebody, unless It rejects this assistance. Of course It can do this, but it is hardly likely. There are those who do, however, and they can become lost in the many swamps and fogs which abound in the lower Astral world. They may wander about for what seems to be years before someone comes to their aid. Of course, they are watched, but no one will approach to give help until they are asked.

"This is a system established on every plane of the grand universe. Every Soul is looked after and cared for, as It enters the plane above. It is sometimes escorted by a spiritual traveler who can open all doors, with only the word needed for the occasion. They pass the Angel of Death, Yama, and go where the traveler feels his charge should be.

"Immediately when one dies on this plane, he or she, is

taken by the messengers of death to the subtle regions where Dharam Raya, the righteous judge, sits enthroned to judge every individual according to his deserts.

"The Christians call these messengers of death, the Angels of Death or the Dark Angels, for dark indeed they are; but in India they are called Yama dutas, or the messengers of Yama, the King of the Dead. This judge is always in court to take care of all comers. There is no waiting, nor sitting in some jail cell.

"No one ever questions the judgment. No comment is made; no oratory for the defense, no pretended righteous condemnation of the prosecution. The prisoner himself makes no complaint and asks no favors. He understands that he is to receive judgment and asks no help, for he must consent to the judgment, the law of the SUGMAD from the highest world to the lowest.

"He is taken to that region, or condition, where he has earned his place, be it good or bad. He will remain there for a fixed time according to the judgment rendered and handed down. After that period has expired, he is then returned to this world, or some other world, to begin life anew.

"This is the routine procedure. He may enjoy a rest in some heaven, or paradise, some pleasant country, perhaps, many times more beautiful and delightful than any portion of this world. There he may remain for a year, a thousand or million years, all depending upon his karma. The higher he goes, the longer the period of his residence there.

"If one's life has been that of a low order, he may be taken to some purgatory, or reformatory, often called a hell—there to endure the punishment earned by him during his lifetime here. He cannot escape regardless—he must meet the appropriate punishments. There is one feature about all of such punishment that must be understood—they are remedial and not vindictive. They are intended for his good, to produce a reformation of character; but they are not

162

eternal as man is often led to believe, especially in the Christian religion. But the law is inexorable. Each one must get just what he has earned and just what is needed to impress upon his inmost consciousness that he must obey the laws of nature or be punished.

"After his period of discipline is over on the subtle planes, he may be required to re-enter earth life in some lower form, to finish his karmic schooling.

"This process of death is enacted upon every physical plane of the universe, and allows Soul to enter into the Astral. But it is not complete on the Astral, for if Soul is to rise higher into the next world by shedding Its astral body; then It goes through a process of death upon it.

"Therefore, on every plane which Soul must enter, after a residence on the lower one, It has to go through a process similar to that on the Earth plane; It drops the body It is wearing at that time, be it an astral or a mental body. If no traveler is there to help It, It must appear before the judge of the so-called dead on that plane and be rendered justice as to where It may go in the higher region.

"This practice is enacted on every plane up to the Sach Khand, where one enters as pure spirit and therefore It never returns to the lower worlds except through the voluntary effort to help others, or for certain experiences needed to keep It in the great world of the SUGMAD.

"We'll leave off here for awhile."

*   *   *

"All right, let's get started again," said Rebazar Tarzs. "Now to finish up the part on eternity which I've been holding back to the end of this particular discussion.

"Certain phenomena occurring in the high world has great interest to us at this point. In the beginning, let me explain it this way. We have those ECK travelers who roam

163

the universes from end unto end—except they do not exactly enter into the real world of the SUGMAD.

"Of course, they enter into the land of Sat Desha, and mingle freely with all the inhabitants there, and go up as far as the ECK, where dwells the first manifestation of the Lord. But they do not go any further than this.

"Within this region where dwells the SUGMAD, ITSELF, there are only a few beings who live and serve IT. These are the Mahavakyis, the Silent Travelers—and so mighty are these great ones that you seldom can confront them. Those who have been fortunate to have come face to face with one of these superior beings have thought they were in the presence of the SUGMAD, ITSELF.

"These Silent Travelers are well named, for they are practically invisible to all eyes outside the world of the SUGMAD. As they come down from the highest region into that of the ECK, instead of taking form like one would think of them doing, these superior beings remain in their cloaks of anonymity.

"These are what we know as the Agents of the SUGMAD — those who travel anywhere through ITS vast empire on ITS business. These strange beings are actually the subordinates of the SUGMAD — in a way they are ITS deputies who carry out ITS will and wishes.

"Now all are subject to the laws of these strange, superior entities for they manifest at any point so desired in the universe and carry out some order, whether it is against the Lord of a certain plane, including the Brahma of the Brahma Lok, or the Soul suffering in purgatory. It is their duty, not to question.

"They are in many forms among the inhabitants of all planes. Here on this earth plane they may be disguised as men, animals, birds or fish, and even rocks if it serves their purpose to carry out the mission of their Superior Commander.

"Much as some of the spiritual travelers know about the SUGMAD, little is known about these Silent Ones, who come and go like the winds of the world. The spiritual travelers have their own agents, as well as the Lords and governors of the various regions of the universes; each in turn reports to his own chief and carries out his desire. But the silent travelers are not responsible to anyone but the Supreme SUGMAD. IT alone gives them their commissions to be carried out—and they must work for IT alone, or be cast out of the heavens into the bowels of the earth, as Lucifer was in the beginning of time.

"These silent ones are in command of the great sound current, in the high heavens, and are to give aid and comfort to the SUGMAD in ITS eternal home. They keep the planes balanced and in order, so that little destruction can come to them, should any of the inhabitants go on rampages and bring about the downfall of planes within planes. They are in charge of time, creativity, space and other mechanical phases of the lower universes.

"They see that the planets in this world are properly hung in space so there will be no collision of them, by being out of their assigned positions.

"They have immense powers, and great wisdom to carry out their missions, and of course unlimited freedom.

"Outside the SUGMAD, these Silent Travelers are the most powerful beings in all the worlds, and next to them are the Spiritual Travelers. The Lords and Governors of all the planes can be powerful within their own domain, but they are subject to the laws which govern them, and even the Brahman, as I have said before, will someday have to be reincarnated again. They are all limited, in power, wisdom and freedom.

"The ECK Masters know when the Silent Ones are around, and they cooperate with them at the level upon which they are working at the time. The ECK travelers are subject to the Silent Ones; they do not have to obey, yet they will because it's realized always that the Silents are direct from the SUGMAD—out of love and respect, they will give their best cooperation, even though at times they wouldn't like to do so.

"So you have three levels of independent workers in eternity, who cooperate in the running of the worlds. First, the SUGMAD, the all Supreme Being, second the Silent Travelers, who are ITS messengers or agents, and third, the ECK Travelers who are both the agents of the SUGMAD and the Silent Ones. The three work together, in perfect harmony and understanding.

"The functions of the Silent Ones are to serve the purpose of the SUGMAD in running the universes, carrying out ITS laws and regulations; the spiritual travelers have the duty of seeing that Souls are returned to the kingdom of the ECKANKAR.

"These are about the only duties that either of the groups have which are in common, otherwise they go their own way and live with their own without coming in contact with one another.

"Quite frequently the Silent Ones appear on earth in some form or other; often they are the shining angels, like those who appeared at the tomb of Christ and told Mary that her lord was gone. Jacob wrestled with one on the ladder of heaven. Occasionally, you will read of a Silent Traveler in a similar manner in the ancient scriptures, or somebody will speak of some strange phenomena happening to them.

"As it stands the Silent Travelers are not concerned with the rulers of planes, Sat Nam, Ramkar, Omkar or Jot Niranjan. These minor gods are only workers within the spiritual hierarchy of the SUGMAD. They are subject to the nature laws of those works within which they are living.

"The Silent Travelers, as I have said, have no such laws hanging over them, and they are free as the winds of the world. Now this is the interest the Silent Travelers hold for you—someday you may become one, for it is the highest point in all of the universes which you can reach.

"You cannot in a sense become the SUGMAD, ITSELF; you can become a part of IT, and you can become a coworker of the SUGMAD. Under no circumstances can you become the Supreme Deity, although religions try to tell their followers that this is true. You cannot do this, regardless of what is told you by a priest or a minister of any gospel.

"You can become a Silent Traveler, which is one of the SUGMAD's closest relations—these strange beings have their home and habitat within the heart of the SUGMAD. Nothing can get any closer than these beings who are without doubt the only creatures who are in direct contact with the Lord God of all the worlds.

"If you are at all interested you may aim your sights at becoming a Silent One. But if you do this, there will be an intensity of training which you have never heard of in your life nor in your many incarnations spent on earth. The training that many lamas are reported as going through would be a child's practice besides what the candidates go through. Many fail to make the ranks of the Silent Ones.

"For example, I will point out that perhaps out of every ten thousand who take the tests and trainings they must go through, one will succeed. Candidates are picked, without their own knowledge, from the higher planes—hardly anyone living on the planes below the Daswan Dwar is ever picked for training. I would say that ninety percent of the candidates have reached the plane of the ECK, before they are even considered. The Silent Ones are not intending to put anyone through the tests and training, who have not finished up their training in the lower world. They know better, for it would mean the loss of a Soul who had gone through the practice of trying to reach the proper plane and suddenly shoved into something much over his head.

"These strange beings are the chosen ones. They intend

to take care of their own, for they have no responsibility to anyone except the SUGMAD.

"To the human heart these creatures look and act cold toward all others, and in a way they are; except for the fact they are running the universes through the administration of the SUGMAD. Each plane has a number of them who are doing their work under the supervision of the top Silent One, like a regular business staff, from the chief executive to the workers.

"These creatures are not bothered with the individual Souls, but concerned only with the mechanics of the universes. They are so busy that nothing else matters to them—to be filled with all the qualities of mercy, kindness and those which serve mankind in another way would be rather out of their field.

"Their chief concern is with the three qualities which I have mentioned several times—Isness, Nowness and Hereness, the trinity of the SUGMAD."

Chapter 9

THE NO-EXISTENCE OF SPACE

The old traveler, Rebazar Tarzs, didn't spend much time in getting into his dialogue this morning after my arrival. He seated himself and began talking.

"Now the next phase of ECK, that mystical philosophy quite unknown to the religions of this earth world and hardly at all to most of its mystics, pertains to matter, space and time.

"Space and time are joint or rather twin aspects of the whole; they are actually members of a materialistic team known as MEST, which when broken down are: Matter, Energy, Space and Time. These constituents are those which make up the physical world—the Pinda, and are represented in the Occult as that of man's physical body. This is the last frontier of Soul, or the lowest to be exact.

"We are discussing matter, space and time in this talk. Energy has been somewhat covered, but it will get full coverage in the next chapter.

"In the beginning let me point out that space actually has no existence. It is hardly anything but a nothingness, a huge hole filled with spiritual energy, the ECK. It is nothing, apart from our perception of objects—and time means nothing, apart from our experience of events.

"Space appears merely as a fiction created by man's own mind—an illegitimate extension of the nature of subjective concepts which help us to understand and describe the arrangements of objects as seen by us, while time appears as a secondary fiction serving a similar purpose for the arrangement of events which happen to us. Time and space are both maya in the modern study of physics and also in philosophy. They are not the same under all circumstances. They are more subjective ideas than objective facts.

"Man's knowledge of the external world cannot be divorced from the nature of the faculties with which we have obtained physical knowledge. The truth of the law of gravitation cannot be regarded as subsisting, apart from the experimental procedure by which we ascertained the truth. Imagine yourself alone in the midst of nothingness and then try to tell me how large you are. It is literally impossible.

"Here are some of the things which you must know about so-called space. First, a straight line may not necessarily be straight; second, a ray of light has weight; third, space is curved; fourth, the universe, even the Pinda world, is boundless yet finite; five, mind creates matter and matter creates space.

"Sixth, every sentient (meaning every experience of sensation and feeling) being is capable of constructing its own universe. Seventh, space and time are not realities. There is no fundamental entity called space existing in itself in which the world is placed, nor is there any fundamental line in which an event occurs. Out of an observer's temporal experience, is constructed time, and out of the same time is constructed space. But there is no underlying time or space with which these can conceivably be correlated. Thus the universe and its creator are neither in time nor space. Eighth, the shortest straight line is an infinite affair. Ninth, the universe is infinite, yet paradoxically small, and tenth, atoms are world systems.

"Eleventh, world systems are atoms. Twelfth, the mind of man is truly omnipresent because all time and space is present in it. Thirteenth, physical qualities in general have no absolute values, only relative to chosen frames of references or codes. Fourteenth, space, time and the physical world of substances have no objective reality, apart from the mental concepts of them that man creates in his mind. Fifteenth, nothing is real except what is in our consciousness and perception, and this, when relative, creates an illusion. Sixteenth, when we view ourselves in space and time, we

170

are quite obviously distinct individuals. When we pass beyond space and time we form ingredients of a continuous stream of the sound current, and seventeenth, everything is relative to human perception. There is no space which is positive, for it is nothingness. Therefore one man's mind is negated by another. Even the travelers, the saints, sometimes do not like the works of another member of their group. Everyone has his own measures.

"One more point to make on this subject. The picture of an electron as a point in space and time fails completely. It has wave-like characteristics, therefore it is called a wavicle.

"An event has many sizes relative to the corresponding standpoints. There are as many imaginary worlds as there are observers with varying interests and purposes, and these worlds appear to change in accordance with the subjective changes in the life of those who experience them.

"When we discard our human spectacles entirely, we find that light and sound are neither waves nor particles. Speaking philosophically, the SUGMAD is neither the Satguru nor the Nirguna, but has the nature of all things.

"When a jiva, or student, as a particle approaches the ECK, he appears to be the SUGMAD, or Satguru. When the student approaches him in the form of a wave by means of self-knowledge, he appears to be the Nirguna, or negative-self. There can be no separation between waves. The nature of light and sound is such that they behave as waves in empty space but like bullets as soon as light encounters matter.

"Soul appears as negative when It sees something other than Itself. Physical space is a matter of inference and construction. The account of an animal given by examining an animal's movements is only an event in the animal's life. The same is the case with events in a man's life. Relativity proves this by equations.

"It has been established that separate component parts

171

of a uniform system of bodies maintain the same position in relation to one another as though the system was stationary. Thus, things inside a swiftly moving railroad coach behave in exactly the same way as when the coach is standing still. In reality, things bear their own measure in themselves and to find the measure of things is to understand illusion, or maya.

"The smallest electron and the largest world which exists, apart from our study of it is senseless. The idea that perception in itself reveals the character of objects is a fond delusion. All that exists is what it is, and this only within the limits of a certain and very small scale. On the spiritual and psychic scale, i.e., from another viewpoint, it becomes something.

"The smaller the reference body, or the reference system, the smaller the world. Space, or nothingness is proportionate to the size of the reference body and all the measurements of space are proportionate to the measurements of the measurement of the reference body. By annihilating somebody's life or mind, his world-experience is annihilated; by the destruction of a jar, that jar's space is annihilated.

"Our measurements are never of space and time but only of the things and the events that occupy space and time. My time measurements depend ultimately on my space measurements and the latter on my ideas of simultaneous action. You depend on your reading of simultaneity in precisely the same way.

"If you built nine boxes of the same measurements but different in forms they would occupy the same space and time, and would be the same objects yet appearing to be different to different observers. In the same way one and the same world appears to be different to different observers. Therefore, every observer lives in his own imaginary world.

"In a dream-experience, earth, roads, mountain surface, denote only forms of empty space; so, in the waking experience also, they are forms of empty space, depending on the position of the observer.

"I, you, he or she are also imaginary forms of waking experience. For instance, a mare cannot become the wife of a man, and woman can't become the wife of a horse, although the mare and woman are both feminine characters. As the waking condition destroys the dream completely, the condition of self-realization destroys the waking experience completely. The body of the observer is also a product of thought just as it happens in dreams.

"For each frame of reference there is a scale of length and a scale of time. Whether a body has taken up energy or not, depends upon the position of his observation. All we need to know is the relation of the other fellow's space and time standards to our own. This is the first thing relativity teaches us. All measures are correct for the time and for the space selected, but one relative measure cannot be applied to understand all events. Therefore, when one thinks that the whole world must move according to his ideas, he assumes a false position. Other persons are also right from their point of view of that time.

"It is hard to give a satisfactory explanation of the theory of space and time in popular language, because the language itself is based on old concepts. All the student can do is become familiar with the new concepts, just as a child gets used to the simple relations and qualities he meets until he understands them. Understanding really means nothing in the world except familiarity and getting accustomed to the concepts.

"The first postulate of nothingness may be illustrated by the familiar difficulty of determining whether a slowly moving train, one is sitting in, or an adjacent one, is in motion. The passenger has either to wait for bumps or accelerations, or he has to look out at some adjacent object which he knows to be fixed, before he can decide if he's moving.

"The second principle is an obvious consequence of the wave theory of light and sound. Just as waves in water once started by a ship travel through the water with a velocity independent of the ship, so, waves in nothingness travel onward with speed bearing no relation to that of the body which originated them.

"Leave off here."

*   *   *

"Okay, now for the second session on the no-existence of space.

"Before starting in on the deeper part of the subject, let me divert to a favorite topic, the fad which man has taken up and tried to work out to form around it a religion—this is reason.

"Reason is a senseless sort of argument that everything works out from logic or deduction according to what the senses make of it. The definition of reason is that it's a statement offered as an explanation or justification of an act or procedure. It's a consideration, motive or judgment inducing or confirming a belief, influencing the will, and leading to an action.

"It is a ground or cause, the reality which makes any fact intelligible to the senses of man. It is supposedly the materialistic power of comprehending, of inferring, of intellectualizing.

"It is to work out, think out, figure out, analyze or conclude about something.

"This is reason. The very thing which Thomas Aquinas, the Catholic founder of Christian philosophy, used to deduct theological thought and start a medieval drive toward the worst piece of thinking in all history. Man has certainly suffered because of his reasoning which is based upon false premises.

"Today this fad has been split into two warring factions, the intellectuals versus the anti-intellectuals. The intellectuals, who are supposedly endowed with unusual mental capacity, versus the anti-intellectuals, who don't believe in intellectualism.

"Now the followers of intellectualism believe in the doctrine that knowledge is derived from pure reason; also, the doctrine that the ultimate principle of reality is reason.

"The anti-intellectuals believe in the doctrine of anti-reason; opposing the intellectual theory, they believe in the doctrine of non-reason. This is a faith in the higher senses, the senses of Soul that make contact with the sound current and become a part of it.

"The reasonists are those who follow Francis Bacon, Descartes, Hegel, Aristotle and others. These are the ones whom the Catholic Church have established as their leaders in the field of thought and metaphysics, thus forming the intellectualism of the church as a basic philosophy. They are: Aristotle, Aquinas, Bernard, Pascal, and a few hundred others who put a materialistic slant to the church's metaphysical theory called Ontology, which is supposedly the science of reality; the branch of knowledge that investigates the nature, essential properties, and relations of being.

"The anti-reasonists are those whom we normally know as the spiritual travelers. They are followers of the doctrine of directly receiving from the SUGMAD and ITS counterparts, the Silent Ones, and of course the ECK. Within spirit or ECK, the great sound current, are the properties of the SUGMAD—Wisdom, Power and Freedom. These are supposedly given to all who will seek them, if they are willing to take the trouble of using the proper techniques of the spiritual exercises.

"The knowledge gained from separating Soul from the body, and moving about in what we know as the Nuri-Sarup, the light body, isn't concerned at all with the reasoning of the mind. Soul learns quickly that It can gain more in fifteen seconds, of knowledge, health, power and freedom, when submerged in the divine, cosmic sound current than by years of trying to reason out something by Its intellect.

"This reasoning out process introduced by the Jesuits in the Catholic Church has completely created a racial aberration among the homo sapiens of this earth plane. Often it looks like a huge, gigantic plot to trap all exposed to what is known as education. Nothing could be further from the real facts.

"Intellectualism is really a trap established by the Kal Niranjan for the Tuza. So many are falling for it, because materialistic education seems to be the only way to knowledge.

"Now I've given this to you for the reason of showing that the materialistic sciences which are a part of intellectualism are a trap to gather all attention to their discoveries. These are, as you know, nothing in comparison with what an ECK traveler knows.

"Take for example what happened a few years ago when the Nobel prize was given to a pair of American scientists at Princeton University for the discovery of the rotation of the atom; clockwise to the right for positive action, and counter clockwise for negative action. When announced through the newspapers, the theosophical society members pointed out that Annie Besant, their renowned leader, had said this in her books in the 1890s, and again early in this century. She was a spiritual traveler.

"All this is concerned with space. The intellectuals are vastly overconcerned with space—but the travelers are not. It is an open hole of nothingness. To the latter, there is hardly a piece of space anywhere. Everything is loaded with atoms, Tuzas and spiritual things, the heavenly wonders.

"The intellectuals are concerned with emptiness, and they are loaded with other materialistic projects made by the hands of men, like human beings living in some housing project, or in the great, empty beehives of cities.

"Now, to the intricacies of nothingness again.

"The wave picture, which I spoke about in my last session, begins to appear as the true picture of reality and the particle picture merely a clumsy object, an approximation of the truth, an approximation obtained by trying to cram force into a frame work of space and time, into a structure which does not admit representation in space and time.

"A wave starts from a moving particle or group of particles growing greater as it moves into the layer of upper strata. As one and the same substance appears from one point of view as a particle and from another as a wave, it is now called wavicle in the language of the spiritual travelers.

"Observers describe events by measures of times and distances made with regard to their frameworks of references. Therefore, such things as length, velocity, energy, momentum are not absolute but relative, i.e., they are not attributes of the physical reality but relations between the observer and what he observes. Consequently, the observed objects are not laws of the physical world but of the observed phenomena. Einstein found that the concepts of length between points in nothingness or events in time didn't as we supposed, represent an intrinsic property of the points or the events. Like direction, it is merely a relation whose value changes with the observer's position relative to the object.

"As we cannot ascertain the position and the velocity of an electron at the same time, it is impossible to compute the future path of the electron. Any interference on our part would change the position of the electron. Everything depends on how you look at it. The visual image will endure as long as we do not change our standpoint, and thus it differs from hallucination. Matter has really a wave structure. Therefore, it will change in quite a definite way when we change our standpoint in regard to it.

"A vista of miles may be represented by an expert artist on a small canvas so that if a man would make an effort to suppress the usual idea of extension and would look at the painting intently, he will perceive the scenes actually extending into miles. No matter how minute the picture on a paper may be, we always feel it to be like its original, so long as the mutual proportion of its contents is in harmony.

"This is also the case in dreams. Extension of space, in dreams and the waking state, is nothing real in itself apart from the mind of the observer. Mathematically, many different kinds of space are conceivable.

"One of the remarkable outcomes is that the difference between a wave and a particle is disappearing. This has to do with something that is neither, and yet shares the properties of both. The difference between a wave and a particle is one of degree, rather than of kind. A group wave of a certain frequency may appear to us as if it were a moving particle of given energy. But it is a clumsy picture. The particle picture tells us that our knowledge of an electron is indetermined. The wave picture, the electron itself, is also indetermined.

"The particle picture assumes that an objective universe exists outside ourselves and tries to depict this objective universe, while the wave picture tries to depict our knowledge of the universe as experienced by us. The wave picture is a picture of knowledge, not of things.

"The mass of an electron is not constant but is a function of its speed, and this again depends on the observer's system of reference. In each mass phenomena where many observers are in the same condition, the statistical laws appear all the more clearly, with the greater number of individuals that cooperate in the phenomena.

"In such cases, we get many pictures but it will be hard to

realize that the two very different shadow pictures are projections of the same object. Accordingly, nothing that varies for different observers can be fundamentally true.

"As stated before, the wave picture provides a representation, not of an objective nature but only of our knowledge of nature. The same electron may be represented by two different wave pictures, not because it is itself different in the two cases, but because our knowledge of it is different in both cases.

"All right. This is enough for now!"

* * *

"Now we'll get started again," said Rebazar Tarzs slowly sitting down on the hard floor again.

"One of the things that is much talked about in spiritual circles is intuition. This is the power of knowing, the power of obtaining knowing without the senses, without recourse to the inference of reasoning; an innate, instinctive knowledge.

"This faculty is connected with the no-thing universe. Ordinarily it is supposed to mean inner-teaching, inner instruction as given by some kind of higher inner self.

"The word intuition means however to look in, to gaze into, see and understand immediately. To know by looking inwardly. In other words to project oneself by looking inwardly and understanding immediately what it is we are seeking. In order to understand the no-thing universe we must rely on intuition, as all ECK travelers do. It is started by joining, or hooking up the forces between Soul within you and the no-thing world within, and without. The working together of the subjective self with the forces of the no-thing world will start working out the kinks between this region and you.

"The forces of the no-thing world will begin to suggest the right course for the outer to take, reason over and adapt for use. The object is to bring the two faculties into balance and give the forces of the no-thing world the edge—but nothing too much, for it would be quite unreasonable

179

to let this faculty rule you completely in this matter-real world; yet on the other hand it knows far more about straightening out the problems of life than you would ever know.

"The idea is not to follow it blindly. Learn to pay attention to it and then use what information it brings to your attention. You have use of it at anytime, anywhere. It's only that the power of the no-thing world is there and must be used whenever you need it.

"What actually happens is that you can furnish the channel for it to flow through your life—and when that channel is open, when there is nothing blocking it—that higher-inner faculty can function readily to tell you something which can't be gained from any amount of outer, man made logic or reasoning.

"Intuition doesn't use words. It existed long before language was invented, and that is why we are cut off, as it were, from our inner selves. We have gone farther down into matter than the inner self has and it can only talk to us when we furnish it with a channel for the no-thing forces to work through.

"The some-thing forces will fight to keep the inner forces from flowing through. The objective will assert itself. You must have a free mind and no upsets going at the time you wish to use it. Any quarrels or arguments will upset the workings of this inner force.

"When you can put the outer to work under the intuition forces and coordinate them together, they will give you a guidance such as you've never had before. The objective misses too much when working alone, especially the help the subjective could give; and the subjective working alone has not a firm hold on the outer world without good training.

"It takes a lot of training to get the inner forces working through you, especially to open the channel and keep it free from the obstacles and aberrations which might clog it. No one will understand this until they start traveling on the path upward into the Far Country.

"Intuition is a basic faculty on this plane. At the foundation of matter lies illusion, a form of perception. When we see or feel ourselves in the world of four dimensions, we shall see that the world of three dimensions does not really exist and never existed. It was the creation of our own fantasy, a phantom ghost, an optical illusion, a delusion, anything one pleases to call it except reality.

"The phenomenal world is simply our incorrect perception of the world. When a man dreams he begins to be conscious of the fact that he is asleep, and that what he sees is a dream, then he wakes up; also Soul, beginning to be conscious of the fact that all visible life is a dream, approaches its awakening.

"Bertrand Russell said, 'When one cosmic time and one persisting space are abolished, we have space-time instead. Our notion of the world structure is changed. There is no cosmic time. We must give up the idea of bodies moving and the talk of events. The unity of a body is the unity of its history, like the unity of a time. Our aspects and interpretations of the universe are constructions of the mind of man. If we could intuit ourselves and other things as they really are, we should see ourselves in a world of spiritual natures, our connection with which we didn't begin at our birth and will not cease with the destruction of the body.'

"Space, or no-thingness is a quality of Soul. The Tuza exists everywhere but through ignorance limits itself to a certain region. Evil consists in transforming something great into something small. We have to remove an obvious limitation.

"All phenomena traveling past us with the velocity of light is called radiation, while the localized events which travel much more slowly or not at all, is called matter. All may be, fundamentally and equally, of the nature of etheric waves. The question is sometimes raised, how would things be regarded by an observer who is himself traveling with the velocity of light? To answer this question, it is pointed out that all things would appear equal. In other words they would appear to be standing still.

"The distinction between ourselves and the outside world is only arbitrary, a practically convenient division between one type of sense impression and another. The group of sense impressions, forming what I term myself, is only a small subdivision of the vast world of sense impressions when involved in the body matter. Obviously, the distinction is only a practical one. The color and form which constitutes for us the needle are just as much sense impressions within us, as the pain produced by its pricks.

"The old dualism of mind and matter, which was mainly responsible for the supposed hostility, seems likely to disappear, not through matter becoming in anyway more shadowy or unsubstantial than heretofore or through mind becoming resolved into a function of the working of matter, but through substantial matter resolving itself into a creation and manifestation of mind.

"Our ordinary thoughts have become space-time bound and can get no grip on concept outside space and time. Our space-time framework proves inadequate for the representation of the whole of nature, or even of this lower world. Therefore, there is absolute necessity for us to secure a state of absence of all thoughts, Nirvikalpa Samadhi, what I call deep trance, in order to experience truth.

"When war breaks out, many men are ready to die for their country. By this, their space-sense somewhat increases, and yet the space sense does not increase sufficiently because the people of other countries remain as their enemies.

"Those only are the wisest men who live for the whole world by loving all the SUGMAD's creatures. Then, the space-time sense is perfect and whole. They have overcome the otherness. They enjoy the fullness of full-space sense. Those who are selfish must die for their country in order to develop this nothingness sense. The spiritual travelers who are unselfish and wise will live for the good of all the SUGMAD's creatures. Spiritual wisdom develops in man the full nothingness sense.

"The will to wisdom is of greater value to humanity than the will to power of the aggressive man.

"The no-space, the nothingness sense depends on the system of reference and the nature of the co-ordinates used.

"If we, who have traveled into the Far Country, told this openly we would be the damned. By this I mean the excluded. Some spiritual travelers have possession of data which is terrible in its aspects to mankind. I say only the travelers know and hold such knowledge.

"The ECK traveler must remain almost silent in this world. The reason being that whenever he speaks, his words are greeted with wild shouts and screams from orthodox religions. The old, invulnerable metaphysical systems, such as Buddhism and Catholicism shake to their foundations. The priests and gurus of all teachings flout and taunt and jeer at the travelers' presence.

"All religions, all philosophical systems, all cosmogonies are created to explain the obvious teachings of life and things. But they have failed, just like we see in the explanation of the no-thing universe versus the some-thing universe.

"Leave off here for a spell."

*   *   *

"To complete this discussion is my promise this afternoon," said Rebazar Tarzs, as a stretch of sunlight beamed through the window and fell upon his shoulder like a bright ribbon of gold. "I'll finish this subject on the no-existence of space, and tomorrow will give you another aspect of the world of the SUGMAD.

"Now the way to the Far Country is through the no-thing universe for all human beings. They must cross the land of nothingness in order to get into the first plane, the Astral region.

"In this region of nothingness, the super-physical regions, are the Sun Worlds, Moon Worlds and the Lightning Worlds. These worlds lie between this physical plane and the astral region. They are merely sub-planes, well described by the Vedas and later the Vedantists who took those scriptures seriously enough to consider them as some of the super superior worlds.

"They really are not very high, but they are worlds of

183

nothingness which the ECK traveler must cross to reach the first pure plane of the astral region.

"The spirit body moves something like this in its journey upward. It leaves the body through the tenth door, the spiritual eye, in the subtle body. At first, Soul looks out through this door, and eventually It goes through it and leaves the body completely. It then steps out into a new world which It has never seen before. This new world will probably be some subplane of the astral zone, but it is a new dimension to Soul.

"There is in this greater universe an almost endless series of sets of dimension, one above the other, like the three dimension world in which we live here, reaching up to the highest worlds. Each set is separated from the one just above it by the difference in the substances, the fineness or coarseness of particle and the different rates of vibrations.

"These differences make one set of dimensions invisible to people living in another set, because the eyes of people inhabiting one region will have a limited range of vision, making it impossible for them to see a region much above or much below their own region, to which they have been adapted. This is the reason we cannot see the astral worlds by or through the physical eyes.

"With the astral eyes, we can see on that plane just as well as we can see on the physical plane with the physical eyes. So, too, with the still higher worlds. With each higher world, or set of dimensions, the light and the beauty increase materially, also the happiness of the inhabitants.

"At the sublime moment when the traveler steps out into the higher world, he begins to realize that he has acquired a vast increase of powers, as well as joy. It appears to him, and it is a fact too, that he can do almost anything he wishes to do. Not only has he increased his powers, but his knowledge and understanding have expanded proportionately.

"At this time, the whole material universe appears as an open book to him, and all dark mysteries have vanished. He finds himself in possession of all knowledge of these lower worlds. He now knows them and has power over them. From here on up, each world gained, gives one complete knowledge and power over the world below him.

"The traveler is now free to proceed on his way to still higher zones. He may not allow himself to be unduly detained in order to enjoy the new world he has just entered. He must proceed always upward, for there will be no ending of the worlds he is seeking.

"Between the physical and the pure astral planes, there are many sub-planes. Vedantic pundits speak of the Sun Worlds first. Then come the Moon Worlds. After that, numerous sub-zones, and finally what Vivekananda calls the Lightning Worlds. This corresponds to the plane of the Sahasra-dal-Kanwal, as it is known to the travelers. It is commonly referred to as the astral region. It is full of light and far more beautiful than this world of the earth.

"It is the region which is commonly considered by many yogis as the supreme heaven. This is as high as they are able to ascend as a rule. The lord of that region they regard as the Supreme Being is only the Kal Niranjan, or Brahm. The travelers speak of him as Kal Niranjan, while most Hindus think of him as Brahm, the supreme God. He is, in fact, regarded as the supreme being by nearly all religions, because they know of nothing higher. Only the great travelers know of the higher regions and the higher deities, on up to the SUGMAD, out of whom all others come.

"At a point between the Sun Worlds and the Moon Worlds and the pure Astral zone, the travelers enter a zone called Ashta-dal-Kanwal. At that point something happens which changes the whole course of his life and also his method of procedure.

"It is the meeting with his own teacher, a superior, experienced spiritual traveler in his radiant form. This is the traveler's Nuri-Sarup or light form. It is your Chiva, or Guru, appearing just as he does in physical life, except that his body is now much more beautiful and full of light, brilliantly illuminated.

"The Chiva receives the neophyte traveler with a cordial welcome and from that moment on the two are never separated throughout the journey to still higher regions, until the neophyte reaches the fifth region, the Sat Nam world. By now he is experienced and can travel upon his own.

"So you see that the Lord of this world, Kal Niranjan, is almost on the human level. He is the God of the no-thing universe, what we are calling space. He is the space God, which the Christians worship, and seem to look for in the sky, a god over the world of nothingness.

"Man cannot conceive of this space world, nor of a space god, for he has personalized his god and made him the protector of his household, life and controller of his events. He doesn't realize that when he prays to a space god, of the nature that I speak about, he is praying to a no-thing to create for him something, or bring about changes in his affairs.

"This stupidity is never recognized, for man is beyond his capacity when getting into the worlds beyond the something plane. It is for certain that he cannot get some-thing out of no-thing, and space just doesn't exist for him, nor anything else.

"Now everything including the Kal Niranjan, God of this universe, is the narcissus, the unconscious beauty of the universe, in the minds of minds. It is the instinct of the Kal to act to exploit the ego. Exhibitionism is the eternal law of what is called evolution. Autoscopy, narcissism and exhibitionism are the motives for all movements throughout the universe.

"Even the genius, the most non-adaptable, who is always at war with his environment, is the great peacock, the show-off and the self-loved individual.

"The principle of this is 'that whatever exists desires an audience.' In everything, including the Kal, and if you do not believe this, read all the holy scriptures, the desire to be seen and loved is most prominent. Everything and everyone desires to tell its story. Of course, this includes the travelers.

186

"Here is where Soul arrives at self-realization.

"You, yourself, are the supreme one in this universe. You are the Kal. You are matter and spirit; being more matter than spirit, you are mainly the Kal. You are always strutting before the pride of humility that dominates you. Your modesty is a secret self-kissing exhibition in the mirror of self-love. Love yourself says the law of nature. I mean by this; love your Tuza and you love the Kal.

"The metaphysical basis of exhibitionism is the strange and incomprehensible inner urge of expression, which is tied into the no-thing universe, space. Theology expresses this urge for exhibitionism. Philosophy expresses it as noumenon becoming phenomenon, exercising an illusion in nothingness.

"Kal invents mirrors. The spaceless seek space in which to move and survey, for space is the ballroom, the peacock alley of the invisible.

"Curse Kal and you are cursing yourself. Praise Kal and you are praising yourself. Thus the Kal, which all mystics and priestcraft oppose, is the inventor of theologies, cosmologies and divine events, with peals of laughter ringing from his throat at their ignorance.

"Even Buddha, who drew the sword against life, came to teach the world that there had better be no world. His cameras were the eyes and ears of his disciples.

"Many seek to become the supreme exhibitionist. Strip away the mask of all earthly dictators and there you will find Kal strutting like the peacock. Strip away the covering of the mystic and you will find the same thing. Even Jesus was the boldest of peacocks who annihilated the yoke of the meek and lowly and said; 'Look at yourselves. You too can be God!'

"Therefore, I say that in the world of space, or no-thing, there are no principles or laws except those of the Kal. There are only the exhibitionists, because the world has made

187

them so. Principles, theories, ideas are the masks of the instincts, the innate craving of the ego-vividness, blown to bits by the winds of the no-thing universe.

"I can only show you that space doesn't exist. It is all in the mind of man—and if he continues to believe that it does, he will live long on this earth planet—in the something universe, until he sees and changes his mind about space. Then he can rise into the higher worlds.

"That's all for now."

Chapter 10

THE TUZASHOTTAMA ENERGY

"The energies of the Tuza are some of the most powerful forces in the God worlds," said Rebazar Tarzs starting his talks in the cool of the early morning shade.

"You will find that Soul operates its own drive like an individual motor in a car. It cannot do any other way, for this is the law of the ECK. All Tuzas must make and use their own energies for their motion, movement and drive through the universes. Nothing else can help them—it must be done on their own.

"Soul uses the sound current as the basic element, out of which the energies It uses can be made to drive Itself onward, or for any action that It undertakes.

"This energy in this universe is called electronic; most scientists are aware of it, and make use of it in our daily living. But Soul can use this for either deadly or peaceful results to Itself.

"It can use electronic beams to knock out another Soul and also to help others. Soul cannot be killed but It can be knocked cold by electronic beams provided they strike It hard enough. Often Souls meet and have fierce battles in which they throw these electronic beams at one another until one is either knocked out or has to crawl away for Its own safety.

"All the electronic energy that Soul has, is manufactured out of the sound current. It does not have storage to carry around Its energy, so It must be able to create this energy and use it immediately. To try and carry it is both clumsy and impractical.

"Soul, knowing that the power of creative words is one of the secrets it possesses, can use these vibrations instantly. Just by the actual calling upon the divine energy

189

through the channel of a secret word, Soul can have it at Its finger tips.

"Every manifestation of life comes from this dynamic energy of the sound current. From the crawling ant to the thunder bolt, from the tidal wave to the solar cycle, everything, including the burning stars in the Milky Way and the flicker of a candle, all take their light and energy from this great central power.

"The pull of gravity, the flash of lightning, the building of thought-forms, and the love of the individual Soul, all come from this current primordial. That which physical science calls energy, which the Orientals call Prana, is only a manifestation of this life of the audible life sound current stepped down to meet material conditions. Like electricity in the air, it is omnipresent and it is also omnipotent. In it lies all energy, either latent or dynamic. It only awaits the proper conditions to express itself as dynamic force, in one form or another. It has many forms of expression, most of which are not yet known to physical science.

"Of course, it has to be stepped down, and at each step down it takes a different character and quality, to which we give names, if we can demonstrate them at all. Most of them science has not yet discovered.

"But every force known, from primal energy, prana, down to electricity and magnetism, the Tuzashottama energy, all are modified to serve the common cosmic and human needs. In the highest region it is all one force, the Supreme SUGMAD, manifested and manifesting.

"The tremendous heat, energy and light of our sun, of all suns, are derived from this stream. Every ray of light in the universe is a phenomenon of this infinite stream of light. Upon its power hangs every star in its orbit. Not a single rose may bring forth its buds without this power and no little child smiles without manifesting this power. Who can comprehend it, or assign qualities? Who can analyze it? We know from its manifestation that it has at least three very wonderful attributes:

"These are: Wisdom—Power—Freedom.

190

"Now, motion and energy fuse and end up being the same thing. Each Soul carries Its own energy or prana about It, just as in a shower of rain. Each Soul carries Its own rainbow about It. If I, the Tuza, change my speed of motion, I create a new ether for myself.

"As all measurements of energy are relative to something, all motions are relative to the Tuza. There is no absolute to the Tuza. There is no distinction between motion and rest in Soul because these are alternate systems of time-space, and a particle at rest, in one of them, may be moving in the others; the difference between unaccelerated and accelerated motion is likewise relative to the system of reference.

"A parrot dies and is reborn as a peacock. He will not generally know that he was a parrot before because his Tuzashottama energy has changed everything, e.g., this time, space, motion and weight.

"This energy is vibratory. It works in vibrations like the shooting of bullets; with speed greater than the eye can comprehend. Light and sound are the basic elements in this Soul energy.

"Light and sound are not parts of the physical things themselves, but are the results of waves of energy flowing out of the ECK as the fountainhead of the SUGMAD. The different vibrations of one thing and another are often the same light and sound rays, yet seen and heard differently. The essence of a thing is an optical or hearing interpretation. What we perceive often as separated from ourselves, really isn't, in the slightest.

"An observer in a rapidly descending airplane actually sees the earth rushing upward and a traveler in an express train actually sees the telegraph poles moving past him.

"It is difficult to see the position and motion of electrons at the same time with the physical eyes. Once though, you step outside the body and look, they are perfectly clear. Inside the body looking through the physical eyes, one cannot see. The more there is a focus on the one, the more blurred the other becomes.

"The same is true when we look at the aspects of the SUGMAD from an earth viewpoint. The positive and negative blur if gazed upon together—separated and viewed from outside the body, they become crystal clear. Man cannot experience both simultaneously, although the sound current contains both aspects within itself on this lower plane.

"Man cannot ascertain the place and motion of Soul at the same instant. It is impossible to compute accurately the energy which Soul will mock up in an instant to either defend itself or move into a higher plane. Both are relative to the position in which that particular Soul wishes to place itself.

"Soul works through the visual image channel to mock-up energy. It uses the Tuzashottama energy for expanding and contracting, through consciousness of the world in which it is operating. It uses itself in the energy field through the three basic attributes of the SUGMAD; wisdom, power and freedom.

"The energy on which the Tuza exists is eternal, and it is necessary to enter into this fluid state and become one with it. Working always in the relative and never in the absolute, it can change, move and give itself certain directive speed that nothing else in the universes of the Far Country can accomplish.

"The law which governs spiritual energies can only come to you by an expansion of human consciousness. This is also true of spiritual experience. The seed must be planted in your mind to receive the dynamic presence of the power and to surrender your mind to its control. It is this surrender and Soul control which brings about the release of the dynamic energies.

"It is the inner energy which you must liberate in order to walk above the ignorant and be of the Godhead. However, often without the guidance of the true inner traveler, there is danger in opening that psychic being concealed within, not usually active; for this being takes over and gives you false energy and failure.

"Philosophy, because of its habit of abstraction, has sel-

192

dom been a power for life. It has sometimes been powerful for high speculation in pursuing mental truth, for its own sake, sometimes for a subtle mental gymnastic in a bright cloud of words and ideas, but generally it has got too far off the beaten track.

"Only the SUGMAD matters, the SUGMAD alone will be the continuing need of the whole being of man. If there is any compulsion to activity, it will not be that of implanted desires nor the forces of nature, but the luminous striving for a greater consciousness ever becoming the sole motive of the whole existence.

"The divine energy of Soul comes in at one time; when mocked up, it leads, compels, instructs and enlightens; then again it may withdraw into the background and seem to leave the being to its own resources. At all times the seeker will be aware of the divine guide and will know that everything is being done for the best.

"This master energy descends upon you, breaks up your present psychological formations, shatters the walls of the ego and gives you greater powers of vision, perception, motivation and perfection. All forms of life that are unable to bear the change of this burning, fiery energy must disappear and all that can bear it will survive and enter into the kingdom of the spiritual worlds.

"The Tuzashottama energy will deal with all that is good for the traveler and for the good of all. Alone, the awaiting universal will must choose, action must change into a dynamic movement of that will, enjoyment must be replaced by the play of a pure, spiritual bliss. All personal will is either a temporary delegation from the ECK, or designated by IT. Even after he is free, the traveler will be in the world, and to be in the world is to remain in its works. To remain in the world without desire is to act for the good of the world in general, for the race, for some new creation to be evolved on earth or for some work imposed by the divine will within you.

"Freedom and truth fulfill its movement in the traveler according to each one's nature. This is the special aspect of the divine energy of the ECK, out of which the Tuza has emerged into action, unlimited by any form of this law or way; for Soul is infinite. You will manifest the divine moments of truth according to the temperament of your being, in any combination of essential attributes that may constitute the form given to your being by its own inner urge. It is this self-nature that men see in you, and not that from the outer.

"We'll leave off here!"

* * *

"The energy of Soul, sometimes known as the master power, is part of the trinity of the ECK, that is: Wisdom, Power and Freedom. As a part of the trinity it constitutes the movement, the action or motion of it.

"And as the Tuzashottama energy it makes up that part of the being which Soul uses when needing action of any kind. Even thought consists of using energy, but on a higher level than on the physical plane.

"So I begin here with wisdom which takes up that part of the trinity that gives right direction to action, and freedom, the quality that gives Soul an opportunity to move and do as wisdom directs. In other words one has more than a limited choice which man believes is freedom—he has the chance to choose his actions and directions without interference from anything or any creature of the SUGMAD.

"Nobody can think of the trinity in the terms of concepts while on this earth plane. It isn't possible for the human mind to grasp these three attributes. They are not shrouded in mystery, but the depths of them are beyond the grasp of human thinking.

"The energy which gives Soul an opportunity to have motion with direction is the basic element of all the universes. Since this is the sound current it must be connected with all things, especially with power and freedom. It has to be linked up with these pair of attributes or it cannot function. It must also have wisdom and must be free to act in any direction that it sees necessary.

"There is one fundamental perception, indispensable to man for gaining wisdom in the many ways of the divine self and that is to see the SUGMAD in ITS essential self and the Truth, unaltered by forms and phenomena.

"Otherwise man is trapped in a net of appearances and will wander confusedly in a chaotic multitude of cosmic aspects. On occasions by seeking to avoid entrapment he will sacrifice all, yet become chained to a small mental formula, or shut up in a limited personal experience, or caught up in a trap of reliving someone else's experiences.

"Of course, this energy is the manifestation of the ECK's creation through spirit, and the key to life's hidden secret is the relation of this spirit with its own existence in the energy forces.

"If man has only an intellectual and metaphysical view on this, then he is seeking in the dark. So you see, what man searches for is not mental truths alone, or truth of thought, but the dynamic truth of a living and revealing spiritual experience.

"Man must awaken the inevitable knowingness and contact the true and infinite presence of the sound current, always and everywhere. That presence must always remain with him as the living pervading reality in which he and all things exist, move and act. He must feel it always and everywhere, concrete, visible and in all things. He must see, feel, sense, contact it in everyway; not merely conceive the SUGMAD and spirit here in this existence but know with the same vividness all existence in God and spirit. This is the fundamental experience which envelops all knowledge.

"This energy is the omnipresent reality, the one existence everywhere; it is a single, unifying presence and not different in different creatures. It can be seen and felt in the completeness of each Soul or form in the universe. The knowledge or experience of it can begin anywhere and express itself through anything, for God is in all, and all is the divine.

"This energy begins to pervade and possess your being and out of it seems to proceed all your impulse to action, all your light of thought and speech, all the formation of your consciousness and its relations, and all relation with other spiritual forms. By the useful efforts of this energy you are no longer the little personal self but that with something of Itself put forward, that which sustains a selected form of Its own working in the universe.

"Since you must live in this world, as long as you have a physical body, and take account of its activities, it is necessary to have the ability to learn what divine truths underlie all things. You must also determine apparent opposition existing between the divine truth and manifest creation, which is the starting point of most spiritual experiences.

"However, at each point of creation you find that you are confronted with a duality, a separation of existence (the positive and negative) which seem to be opposite and their opposition to be the riddle of the universe. Later you will discover they are the poles of one being, Jaram Brahm, connected with, rather by two simultaneous currents of energy, negative and positive, in relation to each other in this world of the Brahm. Their tension is the very condition for the manifestation of what is within the Being; their reunion, the appointed means for reconciliation of life's discords and for the discovery of the integral truth of which you are seeking.

"This is a part of the eternal spirit and also a conscious time-spirit bearing the streams of events, a self-extended spiritual space of nothing containing all things and beings, a spirit substance which is the very form and material of all that seems non-spiritual, temporary and finite.

"You cannot stay in peace or bliss for there would be no solution to the enigma of the SUGMAD, within and without. As it stands now there seems to be a pair of divided states of the SUGMAD. Soon you will learn that this separation is in your consciousness and this truth has immense liberative power, for by it you are no longer bound to ignorance.

The separation is an illusion which can be overcome—it is maya.

"By looking close, you discover there is the ECK in both shadow and light, but not the SUGMAD; it is the ECK who is here with this face of maya. This is the beginning of a growing spiritual experience which reveals to you more and more that what seems to be dark, incomprehensible maya all the time, is no other than the consciousness of the eternal, timeless and illimitable beyond the universe, though spread out under masks of bright and dark opposites for the miracle of the slow manifestation of the divine in mind and life and matter.

"Now you come to the mystery of the Tuzashottama. There are two different energies within you; the inner, silent, moving and observing; the other is the outer energy which pursues its habitual movements, a mass of physical activities, a formation and result of force. This outer energy often enters and captures the inner consciousness of man and no longer does he have a freedom of self, because it acts without his control.

"As man's consciousness deepens he becomes aware that this is only a frontal energy making him reactive to the outer senses. For it is only by the permission of his inner energies that the outer can exist. Hereby, hangs the whole secret of what you are trying to gather from these teachings.

"By the gradual withdrawal of Soul from the outer world and from the outer activities, one can slowly change the nature of his physical self. Eventually Soul will perceive the knower within Itself, and all will become an expression of the divine omnipresence, the ECK, the will and knower.

"It is here that man discovers the two poles of existence of the one being in the Three Worlds, and the lines or currents of their energy, negative and positive, in relation to each other which effect simultaneously, the manifestation of all that is within it.

"It is evident that there is one supreme and infinite energy—the ECK, represented in the two different sides of

Soul on this plane, the inner and outer in relation to each other. All is either prepared or pre-existent in the ECK in being, issues from it and is upheld by its will and presence. All becomes and acts and develops by the energy of the divine in it for individual and cosmic purposes. Duality is necessary in the lower worlds for the manifesting, creating and enabling of the double current of energy which is always necessary for world workings, the two poles of the same being, the ECK.

"On one hand you find the force of matter pushing hard at Soul, while on the other hand you feel the Tuzashottama energy pulling upward out of matter. When there is a complete balance of the two energies in this world and a control of the consciousness, one begins to open to the pull of a stronger power that draws him out of the confused class of ideas and uplifts him into the higher power. He becomes illuminated.

"When the energy from the sound current enters into Soul, every part of the light body is illuminated. Soul is purified and taken out of ignorance. The energy pours in like a current of air, working in all the inner self, dissolving, reshaping, transfiguring all. Bliss will invade Soul and all pain will become divine pleasure.

"Soul will know and understand all within the sphere of the degree of consciousness the ECK has given it, and will no longer need the element of the negative pole of energy, except to sustain itself to live in the earth world, and to have control of the body.

"I will continue with this talk after we have had some tea and refreshed ourselves."

*   *   *

Rebazar Tarzs continued, "One must depend upon this Tuzashottama at all times. By use of the spiritual exercises which I will give later, one will be eventually strong enough to use his own shottama to pass through the gates of death alone.

"Otherwise, he must have a spiritual traveler to help him. He cannot do it alone until he has mastered the knack of leaving the body at will, and without the help of a traveler.

"After he can do this, then his ability to enter the regions above the play of death, as man here knows it, will be greatly enhanced, and he can come and go to those regions above, retaining perfect memory of all he has seen and heard.

"However, this is one of the minor achievements of the neophyte. The samadhi of ECK will take the beginner through to these planes beyond death. Of course, this solves, once and for all, the most serious problem which has ever confronted the human race—the problem of death and what lies beyond it.

"This fact of human experience has not remained wholly unknown to the world's greatest thinkers. Plutarch, for example, said, 'At the moment of death Soul experiences the same impressions, passes through the same process as those who are initiated into the Great Mysteries.'

"This is the exact teaching of the spiritual travelers and it is the common experience of all initiates who have made some advance on the upward path.

"The ECK travelers give their charges the true method by which they can come and go at will between this and the higher worlds, through the Tuzashottama. This is what is called dying daily, or dying while we live—it is a part of the daily routine of the advanced travelers.

"The charges leave their bodies, much in the same way a dying man leaves, except the neophyte does it voluntarily. The process is always under his own control and he can come back into the body at any moment he wishes to return.

Otherwise, his passing out of the body is practically the same as that of the dying man. He thus learns how to use the shottama, what death means, and also what lies beyond death,—even becoming acquainted with the future home to which he is to go, when he finally takes leave of his physical body. He may also converse with friends and family who have long ago left their bodies.

"This achievement cannot fail to interest the neophyte, since it solves the gravest problems of life and destiny. It is one phase of the great work of the ECK travelers. They have broken the seal of death, and so to them and their charges there is no more death. All of this is positive knowledge, not speculation, or guess work. Neither is it the interpretation of any book.

"All the world, the western world in particular, has been accustomed to think that no man knows, or can know, what lies beyond the portals of death. They assert, with apparent finality, that death lands us upon some mystic shore from whence no traveler ever returns. Of course, a few assume that death ends the individual career of man. It is time, however, for men to cease to think of death in such a gloomy mood. In fact, there is no death at all. There is simply a shifting of the scene, an awakening in a new world.

"This, of course, is the matter of using the shottama energy, that which is used by the Tuza. He must do this through mock ups, in order to make the step through the door of death because it is only by the use of his imaginary faculty that he actually gets anywhere.

"Man cannot break through the process of death unless he does it in his mockups. He must set the course, like any other on this physical plane—he cannot leave it entirely up to the traveler who has taken over the spiritual welfare of the neophyte. The traveler can give him so much instruction, and point out the problems of travel in other worlds. He can also show the neophyte how to get out and return to the body at will, but he is not likely to assist him in doing so.

"I point this out in this manner. The traveler isn't going to jerk the neophyte out of his body and shove him up the higher path with force; not likely. Maybe he will occasionally, but not often, because it is not the policy of the traveler to interfere with the development of the neophyte, unless the latter shows timidness or a lack of self-confidence in doing this.

"Drastic actions are used here and there, but as I have said, not as a policy. The spiritual travelers base their work upon the ECK trinity—wisdom, power and freedom. They know that each Soul must learn for Itself how to use the faculty of imagination, for in it lies the secret of the universes, and the trinity. If Soul fails to use it for Its own benefit, then It is crucifying Itself upon the cross of life, the same as the savior did on the cross at Golgotha.

"This is the drama of life. Your imagination is the savior of your universe. Use it wisely—for this is the wisdom of the trinity. Use it directly with the energy of the shottama. Use it freely—this is the purpose of the trinity.

"This shottama is the imaginary image, and the energy by which Soul has the power to act. Under no circumstances can It do anything with it—for the shottama is Its own power, created out of the universal sound current. It is that invisible thread of life upon which Soul travels like the spider that weaves its thread and moves along the thread to the areas it wants to have in its future destiny.

"Now if you remember in your study of physics, there was an assumption which went something like this. The force must establish itself, and the physical object will follow it to that point. In other words, a thought can fix itself at a certain point and the physical body will work out a way of getting itself to this point eventually.

"This is the way Soul operates. It fixes Itself at a certain point or in a certain action through Its imagination, and the spirit body follows the direction. This is a metaphysical law on the higher planes.

"The traveler never loses consciousness when he leaves the body and moves about in the higher regions. Nor does he forget, upon returning to the body again; he has a complete memory of every experience during the absence from his body. Of course this is a bold achievement, the most marvelous of all achievements of man. The beauty of it is, that this accomplishment lies within the power of man through the shottama energy. He requires little, rather only the knowledge of how to go about it, and then an application to the task.

"After one is able to leave his body voluntarily, there is not only no death for him, in the ordinary sense of some dreadful catastrophe, but there is not even a moment of unconsciousness, or a shadow of darkness. One using the shottama energy steps out of his body at will and in full possession of all of his faculties. He knows exactly what he is doing and remains always in full control of the process.

"Of course the ECK travelers leave their bodies when the time comes for them to go. When that time comes, they go as they always have, only at that time they sever all connection with the body and discard it. They go as liberated Souls, rising on wings of power and light. They simply step out of their bodies and go, as one would step out of a close, stuffy room into a beautiful garden.

"When the spiritual traveler leaves the physical plane, he goes where he wishes, for he is the traveler of all higher regions. If he pauses on the astral plane, he uses his astral body there. If he goes on up to the causal plane, he functions there in his causal body. And if he goes up to the third plane, he discards all bodies and from there on up, he acts as free spirit, unlimited and unhindered. As pure spirit, he knows all things by direct perception, without any sort of instrument of contact, such as he was obliged to use on all the lower planes.

"A dying man, of course, breaks all connection with his body when he leaves it; but the spiritual traveler, when he leaves the body as a part of his daily work, leaves a sort of connection with it, so that he may return to it at will. This connection is poetically called in the Bible, the silver cord.

"This cord is never broken by the ECK traveler, or his neophyte, until they are ready to leave the body for all times. Then they of their own will, break this silver cord and pass on up to perfect freedom. This is all there is to that most dreadful thing men call death.

"Now you must remember that every plane has one above it, and in order to reach a farther, upper world, the Tuza must proceed in the same manner as leaving the body on the first plane—the physical one—that is by the use of the imaginary faculty. He must image forth a mockup entry into the higher worlds, and proceed to reach it, by use of the shottama through the imagination.

"This imagination is the true faculty which Soul possesses as its own, and only through it does the shottama proceed. Otherwise, Soul may go for centuries as the victim of Itself—and Its own ignorance.

"We'll leave off here for refreshing the body!"

*   *   *

"We'll continue with the study of death," Rebazar Tarzs said resuming his discussion. "This is in connection with the Tuzashottama, the energy which the Tuza works with in order to make its way through the worlds and uses as a creative force.

"Now I'll talk about the four groups of experiences concerning death. Mankind is divided into these groups or distinct classes because of the typical types of people who experience one or more of the kinds of death explained here.

"The first class includes all who have no spiritual traveler to help them. This, of course, takes in the great bulk of mankind. All of these are obliged to meet the emergencies of death without support of any knowledge of how to use the shottama energy to leave their body voluntarily.

"They leave their bodies unescorted, absolutely alone and helpless, under the law of their own karma. They are to receive payment in full for what they have earned in the life just finished. Of them, the messengers of death ask not when they shall come, neither do they listen to the cries of distress. They are relentless, merciless, operating under the orders of their master, the Negative Power, whose duty it is to administer absolute justice, with no favoritism. As we all know, this class includes the vast majority of mankind. No matter to what religion they may belong, no difference between king or peasant, no matter how good nor how bad; all alike must face the dark angel and follow where he leads. They must go when the hour strikes, whether they are ready or not. None in this class can stay the hand of death, when the inevitable moment arrives. All must face death alone and meet its issues.

"The second class are the ones who have had the initiation from the MAHANTA, but who have done but little or nothing in the way of spiritual exercises.

"This particular traveler will meet them in his spirit body and takes them to that region or locality which they have earned. There he places them in a sort of training school where they make progress under his directions. If they have done wrong, the MAHANTA will guide them through the discipline they must undergo.

"They then continue in their training school until the time comes when they are fit to go into a higher world. But in no case does the neophyte ever go before the judge of death, nor does the black angel of death ever approach him at the time of his physical death. He cannot approach the neophyte of any spiritual traveler, the traveler takes care of his own charges; he is the master of the situation and since he is an embodiment of the ECK, none but the silent ones have any jurisdiction over him. He has the power to do as he likes, and no one can obstruct his path.

"The third class are those who have learned to use the shottama for leaving their bodies, but haven't quite attained the mastership of spiritual traveling. All of this class know the day and the hour when they are to go, long before it comes. The entire process of death is under their own control, and there is never a shadow of difficulty or distress during the process of passing. Neither do they lose consciousness for a single moment. They pass out of the body as easily as one would lay off an old garment. They use the shottama to project themselves.

"They have practiced this daily so the performance is quite familiar. They have visited the region which they are now to live in, so it's like going home again. They break the silver cord, and release the body forever.

"The separation from the physical body now complete, they are free to go where they wish, without bonds of any sort. They go directly to that region, under the escort of a spiritual traveler, where they are to stay for a time, until they are ready for a higher plane.

"These two classes never return to the earth life again, unless they so will and are ordered by the ECK. Generally they are taken upward, step by step, until they reach the highest world of the God realm.

"It is extremely fortunate for any neophyte, if he has been able to reach Sach Khand before he leaves the physical body forever. The way to this is open to all. They can do it, if they will perform the required practice of exteriorization. But actually not many do this. In each and every case, the charges of any spiritual traveler are saved from the monotonous rounds of reincarnation. Their dreary life here is finished.

"The fourth class, which is the last one, are the ECK Masters themselves.

"When the time comes that an ECK Master wishes to leave his body for keeps, he simply lays it down of his own will, steps out of it, as he has done so often; now he breaks the cord and discards the body as an instrument for which he has no further use.

"A chela of his, prepares the body and takes it to a funeral home where it is burned, what you call cremation. The Master has no need for the body anymore, and its destruction by fire is for his own benefit; there could be evil Tuzas who are looking for a body to use. The destruction of it by fire destroys any possibility of this.

"The entire process of the passing of a Master, as well as all circumstances connected with it, are under his own control. There is never a momentary shadow of unconsciousness. He remains a traveler, even through the process of his own death. The ECK Masters are lords of life and death, and therefore nothing can interfere with them because they know the use of the shottama energies.

"After leaving their bodies, they rise at once above all physical, material worlds, above all the lower heaven worlds, and take up their residence wherever they may wish, according to their duties and responsibilities, then enter into the higher duties, as assigned to them by the ECK.

"It may be said that ECK Masters do not generally remain in their physical bodies much, no longer than the usual time allotted to ordinary mortals; however, some who wish to stay have that chance, by immortalizing their physical bodies. Some return and find a body to use—many have lived here for only a few years, and others have been on earth for centuries. It depends upon the traveler and what he wishes to do here.

"In general, they let nature take its course, in all matters physical; although they have plenty of powers to interfere with the usual routine, if they see fit to do so. It is not usually their plan to do so, interfere, that is. They can remain in their bodies for centuries, or even thousands of years, if they wish and deem it wise.

"Many yogis have been known to keep their bodies for centuries, and any high class yogi can do it. But yogis are not spiritual travelers of the highest order. The Masters observe the laws of this world, and carry on their work in harmony with those laws, as closely as possible. Their work is strictly of a spiritual nature, and they do not wish to interfere with the rules governing a country in which they have only a temporary interest. They come to this world for a definite purpose and they stick to that purpose and work as hard as possible.

"After all, what advantage would it be, if they should come for anything other than a spiritual mission? After finishing here, they go on to a higher work, leaving their successors to carry on.

"All ECK Masters have learned the use of this divine energy of Soul. They can mockup energy quickly and use it on the spot, the spur of the moment, for some useful means; mainly for traveling in the ethers, into other worlds, for making greater decisions and for protection. They wear it around themselves like a rainbow, ready for use.

"This is what is known as the magnetic field to the scientists of the earth plane. The field itself is similar to all other fields of the same nature on every plane, and that is the sound current.

"Now Soul needs this energy, the shottama, for its own survival. If it doesn't have it, then it will stay somewhere like a stone, in a semi-lifeless state until another Soul helps it or gives it consideration to get out of its state and use the energy for its own good.

"When man begins to lose this energy he makes the long funeral march downward from the higher planes into the lower regions. This retrogression of the human race is due to the lack of education; his religions have nothing to teach him about the use of the energies to keep him buoyant, and to lift him upward out of this world.

"Man has nothing to live for provided he has not learned the art of using the divine energy. When Soul is without strength or knowledge of its use, It cannot do anything but flounder.

"It is like a motor without the fuel to run it. It simply cannot make any advance until It has the ability to mockup this energy and work through his imaginative faculty, or vice-versa.

"We will stop here and take up another subject tomorrow to discuss!"

Chapter 11

THE SUGMAD OF BEING

Sri Rebazar Tarzs was extremely pleased with himself this particular morning when I entered his little hut in the Hindu Kush mountains, overlooking the wild country of Afghanistan.

Seating ourselves in the hot sunlight outside the hut, the scenery distracted me for a moment, but quickly my attention returned to Rebazar Tarzs as he spoke.

"No problems," Rebazar Tarzs said, starting the morning's discussion, "of greater or of more moving import confront the spiritual traveler than those of the potential awareness of his own consciousness, of the deep significance of the place he occupies in the Far Country as a Tuza, and of the purpose he should first discover and pursue.

"This consciousness of the ECK is the primal metaphysical experience, which, while causing one to penetrate into one's innermost being, at the same time causes one to penetrate deep into the Far Country.

"The Far Country cannot be experienced as one does the physical universe, for man is such a part of the latter that he doesn't see what he is; in fact he aids in its formation, because he is, as it were, an actor in a kind of drama, the variations of which depend on his subjective life expressing its manifold incidents. His affective states are not to be considered as mere accidents, of interest only to himself, to which the universe remains impassive. No, for eventually he becomes the ECK traveler also, penetrates into intimacy with the ECK, participates in the innermost workings of Its life, and gains in the revelation of Its mystery.

"All spiritual science, so the traveler learns in time, is

209

essentially centripetal. It studies the internal thought from the internal planes to the deeper and deeper ones, ever approaching the SUGMAD from which all life proceeds, the one and only Reality.

"The ECK traveler turns away from the world of human sciences which is peripheral and essentially centrifugal and which makes a study of the visible part of the sensual world, the surface upon which, so to speak, thought reflects itself upon itself, in an icy immobility and impersonal intellectuality.

"For ages man has accepted the tradition of the existence of two worlds; one, the world of appearances, the other the world of existences. They have assumed that the knowledge of things link them to his being, and have always assumed that the appearances alone were accessible.

"Everything in the outer is therefore necessarily an appearance. In fact, reality can only be attained within and never without. Man must turn his gaze within in order to begin the most marvelous of all explorations. Happiness comes only from within.

"Only by entering into the divine silence and closing our eyes and ears to the world of illusions can we hear the celestial melody; else we are but yielding to the illusions of the outer imagination and can only reap a harvest of bitter misery. This outer imagination is, of course, maya.

"The discovery of Soul, the real self, is first of all an act of inward retirement; it is termed the going in, penetrating the first step into the God realms.

"We penetrate into an invisible world; but this discovery occasions anguish and it is presumptuous to march to the conquest of this inner world without very definite directions, very precise counsels—hence the necessity, at first, of a spiritual traveler to give the right directions on the royal highway to the Far Country.

"The outward universe withdraws and fades away, as does the most beautiful scenery when the play is intensely dramatic; soon man experiences the joy of the revelation; the universe is no longer an object outside, an enigma to be solved; he no longer contemplates it from without, but from within. Its secret is our secret. This discovery, far from causing a sense of misery, becomes a source of confidence and of light. Man will begin to suffer, if and when he refuses to draw the satisfying waters from this well of happiness.

"After living long in the world as a stranger, he, who takes refuge in solitude, perceives a new world welcoming him and, by and by, he obtains the direct perception of superior planes.

"One of the strange phenomena of the times is that Hegel, the materialistic German scientist, discovered this when he said, 'It is in the heart of my own subjectivity that I discover true reality and not in the motley spectacle displayed before my eyes. It is contradictory to seek for existence outside myself, since outside of myself, I can find only an appearance for me; but I must seek for it in the very depth of my being since I, at least, participate in existence.'

"To understand truth does not demand violence; it needs inward reverence and a willing ear. Truth reveals itself only to those who seek and love it. The great purpose of spiritual training is for Soul to become a co-worker with the SUGMAD.

"This regeneration, this second birth, is what the theologians call the descent of the Holy Ghost. The inner illumination is united to an infinite love for the Divine—this inner flame, this simultaneous love and knowledge, when born, rises and grows until finally through a kind of impersonal ecstasy, our whole being is enkindled with a supreme desire to reach the God worlds.

"We call impersonal that state of intuition in which our thought is no longer divided into a thinking subject and an external world, but rather the outer world is abolished by

211

its integration into our personal consciousness. Our personal consciousness is by no means nullified. Nirvana is not the abolition of personality; on the contrary, it is the completeness of personality.

"The summit of Reality can only be reached through the inner channels. You cannot hope to possess other true riches than those we already bear within us; and we should use them and not neglect them. Alas, they are neglected. So familiar, they no longer appear of any value and we pursue other tawdry chattels whose possession is denied us; we are so weak that the world is sometimes obliged to rebuff us to cause us to detach ourselves from the world.

"The existence of the SUGMAD is a fact and sooner or later all will ardently yearn for IT. Some advanced individuals claim a knowledge of IT. Those who approach this discovery realize that they are among a select, an extremely limited number.

"Up until recently the western world had never been granted the privilege of having the revelations of the spiritual travelers given in a common, universal language. Throughout history the philosophical and spiritual teachings were veiled. That is why such teachings were classified as esoteric, knowable only to a limited number of the initiated.

"The ECK Master is the God-man. A word from him is a word from the ECK. He has no need to help others, for even his presence alone is elevating, inspiring, stirring and life-giving. His company is self-satisfying, and living in his presence is a spiritual education.

"All agonies, miseries, tribulations, taints of world-illness and other negative aspects seem to vanish in his mere presence, and one's doubts are removed. He can awaken through sight, touch, speech and thought. He can transmit spirituality to the neophyte as easily as one offers fruit to another. He is an ever flowing fountain-head of the water of life. A thirsty man only drinks from the water. A thirsty aspirant who has implicit faith in the Silent Ones, the ECK and the SUGMAD, and who is eager to imbibe the teachings and experiences of the spiritual travelers, can drink the divine nectar. The neophyte, who imbibes from his spiritual traveler with an intense degree of faith and deep contemplation, will be immortal.

"Spirituality cannot be taught but caught. Once one has learned the secrets of spirituality at the feet of an ECK traveler and is enlivened with the life impulses received from him, it is no more essential to be in constant physical association with him. He can have inner association with him anywhere, everywhere. He may, however, pay frequent visits, whenever possible, and report on his travels to the Far Country.

"Judging purely from the trend of present events, noting the deep under-current of thought, religious, philosophical, and scientific—it is time for man to come forward with acceptance of the Sound Current, which can uplift him to a high ethical standard of conduct. This would bring a wholesome reaction from the present chaos in morals and standards.

"This will come about by a universal increase in knowledge and an enlightened conscience. At the time this comes about, there will be a separation from the worthless; all systems of religion and philosophy, the wheat from the chaff, a new social order will be established upon the foundation of spiritual, rational and scientific demonstration.

"As flowers and fruit adorn and glorify the plant, so upon this new intellectual, ethical and social foundation a great spiritual evolution will take place. This spiritual quickening will not be caused by the new social order, powered by the Cliff Hangers, but will become the fountain source of the new order. Spirituality is not the flower or the fruit of ethics and social reconstruction; sound ethics and a just social order are good soil out of which spirituality may spring up, when vitalized by the springs of living waters.

213

"It will be the function of the spiritual travelers and their spiritual science, ECK, to supply these living waters by connecting all Souls of the lower worlds with the living sound current.

"We will leave off here for a few minutes."

*   *   *

"Man's first duty is to know himself," Rebazar Tarzs said, starting again. "The ancient sages pointed this out as man's first and primary duty. Worship the gods, if you must; but let your first duty be to find out who and what you are yourself.

"So they wrote over the doors of their temples Gnothe Seauton—know thyself! This is the first command of the ECK travelers. To know oneself, however, in the true meaning of that phrase, as given by the Great Masters, is a very different thing than the meaning given it by modern psychologists.

"Man has a great opportunity to make further progress into the universes, for lying latent in his brain is a capacity one million times greater than he is now using. The materialistic scientists now assert that the average man of today uses only about one millionth part of his brain cells.

"With an awakening of the whole brain, man could achieve miracles that would put the saviors and magicians to shame. But man is too lazy, too bound by dogma and ritual to think of anything other than his own physical comfort. Even the priestcraft has become contaminated, and wish for comforts of the body.

"When man has subjugated his passion, brought his mind under the control of spirit, when Soul stands unfettered and undimmed, it is then, and then only, that he will begin to get some idea of his exalted birthright.

"An ECK traveler can manipulate the forces of nature
214

as a mechanic manipulates the levers of his machine, for he is master of those forces. They must obey him; he is no longer a helpless drifter in nature's vortex.

"Man is a god clothed in rags, a master of the universe, going about begging a crust of bread. He is a king, prostrated before his own servants, a prisoner, walled in by his own ignorance. He could be free. He has only to walk out of his self-constructed prison. None hold him, but himself.

"The ECK traveler always has to contend with three powerful obstacles to reach his goal, and each of these has been almost insurmountable. These three are: Monarchism, Priestcraft and Popular Ignorance. Slowly and steadily the traveler has been obliged to overcome these difficulties every step of his way.

"Religion is supposed to be a friend of man, yet they have been in deadly conflict nearly the entire period of history.

"Priestcraft is now almost an absurd anachronism. It still exists everywhere in strength, but someday it will disappear from the face of the earth.

"Ignorance is also gaining despite the schools and the work of many who are trying to educate the old and young. Alas, they are going at it in the wrong manner—not in the form of showing man how to get out of his body.

"All that physical science knows is that life manifests in certain ways, following certain well attested laws. Scientists do not even try to guess the ultimate causes of life. Only the travelers, having access to the higher planes of being where the phenomena of both mind and spirit can be seen by them, know that without mind and spirit both, no life can manifest on this physical plane, or on any plane where matter is a factor in such manifestation.

"Scientists are loathe to allow the assumption of mind and spirit animating nature. This is no assumption to the travelers, for they can see it working from the higher planes down to this earth.

"Man does not live under a democracy here on this plane; so many of them believe they live under a democratic form of government in your country. But that is a pet delusion, a tale to be told to children, along with other pretty fairy stories. It may be good for the orators, or men seeking office, but it is no more than maya. It appears real because men and women vote to elect their favorites, for there is no real democratic government in the world, and there has never been one. There is nothing but oligarchy, and that mostly an oligarchy of wealth. It is not even an oligarchy of culture.

"So much for generalizations. Now who are the spiritual travelers? They are the co-workers of the SUGMAD, the being of ITS spirit operating throughout the universes, directly under the ECK and the silent ones.

"They have command of all things, but are not the actual supreme ones, although they do have access to the throne of the SUGMAD. They possess control and command over all nature, on all planes, and can come and go as they desire; still they are not supreme in the aspects of the silent ones.

"These ECK travelers have been selected, or elected rather, to serve on the physical plane in a human body. They are the embodiment of what the spiritual ones want—an example for the human race, an inspiration to man so that he may be inspired in lifting himself into higher planes.

"All ECK travelers who come to this world to help others, do so voluntarily—they are surely not appointed by the SUGMAD to leave the heaven world and come below to this ashcan of the four grand divisions of the Far Country, yet they are willing to serve the divine reality in this manner of their own free choice.

"All spiritual travelers are inhabitants of the world of Sach Khand, the home of the ECK—they can live anywhere they please, for example in the world of the SUGMAD,

ITSELF. They do not choose to take up abode there, for the particular reason that it is the perfect world—and they wish to bring all living there, to the highest state.

"Since the ECK travelers are dedicated to the Tuzas in the worlds below, they do not establish residence in the highest region of the universes. They leave that joyous place to enter this world of misery.

"There is complete happiness in the world of the ECK, yet it is not as hard to leave as that of the SUGMAD's domain. The travelers feel that by living here, they are close to the SUGMAD, for direct orders, and at the same time not far away.

"They are willing to perform for the SUGMAD in any part of the universe, even in that terrible, murky place called Hell, which is a part of the lower world below the physical, in one corner of the astral world.

"Hell is a real place, a mockup by the citizens of the earth world, manifested through religions in the hope that the priests could frighten enough members of its particular religion into joining the church and supporting its clergy with a livelihood.

"The business of the spiritual traveler is to make due investigation of all things first, then give his judgment afterwards; or to withhold judgment for further light. Escaping for the time being the limitations of the body, the spiritual traveler journeys in these higher worlds, in full consciousness and then returns to report what he has seen and heard, and otherwise experienced. He proves among many things, that death is only an appearance.

"Travelers explore these higher worlds, going wherever they please, clothed in god-like vesture of light, wisdom, power and beauty, wholly unknown to the common earth man. This is but a glimpse of a real spiritual traveler.

"So many men find it difficult to believe in the spiritual

travelers, because they are not common among people. One of the strangest freaks of the human mind is its tendency to discredit all modern things, especially those relating to religion, and to give emphasis and glory to that which is ancient. It cannot accept that which is right before its eyes; but it will swallow instantly what was written in a book two or three thousand years ago.

"It cannot believe in the living spiritual travelers; but finds no difficulty at all in accepting the story of some adept who lived in dim and distant ages. That men should ever have developed the strange notion that all mastership and all revelation of truth should belong to past ages, is one of the anomalies of history, and one of the most unfortunate.

"The fact that great ECK Masters have lived with us for centuries on earth and are here today, is one of the most important, most cheerful and most hopeful thoughts that man can have. The light of the spiritual travelers is in no way dimmed by comparison with those of the ancient past—in fact many of the ancient masters are still living with us here upon the earth world. There is an adept over seven hundred years old living within a few miles of this mud hut. He is Babaji—the master of Yogda Satsang, and there are several other yoga teachers in the same group.

"I have been asked many times if there is any difference between an ECK Master and the SUGMAD. It is only that the ECK Master is the SUGMAD's representative here on this plane, and through the others. The spirit of the Supreme One is embodied within the ECK Master.

"Now the Master is still responsible to the ECK and the Silent Ones; however, he can travel directly into the highest plane and communicate with the SUGMAD. Seldom does he do this, for he is concerned in his duties with all things below the God world—and this is where he finds all the work to be done, among Souls who need him most.

"He might be called, in other words, the SUGMAD of Being—the little God of the lower worlds, all below the Sach Khand.

"We will leave off here."

* * *

"This being of the SUGMAD, of course, is spirit. This spirit is the ECK. It flows into every man, and each man has that divine spark of imagination which is part of the SUGMAD. I have explained before about this divine faculty and how the SUGMAD wishes to regather it unto ITSELF.

"Life is a controllable thing, but it is through the imaginative faculty that it is controlled. The imaginative image is therefore the only thing to see. This is the manner in which the SUGMAD has His modus operandi, and that is only for the spiritual travelers who are looking at the image of the divine and finding it.

"The ultimate purpose of imagination is to create in us the being of the SUGMAD, well rather I would say, the spirit of the ECK, which is the forgiveness of wrongness, nothingness and somethingness.

"The ECK is, in a sense, the Son of God. Remember that the Christian Bible keeps talking about Christ being the only son of God—and that he is of the trinity, Father, Son and Holy Ghost. This is the ECK. But I will get into this later, for it is worth one whole day of discussion for you.

"The man who is free in the choice of his concepts of images in the use of imagination is well on his way to becoming a spiritual traveler. He has learned the skill, secret and ability of handling himself in the other worlds, whether he is aware of this or not.

"This faculty of imagination is much greater than any man can imagine. What is reality on the other side of the

219

veil of life is imagination on this side—you have little in your images which isn't in existence on the other side.

"What is above is below! Remember that I told you this somewhere back in my talks? Take for example the great astral museum which has all the forthcoming inventions in it that will ever be dreamed of on earth.

"Many inventors like Edison and Marconi were brought here in their light bodies so they could see the future inventions in which they were interested. Back in their bodies again, after awakening from sleep, these men believed that they dreamed these—and after a time they believed that they conceived these inventions, that they were figurations of their imagination.

"Not hardly, but this is the way that all inventions are created in the earth world. No one can think of anything but what it hasn't already been created in the other worlds. This is the reason that man is so far behind in his thought power—he tries to reason and use logic instead of the imaginative tube in his head.

"This isn't the imagination as Webster's dictionary gives it, or the result of some reasoned out idea. The imagination, as I speak of it here, is the divine sense—the use of the third eye to see beyond this world—beyond the senses.

"By sitting in silence and watching the worlds pass in succession before you, then it is possible to see all things. This is the way the spiritual travelers are connected with the Far Country. It isn't actually running out into the distant spaces—or the worlds of nothingness, but it is that ability to bring into focus whatever you wish to see in the other worlds and look at it through the third eye.

"Actually you don't have to travel. You can become like the ECK and see all the worlds by letting your spirit spread out over them. You become the All-Seeing Eye, in other words. Naturally the ability to do this needs plenty of practice and that is why the neophyte should never be discouraged with his practices. Remember that Tulsi Das spent seventeen years in a dark room before he believed that he had mastered this practice.

"Many a lama, in order to find control of the mind, has spent upwards of five years in walled-in rooms which were completely dark. Nobody should think that it is mastered in the matter of months, though it can be done in a relatively short time, mainly through the opening of the third eye and training the visual powers.

"The battle that man fights on any plane is fought out in his imagination. This is the teaching of the ECK philosophy—and it is to be found all through the Shariyat-Ki-Sugmad, the ECK scripture.

"There is only one thing in the world, imagination and all man's deformations of it. It is the gateway to reality. Soul is either the ark of the SUGMAD or a phantom of the earth and of the water. Naturally, it is only a natural organ subject to the senses. The eternal body of man is the Imagination, his spark of the SUGMAD, the Divine Body. The ECK is the leader of all Souls, and we are ITS members.

"By imagination we have the power to be anything we desire to be. Through imagination we disarm and transform the violence of the world. Our most intimate as well as our most casual relationships become imaginative as we awaken to the mystery hidden from the ages. The ECK in us is our imagination. We realize that when we live in imagination, only then can we truly be said to live at all.

"The visual faculty in man is the redeemer, the ECK from heaven, born of man but not begotten of man.

"Imagination's birth in man, rather his awakening to its power and growth, contains the gradual transition from a God of tradition to a God of experience. If the birth of this faculty in man seems slow, it is only because man is unwilling to let go the comfortable but false anchorage of tradition.

"When the imagination is discovered as the first principle of religion, the stone of literal understanding will have felt the rod of Moses and like the rock of Zin, will issue forth the water of psychological meaning to quench the thirst of humanity; all who take the proffered cup and live a life according to this truth, will transform the waters of spiritual meaning into the wine of understanding.

"The ECK, the first true son of God, is not to be found in the writings of man, nor in any external form. IT can only be found in the imagination of IT in whom ITS presence becomes manifest.

"Man is the garden in which the only true son of God sleeps. He awakens this Son by lifting his imagination to the heavens and clothing men in godlike stature. We must go on imagining better than the best we know, for it is all there in the upper worlds, and any man can have it.

"The concept of the imaginative faculty raises fundamental questions. Is imagination a power sufficient to enable man to assume that he is strong? And is it capable of executing the idea?

"Suppose that I desire to be in the Brahm Lok world. Could I put myself in such a state and place and bring about the realization? By all means this is possible, for the imaginative faculty is that body by which the spiritual traveler makes his journey into the heavenly worlds. It is not as you may be thinking, the picture making machine of the mind which does mockups of little things like desires for more money and other materialistic things. No, it is a heaven sent gift which can move the spirit body of man to any world he wishes.

"Does imagination comprehend reason? By reason I mean deductions from the observations of the senses. Does it recognize the external world of facts? In the practical way of everyday life is imagination a complete guide to behavior? Suppose I am capable of acting with continuous imagination; suppose I am capable of sustaining the feeling of my wish fulfilled, will my assumption harden into fact? And, if it does harden into fact, shall I, on reflection, find that my actions through the period of incubation have been reasonable?

"Is my imagination a power sufficient, not merely to assume the feeling of the wish fulfilled, but is it also of itself capable of incarnating the idea? After assuming that

222

I am already what I want to be, must I continually guide myself by reasonable ideas and actions in order to bring about the fulfillment of my assumption?

"Experience has convinced me that an assumption, though false, if persisted in will harden into fact, that continuous imagination is sufficient for all things and all my reasonable plans and actions will never make up for my lack of continuous imagination.

"Truth depends upon the intensity of the imagination, not upon external facts. Facts are the fruit bearing witness of the use or misuse of the imagination. Man becomes what he imagines. He has a self-determined history. Imagination is the way, the truth, the life revealed. We cannot get hold of truth with the logical mind. Where the natural man of sense sees a bud, imagination sees a rose full blown.

"Truth cannot be encompassed by physical facts. As we awaken to the imaginative life we discover that to imagine a thing is so, makes it so; that a true judgment need not conform to the external reality to which it relates.

"The imaginative faculty does not deny the reality of the sensuous outer world of Becoming, but man needs to know that it is the inner world of continuous imagination that is the force by which the sensuous outer world of Becoming is brought to pass. He needs to see the outer world and all its happenings as projections of the inner world of imagination. Everything is a manifestation of the mental activity which goes on in man's imagination without the sensuous reasonable man being aware of it.

"It is necessary to realize that every man must become conscious of this inner activity and see the relationship between the inner causal world of imagination and the sensuous outer world of effects.

"We will stop here for refreshments."

*   *   *

"It is a marvelous thing to find that man can imagine himself into the state of his fulfilled desires on the higher

223

planes and escape from the jails which ignorance have built.

"Until man has the sense of ECK as his imagination, he will see everything in pure objectivity without any subjective relationship. Not realizing that all he sees is a part of himself, he rebels at the thought that he does not see the conditions of his life as they are related to his own mental activity. Man must firmly come to believe that reality lies within him and not without.

"Although others have bodies, a life of their own, their reality is rooted in the earth world; you are rooted in the world of the SUGMAD.

"The world presents different appearances according as our states of consciousness differ. What man sees when he is identified with a state, cannot be seen when he is no longer fused with it. By state is meant all that man believes and consents to as true. No idea presented to the mind can realize itself unless Soul accepts it. It depends on the acceptance, on the state with which you are identified, how things present themselves. In the fusion of imagination and states is to be found the shaping of the world as it seems. The world is a revelation of the states with which imagination is fused.

"It is the state from which we image that determines the world in which we live here or in the God realms. The rich man, the Tuza in hell, the thief and half a dozen others are what they are by virtue of the states from which they view the world. On the distinction between these states depends the distinction between the worlds of men and the spiritual travelers. Individually, there is a vast difference in the worlds of spirit and men. It is not the actions and behavior of the good man that should be matched but his point of view. Outer reforms are useless if the inner state is not changed. Spiritual success is gained not by imitating the outer actions of the successful but by the right imagination, right actions and right deeds.

"If we detach ourselves from a state, and we may at any moment, the conditions and circumstances to which that union gave rise, vanish. Determined imagination, thinking from the end, is the beginning of all miracles.

"The future must become the present in the imagination of the one who would wisely and consciously create circumstances. We must translate vision into Being, thinking of into thinking from.

"Imagination must center itself in some state and view the world from that state. Thinking from the end is an intense perception of the world of fulfilled desire. Visualizing from the state desired is creative living on any plane in the Far Country.

"Ignorance of this ability to imagine from the end is bondage. It is the root of all bondage in which man is bound. To surrender to the evidence of the senses underestimates the capacities of Soul. Once Soul accepts imagining from the end as a creative principle in which he can cooperate, then he is redeemed from the absurdity of ever attempting to achieve his goal by merely thinking of, in hopes of entering into another world.

"The whole of life is the appeasement of spiritual hunger, and the infinite states of the world are purely a means of satisfying that hunger. The principle upon which each state is organized is some form of hunger for the full life, some passion for spiritual traveling to even higher levels of experience.

"The only desire that man can rightfully have is a right and natural craving to enter into the state of consciousness which will allow him to enter into the Far Country.

"The spanning of the bridge between thinking of-desire, and thinking-from satisfaction is the utmost ultimate secret. We must move spiritually from thinking of the end to the thinking from the end. This, reason can never do. By its nature it is restricted to the evidence of the senses; but imagination has no such limitations.

"Desire exists to be gratified in the activity of the imagination, while satisfaction is in existence because it is the activity of the imagination. Through imagination man escapes from the limitations of the senses and the bondage of the mind.

"So you see imagination carries man over the worlds,

where reason holds him immobile. He, who can think from the end, has no limitations. He creates the means and fashions his way out of limitation into the ever greater mansions of the Far Country. It does not matter what he has been or what he is. All that matters is what he wants to be in the spiritual country.

"He knows the world to be a manifestation of the spiritual activity which goes on within himself, so he strives to determine and control the invisible spirit, which we call the ECK. He does this by controlling the ends from which he thinks, lives and dwells in.

"In his imagination he dwells within the ends which he believes is his proper place in the heaven world, confident that he will dwell there in the spiritual body, as the traveler does when he goes out into the higher regions.

"He puts his whole trust into the feeling of the spiritual wish fulfilled and lives by committing himself to this state, which the arts of fortune have placed before him. He puts himself in the ready state of moving in the waters of imagination, knowing that every spiritual state existent is awaiting him, for he has learned to think from the end and is indifferent to merely reasonable probabilities, confident that through continuous imagination his assumption will harden into fact.

"Therefore, life is a controllable thing. Man experiences what he pleases, once he realizes that he has been given the divine gift for his own use and that he is what he is, by virtue of the state of consciousness from which he imagines and views the world.

"So, it is man's constant attitude which makes him master of his own destiny and captain of the universe in which he lives; and lord of all universes, should he desire to be.

"Soul is as real in the world of subjective experience as man's outer physical body is real in the world of external realities, but Soul expresses a more fundamental part of reality. This existing inner body must be consciously exercised and directed. The inner world of spirit and feeling to which Soul is attuned has its real structure and exists in its own higher space.

"There are two kinds of movement, one that is according to the outer body and another that is according to the inner, to the Soul body. The movement relative to Soul is casual, to the outer body compulsive. The inner movement determines the outer which is joined to it, bringing into the outer a movement that is similar to the actions of the inner body. Inner movement is the force by which all events are brought to pass. Outer movement is subject to the compulsion applied to it by the movement of the inner body.

"Whenever the action of the inner body matches the actions which other bodies must take to appease desire, that desire will be realized.

"To realize the desire of traveling in other worlds, an action must be started in your imagination, apart from the evidence of the senses on whatever plane you are living, to involve movement of Soul and imply fulfillment of your desire for spiritual traveling. Whenever the inner action matches the outer action to appease desire, that desire will be realized.

"The journey is in yourself. You travel along the highway of the inner world. Without this inner movement, there is little you can do, nor anywhere you can travel, for it is the secret of all things. Without inner movement it is impossible to bring forth anything.

"Inner action is introverted sensation. This inner action orders all things according to its nature. Spiritual action only acts if it's acted upon through the imagination. Only by centering Soul, the real self, in the center of the imagination and projecting it to that place or situation, anywhere, be it here on this physical plane or in the Far Country, can Soul fulfill its mission of being in the SUGMAD.

"I cannot find myself, nor can you find yourself in anything other than this divine faculty which the SUGMAD has placed within each of us, ages ago when ITS supreme imaginative eye was broken into uncounted pieces and found by the men of the lower worlds.

"All situations, whether human or spiritual, are already made states. All aspects of life, drama, plot, circumstance, and, of course, place are in existence whether we believe it or not. They become overpowering reality when we are in them, be they on this plane or in the Far Country.

"Truth is common to all men, but the consciousness of it and much more, the self-consciousness of it, is another matter. Man needs to study this phrase carefully to understand what lies between himself and the heaven world.

"I will take this up today for our last discussion. Meanwhile try to digest what I have told you here."

Chapter 12

THE PHILOSOPHY OF ECKANKAR

That morning we sat down for the last discussion on ECK, the sun gleamed over the world like a bright, golden disk high in the sky.

The haze hung over the Hindu Kush where the wild peaks shone like silver cones in the cobalt sky, and the gorges were every color imaginable in the morning light. It was a day for rejoicing, a day for beauty as if this was the world above. There was a hint of sadness in the soft wind blowing from the high range where the glaciers gleamed like glittering diamonds.

The visits with Rebazar Tarzs were coming to a close this day and soon the pleasure of the task would be gone. It was a depressing mood, and he caught it instantly.

"The day comes and goes on this planet," he said softly, while dropping upon the ground floor inside the hut and spreading his deep red coat over his feet. "It is a world that has changes, for the day dawns and swiftly passes into night, and light comes again, in a succession which seems endless, but always there is the changing. You never find this in the high worlds of the Far Country.

"What need do you have to rest in eternity? None, for there is no body which will ever tire; fatigue is as unknown as the thing you call disease in this world.

"Disease is nothing more than the tiny microscopic bacteria eating at the flesh body. They are the cannibals. Man cannot compete with them. They attack him in every way and shape, yet he seems to think they are his fate, that the gods are punishing him for some misdeeds, and usually his means of getting rid of them is to pray or offer sacrifice in ritual to his favorite deity. It sounds ridiculous but that is the way it is, and whether you believe this or not, it needs nothing more than observation with a detached attitude on mankind to verify the statement.

"Well, it is so, but to get down to the subject of today is necessary for we are going to discuss the Philosophy of ECKANKAR which you have been thinking about for a long time.

"The philosophy of ECKANKAR is that branch of the ECK sound current which embraces the science comprising ethics, aesthetics, metaphysics and the knowledge of the underlying principles of the trinity; wisdom, power and freedom, as you already know.

"This consists of a lot of points which I have just mentioned, but mainly four things, which are, and I repeat, ethics, aesthetics, metaphysics and principles of the trinity. Broken down, the major points begin with the ethics of ECK.

"Now I've gone through a lot of this and won't repeat my grounds again, when I spoke of the parts of the mind, the four Antishkarans, and the five perversions of the mind. These five were Kama, meaning lust; Krodha, meaning anger; Lobha, which is greed; Moha, attachment; and Ahankara, which is vanity, the last of these deadly five.

"Then I discussed the five passions and their remedies, which were Kama, whose opposite is chastity, continence; Krodha, which has the opposite of Kshama, forgiveness, tolerance; Lobha, matched by Santosha, contentment; Moha, opposed by Viveka, which is discrimination; Vairag, which is unattachment, and last, Ahankara, whose opposite is Dinta, humility.

"All mankind is divided into two groups — Manumukhs and Gurumukhs. This means those who follow the dictates of their own minds, and those who follow the MAHANTA, the Living ECK Master. The Manumukh follows the mind, obeying its every whim, doing just what he likes. He is a slave to the mind and its passions. But the man whose face is always toward the ECK Master is the free man, one who is developing his own powers to the greatest extent possible.

"He is not under the ever-grinding wheel of birth and death, the grinding wheel of desire and karma. This sublime achievement is accomplished by the practice of using the sound current in one's life. The ECK Master shows him the way, and no one has ever done it alone in the beginning. There has to be the spiritual traveler and the practice, called the ECK, the regenerating Bani, the audible life stream. There is positively no other cure for the perversions of the mind—none but the voice of the ECK ringing through Soul. When that holy symphony is heard, these passions lose their power and drop away, and the high ethics of the SUGMAD comes into the life of Soul. One must become absorbed in that luminous reality, and must forget all else. That reality gives strength and will, until man becomes more than just a mere flesh and blood animal. He becomes a living thing, a living power, reborn and exalted. All these perversions disappear, and he finds real wisdom and freedom. Just as the five passions may be regarded as the five black angels of death, so the five virtues may be considered the five white angels of life.

"Ethics are good, but there is nothing unique in the goodness of man. All religions are loaded with ethics, and the same ideas are taught mankind century after century in many varying forms. But frankly, ethics never yet has opened the way to the inner kingdoms. Ethics may clean the mind and prepare the way to knock at the inner door, but it can never open that door. This can be done only by one of the great spiritual travelers.

"Ethics as taught by all religions is obsolete. Any group teaching ethics alone has very little to offer the hungry seeker after spiritual light, except that which is common to all religions.

"All religions consist of five basic elements. They are: (1) superstitious assumptions, (2) emotional extravaganzas, (3) ritualistic ceremonies, (4) metaphysical speculations, (5) ethical principles.

"Ethics is a means of mind cleansing: although not a perfect means, at best it does prepare one to start on the path of God-realization. When one reaches this God-realization, he becomes a spiritual traveler, is united with the sound-current and with it, becomes a self-religious person.

"When man has gained this inner experience, he has the dynamic life within himself to meet all temptations successfully and live the life called for by the finest code of ethics. To make morality a means of attaining religion is to work backwards. Ethics is a means of getting to this state through preparation of the mind, nothing else. It is neither religion, nor the soil out of which it grows. Genuine ethics is the fruit of the trinity, wisdom, power and freedom, and this is the life-giving fruit of the great sound current. Ethics never form the basis of a universal philosophy like ECK-ANKAR, for ethics can never create wisdom, power or freedom.

"For the Christian, ethics are supposed to generate love, but this is untrue, for you have witnessed the strange phenomena of an intense religionist manifesting great hatred. Ethics are the best that any historic religion has to offer. Take ethics out of Christianity and it would fold immediately because its theories about God, heaven and spiritual liberation are quite worthless, because they are not founded on knowledge. Take out of any religion its code of ethics, and it would not survive a single month, except in those forms where they value ceremony for its psychological effect.

"One of the ways to make spiritual headway on the path to the SUGMAD is to always ask yourself, when in doubt about any action—Is it true, is it necessary, is it kind?

"This is one of the most inflexible of all laws for such as seek spiritual advancement. Let no one imagine that he can ignore this law and still make headway on the upward path. It cannot be done. The path of the trinity leads to enlightenment and liberty and the Far Country; but the ways of the five passions lead to the lower pits of hell.

"Ethics are also tied in with good and bad karma, as you know. The underlying principle is that every act performed must be followed by its natural and legitimate results. This is a law so universal that it is amazing all men have not grasped its general significance and applied it in ethics,

232

the same as in mechanics. It is recognized in physical science; any student picking up a book on physics, discovers the working of the same law in every problem confronting him.

"The law of karma is the underlying principle of personal responsibility. It is a well known law of physics that action and reaction are equal, but opposite in direction. This is the law that brings back upon the doer, in spite of himself, the legitimate results of his own conduct. He must gather the fruit of his own reactions. This reaction he cannot possibly escape. Hence every action performed has its double karma, based upon this law of action and reaction—it affects the recipient and it returns upon the doer. The doer is always a recipient of the same act. So action and reaction are the dual forms of karma.

"This is the basis of ethics, whether you understand it or not. There is no need to go into lengthy details about this universal law. It is a silent worker in the empire of man and matter, but in the higher universes where spirit governs all, there is no karma—because the higher law of wisdom, power and freedom supercedes all other laws.

"Do not be misled by the old, but erroneous maxim 'The greatest good to the greatest number.' This is one of the most unfortunate slogans that ever gained recognition. It sounds plausible, but it is completely misleading. This saying has been used for centuries to justify murder in the name of society. Nothing can be moral or good, if a single individual has to be sacrificed to gain it. Who is going to make good to the victim? Who shall compensate him for the deprivation of his natural rights? If a man misuses his liberty, or his privileges, he may forfeit that liberty or those privileges; but by no means, nor upon any sort of pretext, can he be deprived of his life. If society reverts to the law of Moses to justify the murder of a criminal, where is its boasted Christian ethics?

"Mental superiority produces no real civilization. Culture, literature, art, do not make civilization. Refined tastes do not make civilization. There is a vast difference between aesthetics and ethics and ethics in its highest development,

233

does not consitute civilization. Wisdom, power and freedom make civilization and these three are of the essence of pure spirit. Spirituality is always abundant in every Golden Age.

"This is what makes it golden!

"We will leave off here."

*   *   *

"The second aspect of the philosophy of ECKANKAR," said Rebazar Tarzs, "is aesthetics.

"Now in order to understand what I am going to speak about, it's best to first explain the word, aesthetics. It is that branch of philosophy dealing with the beautiful, chiefly with respect to its essential character, tests by which it may be judged, and its relation to the human mind. It is also a branch of psychology concerned with the sensations and emotions evoked by the fine arts and belles-lettres, mainly the beauty of the scriptures.

"Beauty of the spiritual senses has always been among the highest perceptions of Soul. It consists in the qualities of beauty, harmony, and rhythm. Many words are used in order to describe the sensations of this perceptive faculty.

"Those who have reached the world of Daswan Dwar, that plane called the third region—actually the first in the Omkar area, are called the Parahansas, the swans, birds of beauty and cleanliness. Before this the Tuza is likened to a crow.

"The faculty which discerns beauty, form and color, is one of the four faculties of Antishkarans, consisting of manas, buddhi, chitta, and ahankar. Of these four faculties, chitta represents the beauty quality of the inner self.

"This is the faculty aroused when one has that experience called the God-Realization. The beauty of all the universes flows into him. This God-Realization is an individual experience. It is a realization of beauty, of aesthetics. No man can really explain what aesthetics can be.

"It is an experience based upon a relation between things and individual intelligence. Aesthetics is an experience of joy springing out of that relation. It is a step toward the

234

final realization of reaching the world of the SUGMAD. In essence, aesthetics is a form of wisdom, power and freedom, for it is a ray of light from the infinite heart of things. It is a light, the sound of the audible current and joy existing only when Soul finds Itself in the infinite.

"All MAHANTAS explore the higher regions, going where they please, clothed in a god-like vesture of light, wisdom, power and beauty, wholly unknown to the common earth man. To glimpse a real spiritual traveler, one must look at him through the chitta faculty. To fully understand a real traveler, one must himself become a spiritual traveler. Can you say that the insect comprehends the physical man?

"Now as I told you previously, the chitta faculty is that function, or faculty which takes cognizance of form, beauty, color, rhythm, harmony and perspectiveness. It enjoys those things and what it doesn't like, it rejects.

"It receives its impressions through the third eye, the faculty of seeing for the Soul body.

"When living in the human body, he who has developed this mode of action to its highest will be engaged in the highest forms of thought activity, such as philosophy, literature, music and art. This part of the mind is that section of it lying closest to the spirit self—it is called the nij-mind. I am not certain if I discussed this with you before—briefly, it is a sort of pilot, or gyroscope, whose function is to receive the impressions of Soul and pass them on to the subordinate minds for their regulation.

"This mind is concerned with the aesthetics of life, and will deal in this quality unless Soul demands it do otherwise. Soul looks upon and seeks beauty on the other planes all the time.

"It is an illuminating fact that all intelligence, light and power come from Soul. This statement is without qualification. It is literally and universally true. All light, all intelligence, harmony, rhythm, beauty, wisdom, love, morality and power, come from the Tuza. They are all derived from the spirit and are all imparted to the mind by the spirit, just as the electric current gives power to the bulb to make it incandescent.

"The Tuza in turn receives it from the sound current, that magnificent powerhouse flowing out of the ECK, the first manifestation of the SUGMAD in the worlds below. This ECK is full of beauty and rapturous wisdom which can be gathered only by those who are in tune with it.

"This faculty is tied in with the imaginative faculty so closely that it's often hard to distinguish the two. Take for example, he who sees the beauty in anything progresses faster than those who do not. If a man thinks of winter as only summer sleeping, or that caterpillars are butterflies immobilized, that the storm is only the other face of the clear sky, he is living in the world of aesthetics.

"When man desires to change so that he may enter into the higher worlds, he enters into a new longing and will eventually arrive at that stage of spiritual progression called the spiritual traveler, one who can roam the worlds at his own desire.

"Without imagination man remains a creature of the earth dust, a materialistic thing. Man either goes forward in his imagination or remains a prisoner of his senses. He is free to soar like the eagle or remain upon the earth as does the worm and make his home within the dirt.

"The imagination faculty and the chitta are so much one another that when the illumination comes to a man, he is never, the first time, certain that it is something of his imagination or reality. His imagination working in harmony with the other faculties of his inner self does bring about illumination; often he has a degree of illumination which comes to him as result of purity alone. These are natural spiritual travelers; although they are often the result of their religious training, many are known in the church as saints. A degree of illumination of this nature is called Prathiba. This is the illumination of the supreme genius, the great poet, the superb artist, the benevolent philanthropist. But such people are born, not made by their own thinking.

"The above class are closely related to those who are said

to radiate a light and a knowledge, the Dharma Megha. Soul appears naturally to be clothed in brilliant light. This is sometimes spoken of as a cloud of virtue. Such a great Soul, wherever It goes, is clothed in this mantle of glory. It can be seen by all who enjoy astral vision. But these are very rare among the inhabitants of this planet.

"This Dharma Megha is a king of samadhi, an absorption of the mind into the object of contemplation, with complete detachment, particularly detachment from the love of this world, from worldly desires, the Vairag.

"Such a person is said to radiate a light like a mantle of glory. While in this state, the mind is freed from activity, inwardly or outwardly, through perfect Vairag, detachment.

"So to know the truth you must live with the truth; to live with the truth your inner actions must fulfill, rather match the actions of your fulfilled desire. Expectancy and desire must become one. Your outer world is only actualized by inner movement; it is through ignorance of the law of the spiritual path that those who take to warfare are perpetually defeated.

"This inner war between the negative power versus positive power goes on forever, racking the mind and body until both are eventually destroyed forever, and the Tuza must dwell somewhere in the astral until It becomes convinced that It can take over and control Its own destiny. The discipline given It will be hard and long, until It accepts the understanding of the spiritual traveler's goal for It.

"The whole manifested world is present to show us what use we have made with the Word, the ECK—the creative power of the ECKANKAR.

An uncritical observation of the inner world will reveal to us the ideas from which we view the world. Inner motion mirrors the imagination of man, and his imagination mirrors the state with which he is fused. If the state with which he fused is the cause of the phenomenon of his life, then he is relieved of his burden of wondering what to do. He has no alternative but to identify himself with the aim of reaching the Ocean of Love and Mercy.

"It is possible to resolve every situation on any plane of the Far Country by the proper use of imagination. The task therefore is to think in terms of aesthetics, not the improper kind which is a false picture of the pseudo-goodness of all, but the truth, the reality in which man must dwell when he becomes a spiritual traveler.

"Therefore, imagination is the word of the SUGMAD, projected through the ECK, for man to dwell in the beauty of all things. This imagination is the coin of heaven, and it advances all Souls into events, situations and positions in life. It is only what is done now that counts.

"Be therefore, wise in choosing what you are thinking, saying, or expelling from the Tuza, because it will manifest itself somewhere in the universes and eventually return to you the results. Thought can also be karma as well as physical action.

"This I am going to take up in the study on the metaphysics of the ECK, which is next after we stop to refresh ourselves with tea."

*   *   *

Rebazar Tarzs said, "Now for a brief discussion on the metaphysics of ECK. This is a study of the abstract, the abstruse, that division of philosophy which includes ontology, the science of being, and cosmology, the science of the fundamental causes and processes in things; in a looser term, all of the more abstruse disciplines, and in a narrower sense, Ontology alone.

"What is Ontology? If I have already explained it, I will do so again. Ontology is the science of being or reality; the branch of knowledge that investigates the nature, essential properties and relations of being.

"The metaphysics of ECKANKAR is the study of the spirit which we know as the sound current. This is the whole of cosmology, and the fundamental cause and process of all things in the worlds of the Far Country. It cannot be otherwise, for it is so destined that in making all the worlds the SUGMAD used ITS only begotten son, the ECK, the highest crown worn by all men.

"Jesus became known as the Christ; Prince Siddhartha, became the Buddha. So the SUGMAD made ITS manifestation in what is known to us as the ECK, and when man reaches this height, he becomes a Christ, Buddha or MAHANTA, what we know as the ECK, the shining one.

"It must be understoood that the knowledge of ECKANKAR is not a slow product of evolution, an accumulation of learning, gathered during long ages of study. It is not the sum of knowledge accumulated in libraries, to be memorized by students nor a record of acquired information. The knowledge of the ECK, known by the spiritual travelers, is unique. Every traveler gains the whole sum of metaphysics, anew, during his travels. His knowledge of the ECKANKAR is gained by a definite line of individual endeavor and personal experience. It is not something gathered up by him from many sources, but is gained from within himself by the expansion of his own consciousness. Any man may gain this development and this metaphysical knowledge, provided he has the scientific method of the spiritual travelers. In the light of this illuminating fact, one of the assumptions of the worldly knowledge disappears—that a definite certain knowledge of the ECKANKAR cannot be acquired.

"The most common concept of the SUGMAD is that of a creator. Man can only think of a creator as doing something, so he pictures the Christian God as creating and managing the universe. He is obliged by the urge of his mind to account for things as he finds them, at least to try; and the natural conclusion is that some power created them.

"The curious query of whether man created God, or God created man is always debated. History has proven that man created God, but logic assumes that God created man. Both logic and history are unreliable. The gods of man sprang out of his imagination. If you study the religions of the world, you will find that every God represented in them is so like man in character that their parentage is quite unmistakable. To the careful student of history there is nothing more clear than the fact that mankind has been busy constructing gods after his own image.

"The Christian Bible says that God created man in his own image and likeness, and man flatters himself that his God is not greatly superior to him. If true then, it is no compliment to the Christian God to have a few billion creatures, like himself, rushing around this earth in the terrible mess created by themselves.

"The world is full of gods who are claimed to be related to man in image and likeness.

"Too many gods, anyway, like too many cooks spoil the broth. So much depends upon what one means by the word, God. Here, in fact, is the very heart of the question of the metaphysics of ECK. The big discussion about God and the gods in this world is mostly a display of words and vanity. Seldom does any priest know the subject he is trying to discuss when the talk comes around to the highest reality.

"The Christians have taken a man called Jesus, as an historical figure and clothed him with all the characteristics of man, plus some divine qualities; he is equal to the Father, and Spirit—they put three qualities in him, God, man and spirit. A pretty tall order when you think about it. The reason for this is that man's imagination cannot think of anything being above himself; so he made God a man. Knowing that man wouldn't follow man, he had to give him some divine qualities, and so made him omnipresent by making him spirit.

"This is what all followers do with those higher than themselves in knowledge. Remember that any spiritual traveler who is known to men, had certain qualifications others do not have. They have: first, longevity, second, omnipresence, third, ability to travel in any world of the Far Country, and fourth, the protection of the divine power which ordinary

240

man cannot even comprehend. Of course they have also, wisdom, power and freedom.

"No man ever gained the latter—wisdom, power and freedom by a process of logic, by ratiocination, reading books or attending lectures. Yet these are the methods employed by the majority of mankind. The ECK travelers solve all of their problems by methods exact and exacting, as in mathematics. They get their wisdom by spiritual sight and hearing. Even after they have proved a proposition, they establish no authority, except that of truth itself. Authority hampers truth, throttles free investigation. It, in itself, is an enemy to progress. The system by which one learns under a spiritual traveler makes personal experience the final and only court of appeal. Its processes are simple and direct. They can be understood by the most ordinary intelligence, and for that reason intelligence need not play a part in it.

"Asceticism is one of the more regrettable features of modern degeneration and a radical departure from the pure teachings of the spiritual traveler.

"It has been practiced by men of nearly all countries and religions, in the mistaken notion that it will aid them in acquiring spiritual perfection. Buddha practiced it in extreme forms, until he almost lost his life, and when he gave it up, his old friends condemned him. Medieval Christians practiced it. Vast numbers of Indian yogis have practiced it, and many are doing so today. But the travelers have never taught asceticism and they do not teach or practice it today. The path of the ECK travelers is for all mankind and as such it must be available to all men in all walks of life.

"Those who practice asceticism are seeking desperately for their release from material bondage, but they seek in the wrong way. They do not know the path of the travelers.

"Now in order to make the first step upon this path into the Far Country, man must first find the Living ECK Master. He is never too far away and always watching to see when

241

one is opened for the opportunity. When this is done, he finds one readily, as if suddenly coming upon a pile of wealth sitting in the turn of the road, and nobody around but himself to claim it.

"He cannot get anywhere unless he finds the MAHANTA who will take him under his wing to teach him how to travel the royal highway to the SUGMAD. He will gain understanding of the principles, rituals and occult knowledge, but not until he comes in contact with a spiritual traveler does he start on the upward road.

"The Master gives him the initiation, dips the Tuza in the ECK, like the mother of Achilles did her son, in the river Styx to make him immortal. After this he gets down to work practicing the techniques given him by the Master.

"He chooses a room free of all noises and interruptions. At fixed hours he sits with the body erect and comfortable. He keeps his thoughts centered in the fore of his head, and inside it at the Tisra Til, the third eye. He simply thinks of this center imagining himself there, and the attention is held here continuously and without wavering. The mind must be perfectly motionless.

"Think only of your friend, the MAHANTA, who is going to be with you and help you travel the inner worlds of the Far Country.

"After awhile, the MAHANTA appears to him, in the Tisra Til, and beckons. Clad in a white, shining spiritual coat, the traveler takes you by the hand and you step away from the body in your Nuri-Sarup, the astral body.

"At this sublime moment you have stepped out into the higher world. At once you begin to realize that you have acquired a vast increase of powers, as well as joy. It appears to you, and it is a fact too, that you can do almost anything you wish to do. Not only have you increased your powers, but your knowledge and understanding have expanded proportionately. At this time the whole material universe appears as an open book to you, all dark mysteries have vanished. You find yourself in possession of all knowledge of the lower worlds. You now know them and have power over them. From here

242

on up, each world gained, gives you complete knowledge and power over the world below you.

"This is what the ECK traveler is showing you; the way to climb the upward path into the Far Country.

"We will leave off here for some tea."

*　　*　　*

Rebazar Tarzs began again, "The principles which live behind the trinity are the most important aspects of the philosophy of ECKANKAR.

"The trinity is—wisdom, power and freedom. These are age old principles but hardly any religion or philosophy includes them as a trio; the usual trinity being wisdom, love and power, or father, son and spirit.

"These actually represent various aspects of the sound current. The wisdom aspect is that part of the current which carries the great knowledge of all things within it—and once contacted by the traveler never again does one have doubts of anything concerning the Far Country. All things are his in the way of knowledge—he reaches the pinnacle of the peak in wisdom, in knowledge, and ways of learning.

"Wisdom is the highest quality which Soul can develop within Itself. Once It has wisdom then all other things are possible, for It knows where and how to find all the things of life, all Its desires in the lower worlds are forgotten. It no longer wishes for anything for it is foolish to do so.

"Man is the highest form of creation on this plane and he is a sojourner here. The wisdom that he learns in his material existence is only a speck compared to that in the innumerable worlds of light and sound beyond.

"Wisdom, as the mother of all truth, can guide him into these worlds provided he listens to her. Power is his source of motion, and the instrument to gain that divine energy to control all life on any plane in the Far Country. Freedom is that liberation from all obstacles and the opportunity to live a full life in the spiritual worlds.

243

"Wisdom also goes with a good mind, purity and perfection. Power goes with the supreme will, manifested in all worlds, and with creativity. Freedom goes with immortality, with single-minded devotion to the cause of the SUGMAD.

"While the ECK gives Soul wisdom when It is dipped into the immortal river of heaven, IT also gives Soul divine creativity, power, the ability of sustaining all things in life. At the same time IT gives a love of motion, which is freedom from hindering dogma and ritual.

"What I am trying to say here is that all of these qualities of the SUGMAD which are latent in Soul are actually so great that we are unable to find words for them. The system which I have laid down for you to follow, leaving the body at will, traveling through the universes, is the exalted ideal of all spiritual systems. It lays stress upon the unfoldment of spiritual wisdom, power and freedom. It shows the lofty vision of the spiritual traveler, and once this is revealed, none want to turn back.

"Too many touch the first plane, believe that they have met God, and this is the end of their journey into the heaven world. 'Tis a shame but such self-deception is incredible. It is likely they believe that God commands them to do something, and listening to this false voice often ruins their lives and others.

"The man of wisdom, power and freedom is hardly a tender man, but he may be a gentle one. This gentleness gives strength, but the materialistic critic will hardly believe this; in fits of rebellion he points out that this is a weakness, a feminine virtue, and not fit for earthly strength.

"Once man enters into the ECK and is submerged in ITS life giving forces, then he knows the falsity of this attitude.

"When he is truly submerged into the sound and becomes a part of it, the spiritual traveler finds himself at one with the world universe of universes. He is the supreme one in the infinite, limitless, the whole of spiritual existence. He becomes the center of the Far Country, the master of all things, the ECK, the Son of the SUGMAD.

244

"In finding wisdom, one finds wisdom of the highest order. You can say that the Supreme Being is wisdom, power and freedom; that IT is omnipresent, all pervading. You, as the spiritual traveler are exactly the same, except as to your physical limitations. Spiritually, you have no limitations. But the body is not the traveler, it is only a covering, one of your ready instruments. You may, at will, leave this body and work upon any of the higher planes; each plane, as you ascend, gives you greater freedom and scope of power.

"The living ECK Master has no limitations, being one with the SUGMAD. Only the materials through which he works limit his actions; in like manner they limit the actions of the Supreme Being, ITSELF. Can the SUGMAD converse with you, as man with man, without first becoming man? The omniscience of the SUGMAD may not be able to express itself through the physical brain of the traveler, but the traveler may, in single moments, rise to the regions of the worlds far above the sphere of brain activity, where his consciousness automatically expands, even to the limitless. When he returns to this plane, he will remember just as much of it as can be brought within the compass of brain action.

"The duties of all spiritual travelers consist of connecting Souls with the ECK, the sound current, and taking them out of this world to their own place in the Far Country, where they have earned their stay.

"Second, the traveler has to teach the way to all who are willing to listen. He alone has the kingdom of heaven within. He alone can guide the wandering Soul to the open door of heaven, and help him enter into it.

"Third, the traveler is to bring light and sound into the world, that all may profit by it. Not simply his followers but all people and the whole world. This is a part of his secret world. None may follow him into the secret chambers of his retreat and see all the features of the great work he is doing. There is not a living being in all the world who does not receive benefit from the spiritual travelers.

"These travelers know of the SUGMAD because they have made experiments and have the proof. The travelers know that there is a supreme and all-sustaining One, whose chief attributes are wisdom, power and freedom.

"Now, man was created by an infinite good, and he must derive his own good qualities from that infinite good. We must concede, as a matter of fact, that he himself has created most of the gods and devils, known to history; yet in spite of this, the Supreme Reality stands out far above all this sham and exposure. Man is the sum of all goodness, but sooner, or later, we have to settle the problem of where he got his evil propensities.

"These are painfully manifest. They must be explained. Shall they be attributed to the same infinite power we call the SUGMAD? If man didn't get his evil qualities from the SUGMAD, the author of all good, where did he get them?

"This can be explained by pointing out that evil exists only in the lower worlds. All people should know this, but they do not understand why and how they were subjected to evil in the first place. I go back to the discourse on the mother goddess, the feminine principle, the destroying principle of all things—not in the sense that man usually believes, for destruction is necessary in this world. The Kali must exist or man would be over populated; nature would never be in the balance. Does that explain the two opposites in the lower worlds? It should.

"All ECK travelers agree, and all of the inhabitants of the higher worlds say, that there is one supreme infinite essence, which is called the ECK; it is composed of pure spirit substance; and the SUGMAD, in the form of the manifested ECK resides in and permeates the supreme regions, from whence, as ITS headquarters, IT projects ITSELF into and permeates all regions throughout creation. IT is in no way limited except in the manner of form which IT must take in order to exist in certain worlds, other than ITS own.

"That form is only an infinitely small fragment of IT-SELF. IT is universal spirit, moving forth in a living stream. vibrating through all worlds, entering in and vitalizing all that exists. IT is the dynamic life of everything that lives. IT is impersonal, universal, all-permeating, omnipresent, and all-sustaining. IT is the life, the very existence of all. IT is existence absolute.

"To this all-embracing, all-sustaining essence, no name can be applied other than what we know, the ECK, the voice of the SUGMAD. There is a universal agreement among the world's greatest spiritual thinkers that the supreme power is seeking to find those who are willing to enter into it and become one with it, and that in it, one finds wisdom, power and freedom.

"This is the highest ideal of Soul ever conceived or formulated in the thoughts of the ECK travelers. And this is the finding of the great ECK Masters.

"With this I end these talks!"

Glossary of ECKANKAR Terms

Words set in SMALL CAPS are defined elsewhere in the Glossary

ARAHATA. An experienced and qualified teacher for ECKANKAR classes.

CHELA. A spiritual student.

ECK. The Life Force, the Holy Spirit, or Audible Life Current which sustains all life.

ECKANKAR. The Ancient Science of SOUL TRAVEL. A truly spiritual religion for the individual in modern times, known as the secret path to God via dreams and Soul Travel. The teachings provide a framework for anyone to explore their own spiritual experiences. Established by Paul Twitchell, the modern-day founder, in 1965.

ECK MASTERS. Spiritual Masters who can assist and protect people in their spiritual studies and travels. The ECK Masters are from a long line of God-Realized Souls who know the responsibility that goes with spiritual freedom.

HU. The secret name for God. The singing of the word HU, pronounced like the man's name Hugh, is considered a love song to God. It is sung in the ECK Worship Service.

INITIATION. Earned by the ECK member through spiritual unfoldment and service to God. The initiation is a private ceremony in which the individual is linked to the Sound and Light of God.

LIVING ECK MASTER. The title of the spiritual leader of ECKANKAR. His duty is to lead Souls back to God. The Living ECK Master can assist spiritual students physically as the Outer Master, in the dream state as the Dream Master, and in

249

the spiritual worlds as the Inner Master. Sri Harold Klemp became the Living ECK Master in 1981.

MAHANTA. A title to describe the highest state of God Consciousness on earth, often embodied in the Living ECK Master. He is the Living Word.

PLANES. The levels of heaven, such as the Astral, Causal, Mental, Etheric, and Soul planes.

SATSANG. A class in which students of ECK study a monthly lesson from ECKANKAR.

THE SHARIYAT-KI-SUGMAD. The sacred scriptures of ECKANKAR. The scriptures are comprised of twelve volumes in the spiritual worlds. The first two were transcribed from the inner planes by Paul Twitchell, modern-day founder of ECKANKAR.

SOUL. The True Self. The inner, most sacred part of each person. Soul exists before birth and lives on after the death of the physical body. As a spark of God, Soul can see, know, and perceive all things. It is the creative center of Its own world.

SOUL TRAVEL. The expansion of consciousness. The ability of Soul to transcend the physical body and travel into the spiritual worlds of God. Soul Travel is taught only by the Living ECK Master. It helps people unfold spiritually and can provide proof of the existence of God and life after death.

SOUND AND LIGHT OF ECK. The Holy Spirit. The two aspects through which God appears in the lower worlds. People can experience them by looking and listening within themselves and through Soul Travel.

SPIRITUAL EXERCISES OF ECK. The daily practice of certain techniques to get us in touch with the Light and Sound of God.

SUGMAD. A sacred name for God. SUGMAD is neither masculine nor feminine; IT is the source of all life.

WAH Z. The spiritual name of Sri Harold Klemp. It means the Secret Doctrine. It is his name in the spiritual worlds.

INDEX

A

Aaron's Rod, 96
Achilles (heel), 59, 242
Action and reaction (dual forms
   of karma), 233
Acts of the Apostles, 140
Adonai, 27
   Definition, 27
Adoration (Ray), 130
Advaita ECK force, 24
   Definition, 24
Aesthetics (ECK), 230, 234-238
Agam (Inaccessible), 26, 126
Agam Lok, 13, 73
Agam Purusha, 27, 125
   Definition, 27
Ahankar (execute orders), 80
   Definition, 81
Ahankara (vanity), 52, 53, 230,
   234
Akal (timeless), 26
Akal Purusha (Sat Purusha), 27
Akashar, 26
   Definition, 27
Alakh, 126
Alakh Lok, 25
   Definition, 25
Alakh Purusha, 27, 125
   Definition, 27
Alexander the Great, 49, 50
All-Seeing Eye, 220
Allah, 28
   Definition, 28
Allah of Mohammedans, 126
Ameretat (immortal life), 114
Amesha Spenta (Holy immortals),
   114

Anami (without name), 26
Anami Lok, 13
   Definition, 73
Anda, 14, 106, 159
Angel of Death, 161
Angels, 90
   Definition, 90
Angels of death (five black), 231
Angels of life (five white), 231
Anger (Krodha), 51
Annapurna (mountain peak), 29
Anti-intellectuals, 175
Anti-reasonists, 175
Antishkarans, 80, 102, 234
   Definition, 80
Aquinas, Thomas (Catholic
   founder of Christian
   philosophy), 130, 174, 175
Arhirit (city), 21
Aristotle, 130, 175
Armaiti (perfect piety;
   single mindedness), 114
Artha (prosperity), 105
Asha-Vahista (supreme will), 114
Asana (physical postures), 143
Asceticism, 241
Asgard (Scandanavian name for
   Far Country), 9
Ashta-dal-Kanwal (center—
   zone), 103, 185
Ashtang Yoga, 143
Astral, 163
Astral body (Nuri Sarup), 75
Astral City, 15
   Definition, 15
Astral eyes, 184
Astral Light, 143, 149

251

E

Earth Mother (Kali), 89
Earth Plane, 163
ECK, 8, 16, 24, 34, 35, 36, 38,
    56, 59, 61, 62, 63, 74, 76, 78,
    79, 81, 82, 83, 84, 87, 97, 108,
    112, 113, 114, 115, 121, 126,
    127, 130, 132, 134, 136, 137,
    138, 140, 156, 160, 164, 171,
    175, 193, 195, 198, 209, 212,
    213, 214, 216, 217, 218, 219,
    220, 221, 222, 224, 226, 229,
    242
Adepts, 93
All-embracing, all sustaining
    essence, 247
Audible Life Stream, 141
Become filled with, 141
Being the ECK ITSELF, 34
Chela, 7, 8
Consciousness of the, 209
Current, 46
Divine, 135
Divine energy of the, 194
Gives and sustains life, 114
Great travelers of, 113
Has ten rays or forces, 129
Heavenly, 141
Highest of all Spiritual
    powers, 114
Initiate of, 97
Is in both shadow and light,
    197
Knowledge of the, 239
Law of the ECK, 189
Leader of all Souls, 221
Manifested, 246
Marg, 57
    Definition, 57
Master(s), 7, 13, 17, 29, 31,
    36, 44, 63, 67, 69, 73, 120,
    124, 142, 206, 207, 218, 247,
Master has three almost
    insurmountable obstacles, 215

Master is embodiment of the,
    205
Master is the God-man, 212
Master power and spirit, 139
Metaphysics of the ECK, 238
Music of the ECK, 112
Music of the spheres, 158
Mystical philosophy of, 169
Often known as Sat Nam, 125
One supreme and infinite
    energy, 197
Penetrates into intimacy with
    the ECK, 209
Philosophy, 221
Philosophy of Sound Current,
    137
Plane of the ECK, 167
Power, 24, 55, 130
Saints, 23
Samadhi of ECK, 199
Scripture (Shariyat-ki-
    Sugmad), 221
Seeks union with, 143
Spirit of all things, 114
Spiritual energy, the ECK, 169
Spiritual exercises of ECK,
    102
Spiritual liberation, only the
    ECK, 138
Sraosha (or ECK), 115
Supreme infinite essence, 246
Supreme Spirit, 138
That formless fluid, 129
The first true son of God, 222
The great sound current, 175
The highest crown worn by all,
    239
The infinite light and sound,
    129, 138
The land of, 133
The path of, 131, 133
The positive power, 125
The regenerating Bani, 231
The sound current, 140, 230,
    231, 246
The Supreme, 153

Grinding wheel of desire and
    karma, 230
Guda-chakra (See: Mulchakra),
    101
Gurumukhs(follow Mahanta),
    230
Gyatri, The, 96
    Definition, 96

H

Hammurabi's Code, 31
Hansni Tunnel, 22
Happy Hunting Ground (Am.
    Indian for Far Country), 9
Happy Isles (Greek for Far
    Country), 9
Hatha Yoga, 142
Haurvatat (absolute wholeness,
    perfection), 114
Heaven (Christian—Far
    Country), 9
Heavenly Kingdom, 7
Heavenly worlds, 156
Hegel (Materialistic German
    Scientist) 130, 211
Hell, 217
    Definition, 217
Hell, lower pits of, 232
Hereness, 153, 154
Higher worlds, 137
Himalaya Mountains, 29
Hindi (language), 27
Hindu Brahman rulers, 32
Hindu philosophy, 145
Hindu religion, 150
Hindu trinity, 154
Hindu Kush Mountains, 29, 49,
    109, 149, 209, 229
    Description, 29
Historical figures, 12, 49, 50
Holy Ghost, 140, 211, 219
Holy immortals (See.
    Ameshspenta), 114
Holy Spirit, 140

Holy symphony, 231
Home of Truth, 22
    Definition, 21, 22
How does one find God?, 58-67
Hrida chakra, 102
Human consciousness, expansion
    of, 192
Hungry seeker, 231

I

Ida and Pingala, 99
Ignorance, 32, 215, 225
Ignorance of the law, 237
Illumination (Prathiba), 236
Illusion(s), 210
Imaginary (Faculty), 200, 201
Imaginary image, 201
Imagination Faculty
    (Imaginative), 42, 43, 203,
    219, 220, 221, 222, 223, 224,
    225, 226, 227, 236, 237, 238,
    239
    Definition, 43
Imagination, illusions of, 210
Imagination's birth in man—
    is his awakening, 221
Imaginative eye (supreme), 227,
    228
IMMORTAL TUZA, THE
    (Chapter title), 69-88
Immortality, 159
Immortality, Waters of, 49
Indian Yoga Systems, 144
Indian Yogis, 241
Individual Soul energy, 145
Indri chakra, 99
    Definition, 99, 102
Infinite One, 27
Initiates, 199
Initiation, 242
Inner body (soul), 227
Inner door, 231
Inner energy, 192
Inner experience, 232

Inner illumination, 211
Inner kingdoms, 231
Inner movement, 227
Inner traveler, 192
Inner worlds, 227, 237, 242
Intellectualism, 176
Intellectuals, 175, 177
Intelligence ray, 130
Intuition, 179-181
Inventors (Edison and Marconi), 220
Ion, 21
Ionosphere region, 21
Isles of the Blessed (Greek Far Country), 9
Isness, 150, 151, 153, 154
Isness or the Nowness, The, 150
Isness of the SUGMAD, 150
Isness, Nowness and Hereness, 157, 168
Isness, the creative moment, 153
Isthul Sharir, 75
Definition, 75
IT, ITS, ITSELF (SUGMAD), 25-28, 40-44, 55, 70, 118, 119, 121, 122, 129, 134, 136, 196, 219, 221, 222, 246, 247
Being infinite, is without will 129
Cannot be direct creator, 129
Emanations on Rays
IT can only be found in the imagination of IT, 222
IT makes ITS own laws, 190
What IT is like, 109

J

Jacob (on ladder of heaven), 166
Jaram Brahm, 196
Jehovah of Jews and Christians, 126
Jesuits in Catholic Church, 176
Jesus, 32, 40, 93, 119, 124, 139, 140, 187, 239, 240
Jewel is in the Lotus, The, 96

Jhankar, 20
Definition, 20
Jivan Mukti (life everlasting), 142
Jnana, 104
Definition, 104
Judaism, 40

K

Kabir, 10
Kailash (mountain), 18
Kal, 186, 187
Kal, lord of karma, 56
Kal Niranjan, 89, 125, 130, 131, 176, 185, 186
Kal power, 130
Kal Purusha, 27
Definition, 27
KALI, THE WORSHIP OF (Chapter title), 89-108
KALI, 246
Annapura, 95
Chandi, 95
Durga, 95
Earth Mother, 89
Feminine Principle, 91-93
Gauri, 95
Goddess of Fate, 106
Kali the Black, 95
Moon Mother, 106
Mother Goddess, 90-91
Mother India, 94
Mother Nature, 106
Parvati, 95
Saktis (Saktas), 94
Sex Goddess, 91
Temple of, 94
The Vampire (blood cult), 94
Uma, 95
Worship of, 89, 94, 95
Kama (Lust), 51, 105, 230
Definition, 51, 105
Karakoram Range, 29

Man is a small universe, 100, 101
Mana(s) (the mind), 14, 234
Manas (receives and tastes), 80
    Definition, 80, 81
Mansarover, 19, 59
    Definition, 19, 59
Mantra Yoga, 143
Manumukhs (obey the mind),
    230
Mariolatry, 94
    Definition, 94
Masculine principle, 34, 35, 107
Masonic Order, 136
Master(s), 120, 134, 142, 144,
    242
Matter or Nature (ray), 130
Maya, 93, 145, 169
McWilliams Law, 155
    Definition, 155
Medieval Christians, 241
Medusa (Egyptian God), 94
Mental superiority, 233
Mer (mountains), 18
Mersumer Kailash (city), 18
Messenger of death (Angel of
    Death), 162
MEST (Matter, Energy, Space
    and Time), 169
Metaphysics (ECK), 230, 238-
    243
Microcosmic Centers in body,
    101-103
Milky Way, 190
Mind, 80-87, 132
Mind and Soul, 139
Mind body, 75
    Definition, 75
Mind of man, 188
Mockups, 200, 203
Moha (attachment), 52, 82, 230
Moksha, 105
    Definition, 105
Moon Worlds, 183, 185
Mother, the Divine, 105
Mother, Earth (Kali), 89

Mother Goddess (Kali), 90, 91,
    107
Mother(s), Great, 107
Mother, Virgin, 91, 92
Mount Olympus, 27
Mountains of Far Country, 18,
    22
Mountains of Physical Plane, 11,
    29, 49
Mudra exercises, 143
Mukam Taq, 159
Mulchakra, Muladhara or
    Guda-chakra), 101
    Definition, 101
Musical Life Current, 137
Mystics (those who sought IT),
    36

N

Nada (Vedas) (Primal music
    of universe), 136
Nada Brahm (Word of Brahm;
    primal Nada), 136
Name of the SUGMAD, In the,
    54-58
Names for Far Country (other),
    9
Negative and Positive, 196, 197,
    237
Negative Lord of the Universe,
    132
Negative pole of energy, 198
Negative Power(s), 87, 126, 156
Neophyte, 200, 201, 203, 212,
    213
Newton's Law of Motion (relat-
    ing to the mind), 61, 87
Nietzsche, 120, 131
Nij-Dham, 26, 159
Nirala, 26
    Definition, 26
Nirankar (without body or
    form), 26
Niranjan, Jot, 14, 166
    Definition, 14-15

T

Tabriz, Shamus-I-, 10
Tantra, 104, 105
Tantras, 96
  Definition, 95, 96
Tantric Cult of Kali, 104
Taoism, 30
Tarzs, Rebazar, 7, 10
  Title: Great Master of
  ECKANKAR, 7, 10
  Personal description of:, 11,
  19, 70, 89, 129, 149, 169, 179,
  183, 209, 229
  Description of home of
  Master:, 10, 11, 12, 29, 49, 69,
  109, 149, 209, 229
Tenth door (spiritual eye), 184
THAT ALONE EXISTS
  (Chapter title), 109-128
Theosophical Society, 176
Third eye (Tisra Til), 235
Three Worlds, 197
Thor (See: Norseman), 28
Time and space, 169-174
Tirich Mir(mountain peak), 29
Tisra Til (third eye), 102, 103, 242
Traveler in Far Country, 44-48
Trikuti (Brahm Lok), 104, 125
  Definition, 104
Triloki (three worlds), 125
Trinity (ECK)—Wisdom, Power
  and Freedom, 230, 243-247
Tropopause, 16
Troposphere, 16
Truth, 195, 196, 211, 228, 237
  Definition, 211
Tunnels in Far Country, 22
Tulsi Das (Explorer), 10, 220
Turiya Pad (Astral plane), 14, 145
Tuza (the Soul), 70, 138
  150, 152-154, 156, 176, 177,
  181, 189, 191, 200, 203
  Definition, 70,76
TUZA, THE IMMORTAL
  (Chapter title), 69-88

(The) Tuza is immortal (Soul),
  71
TUZASHOTTAMA ENERGY,
  THE (Chapter title), 189-208
Tuzashottama energy, 145, 190,
  191, 192, 193, 194, 198, 199,
  203
Tuzashottama, the mystery of,
  197
  Definition, 197

U

Understanding of eternity, 158
Universal mind, Home of, 17
  Definition, 16, 17
Universal sound current, 201
Using the Shottama energy, 200,
  202

V

Vadan (Sufis), 136
Vairag (mental detachment),
  59-65, 230, 237
  Definition, 61
Valhalla (Scandanavian Far
  Country), 9
Vanity (Ahankara), 52
Vedantic pundits, 185
Vedantists (Vedas), 13, 145, 183
Virgin Mary, 93, 94
Virgin Mother (Kali), 91, 98
Vishnu in Hindu trinity, 151
Viveka (discrimination), 62, 63,
  230
Vivekananda, 106, 185
Voho-Mano (good mind; divine
  wisdom), 114
Voice of Silence, 136
Voltaire, 131

W

Waters of Immortality, 49
Wave picture(s) (the electron),
    155, 156, 177, 178, 179
Way to God, the, 30, 31, 32
Wheel of birth and death, 142,
    230
Wheel of transmigration,
    liberation from, 141
Wisdom, 243
Wisdom force, 129
Wisdom, Power and Freedom
    (trinity), 130, 139, 175, 190,
    192, 194, 234, 241, 246
Word of Power, 96
    Definition, 96, 97
Word, the, 139
World of Aesthetics, 236
World of the SUGMAD
    (entering the), 38, 39
WORSHIP OF KALI (THE)
    (Chapter Title), 89-108

Y

Yahveh, 27
    Definition, 27
Yama, King of the Dead
    (India), 162
Yang (male principle), 91
Yang and Yin, 91
Yin (female principle), 91
Yoga, 143
Yoga (Patanjali system), 99
Yogi system (Yogi; yogis)
    (system of yoga), 144, 146

Z

Zarathustra (Ormuzd), 28
Zen Buddhism, 51
    Definition, 50, 51
Zenith, 133
    Definition, 133

How to Learn More about ECKANKAR

People want to know the secrets of life and death. In response to this need Sri Harold Klemp, today's spiritual leader of ECKANKAR, and Paul Twitchell, its modern-day founder, have written special monthly discourses which reveal the Spiritual Exercises of ECK—to lead Soul in a direct way to God.

Those who wish to study ECKANKAR can receive these special monthly discourses which give clear, simple instructions for the spiritual exercises. The first annual series of discourses is *The ECK Dream 1 Discourses*. Mailed each month, the discourses will offer insight into your dreams and what they mean to you.

The techniques in these discourses, when practiced twenty minutes a day, are likely to prove survival beyond death. Many have used them as a direct route to Self-Realization, where one learns his mission in life. The next stage, God Consciousness, is the joyful state wherein Soul becomes the spiritual traveler, an agent for God. The underlying principle one learns is this: Soul exists because God loves It.

Membership in ECKANKAR includes:

1. Twelve monthly lessons of *The ECK Dream 1 Discourses,* with such titles as: "Dreams—The Bridge to Heaven," "The Dream Master," "How to Interpret Your Dreams," and "Dream Travel to Soul Travel." You may study them alone at home or in a class with others.
2. The *Mystic World,* a quarterly newsletter with a Wisdom Note and articles by the Living ECK Master. In it are also letters and articles from students of ECKANKAR around the world.
3. Special mailings to keep you informed of upcoming ECKANKAR seminars and activities worldwide, new study materials available from ECKANKAR, and more.
4. The opportunity to attend ECK Satsang classes and book discussions with others in your community.
5. Initiation eligibility.
6. Attendance at certain chela meetings at ECK seminars.

How to Find out More

To request membership in ECKANKAR using your credit card (or for a free booklet on membership) call (612) 544-0066 between 8 a.m. and 5 p.m., central time.

There May Be an ECKANKAR Study Group near You

ECKANKAR offers a variety of local and international activities for the spiritual seeker. With hundreds of study groups worldwide, ECKANKAR is near you! Many areas have ECKANKAR Centers where you can browse through the books in a quiet, unpressured environment, talk with others who share an interest in this ancient teaching, and attend beginning discussion classes on how to gain the attributes of Soul: wisdom, power, love, and freedom.

Around the world, ECKANKAR study groups offer special one-day or weekend seminars on the basic teachings of ECKANKAR. Check your phone book under **ECKANKAR,** or call **(612) 544-0066** for membership information and the location of the ECKANKAR Center or study group nearest you. Or write **ECKANKAR, Att: Information, P.O. Box 27300, Minneapolis, MN 55427 U.S.A.**

☐ Please send me information on the nearest ECKANKAR discussion or study group in my area.

☐ Please send me more information about membership in ECKANKAR, which includes a twelve-month spiritual study of dreams.

Please type or print clearly   941

Name _____

Street_____ Apt. #_____

City_____ State/Prov._____

Zip/Postal Code _____Country_____

(Our policy: Your name and address are held in strict confidence. We do not rent or sell our mailing lists. Nor will anyone call on you. Our purpose is only to show people the ECK way home to God.)